The WORKING PARENTS

cookbook

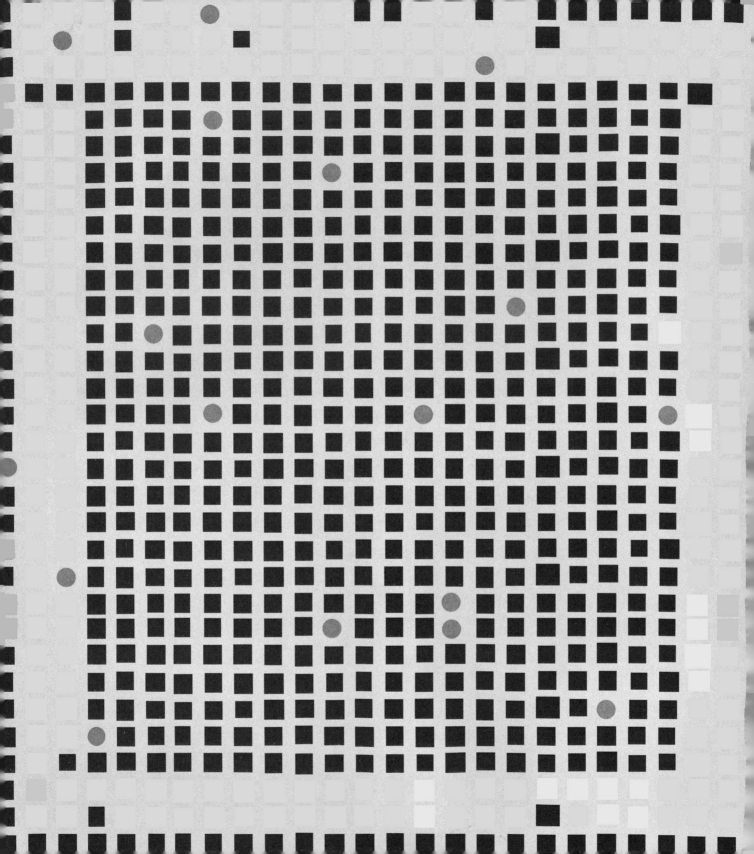

The
WORKING
PARENTS
cookbook

more than **200 RECIPES** for great family meals

By

JEFF and **JODIE MORGAN**

CHRONICLE BOOKS
SAN FRANCISCO

Library of Congress Cataloging-in-Publication Data available.
ISBN 0-8118-3685-1

Manufactured in Canada.

Designed by Werner Design Werks, Inc.

Distributed in Canada by Raincoast Books
9050 Shaughnessy Street
Vancouver, British Columbia V6P 6E5

10 9 8 7 6 5 4 3 2 1

CHRONICLE BOOKS LLC
85 SECOND STREET
SAN FRANCISCO, CALIFORNIA 94105
www.chroniclebooks.com

ACKNOWLEDGMENTS

The list of friends and family who supported this project with their palates, recipes, and encouragement is long. First and foremost, we need to recognize our daughters and primary sources of inspiration, Skye and Zoë, without whom we would never have written a book such as this one. They have taught us the value of patience and the importance of being flexible. Since they were old enough to chew, Skye and Zoë have shown us that children can be just as appreciative of culinary subtlety and variety as grown-ups.

Other children and adults who shared their recipes and tested ours include Scott Snowden and Joann Ortega, the Brandl family, Chelsea Tipp, Steven Rothfeld and Susan Swan, Barb and Jayson Woodbridge, Jan Morrissey, Nicki King, Stevie Weevie Goldfinger, Rick and Hana Yoshimoto, Inge Judd, Leslie Tschida and Danielle DiMercurio, Karen Hatten, Martha Vierra, and Lord and Lady Butler.

Our butchers Matt, Victor, Les, Jorge, Enrique, Dylan, and Julio were invaluable for their aptitude with a knife and their guidance in the ways of meat and fish.

Thanks also go to our editor, Bill LeBlond, whose clear vision helped transform this project from an idea to reality, and to his associates at Chronicle Books: Amy Treadwell, Jan Hughes, Doug Ogan, Vanessa Dina, Steve Kim, and Sharon Silva.

Table of Contents

INTR⊙-
DUCTION

balancing **WORK,**
FAMILY, and
MEALTIME

Every parent is a working parent, whether gainfully employed or not. Like jugglers, we keep many balls in the air. And despite our workday requirements, we still find a way to take care of our children. We shop for them, cook for them, and drive them to doctors, dentists, piano lessons, soccer and softball games, play dates, and numerous other daily destinations. Maybe that's why we're more tired than hungry at dinnertime!

But regardless of how we feel, a household full of grumbling tummies must be fed. This book is designed for parents—married or single—with busy days, finite budgets, demanding children, and a keen desire to eat well. It offers some two hundred recipes and a wealth of ideas to ease the stress of providing nutritious and appetizing meals at home.

Many of the dishes featured here require no more than 15 to 30 minutes of preparation. Most take less than one hour. Suggested preparation and cooking times are noted at the top of each recipe. However, easy doesn't always mean fast. Some recipes call for extended time in the oven or on the stove top. We call that "free time." While our oven is working in the kitchen, we're not.

The Working Parents Cookbook is not about cooking only for kids. It's about cooking for families—both children and parents. At our home, our daughters have learned to appreciate our tastes, even though they don't like everything we like. Their own tastes diverge, too. But, more often than not, we all happily eat the same thing for dinner.

Although we have been associated with the food and wine industry for many years, we are not professional chefs. We do not possess the latest in kitchenware, the fanciest stove, or a cadre of assistants to help us chop, mix, and carve. Nonetheless, we appreciate fine professional cooking, and over time we have created equally interesting meals in our home kitchen. For us, the secret lies with fresh ingredients and recipes that fit our culinary abilities and limited time. Eating well does require planning. But at the end of the day, we find there is nothing better than a family meal to balance work and lifestyle.

Unfortunately, many families don't share this experience. In their book *Joined at the Heart* (Henry Holt & Company, 2002), former vice president Al Gore and his wife, Tipper, inform us that as many as two-thirds of American families no longer eat dinner together on a regular basis. The increasing demands of office, homework, commuting, team sports, and

SLOWING DOWN: DINNER BY COURSE

We may cook fast, but we don't eat fast. Sure, a quick snack or meal is better than no meal at all. And we do, on occasion, find ourselves rushing through mealtime to race off to some destination, especially in the morning. But dinner is an opportunity to relax with our families and share accounts of daily experiences, so we like to linger at the table.

At our house, we've found that eating in courses naturally slows us down and encourages conversation along with good digestion. After all, a three-course meal is impossible to eat in ten minutes. But we still keep it simple. Our opening numerous other activities have taken their toll on what was once a daily expectation—the family dinner.

But it needn't be this way. Providing food for ourselves and the ones we love should be a welcome reprieve from the rigors of the day. Additionally, mealtime offers emotional as well as nutritional nourishment. As we share a meal, we share quality time together, and improve the quality of our lives.

How do we do it? That's what this book is all about. We hope our recipes, collected and developed while raising two wonderfully challenging children, will provide you with a diverse culinary repertoire to make family meals as pleasurable in your own home as they are in ours.

course is usually a green salad or some kind of garden dish. This is like a warm-up that eases us into dinner. We follow with the main course—possibly pasta, or maybe an omelet, chicken, fish, or meat, plus a side dish. Dessert or cheese rounds off the meal.

However, we don't chain our kids to the table. If youthful energy requires some up and down movement, we see no harm in it. Nevertheless, we discourage telephones and television at dinnertime. They quickly take the focus far away from family.

Chapter **1**

Eating WELL

Eating HEALTHY

There are more books touting recipes for healthy eating than we care to count. Some promote low-fat diets, while others advocate high protein and low carbohydrates. Still others lean toward vegetarianism. Most of them offer good—or at least interesting—ideas on nutrition.

But many of them suffer from a narrow focus that overlooks the very essence of our omnivorous nature. In other words, we are designed to eat just about everything. And with today's markets serving up an unprecedented wealth of fresh fruits and vegetables, grains, dairy products, fish, and meats, it strikes us as downright silly not to take advantage of the culinary bounty at our disposal.

The key is balance and moderation. Without them, we face a new generation of children and adolescents who are twice as overweight as youths were in the early 1970s. A 2001 report from the Office of the Surgeon General of the United States indicates that 13 percent of American children and adolescents are considered obese, as are nearly 60 percent of their parents.

To help us in our quest for better nutrition, the federal government issues guidelines such as the Food Guide Pyramid, which was released in 1992. It was developed in response to studies that showed a link between high-fat diets and such ailments as heart disease and high blood pressure. To its credit, the pyramid is based on the so-called Mediterranean diet, somewhat similar to what is traditionally eaten by the Italians, Greeks, Spanish, and French. So it can't be all bad, right?

However, the pyramid falters by not featuring many other ethnic dining traditions, such as those of China, India, and Japan. Serving recommendations can be confusing as well. They would have us snacking on fruits and vegetables three to five times daily, and starches like bread and pasta some six to eleven times each day. That may not work in our busy, active days. As a result, numerous revised versions of the pyramid have been developed, and many offer useful insights.

We take a simpler approach to nutrition. Instead of a pyramid, we propose more practical and flexible nutritional guidelines built around three meals a day, with a few snacks when possible. The key ingredient in our diet is simply "real food," that is, food that is minimally processed, if processed at all. As a nation, we eat too many simple carbohydrates, like sugar and white flour. These are rapidly absorbed into our bodies and then converted mostly into fat. By contrast, complex carbohydrates,

**LITTLE HELPERS:
KIDS IN THE KITCHEN**

Sometimes it may seem like more trouble than it's worth to have your kids in the kitchen. But it's never too soon to introduce them to the pleasures of cooking. Not only is preparing food fun, but it's also a way to encourage children to explore foods that they might not otherwise be predisposed to investigate. With each success in the kitchen, your child's sense of confidence will grow.

TIPS TO REMEMBER

Keep sharp knives away from small children. Allow them only to cut soft materials with small, serrated knives. The handles of pots and pans should never extend out over the front of the stove or another burner. (This is a good idea for grown-ups, too.)

Do not store wooden spoons near lighted burners. And if you cook with stainless-steel spoons, don't leave them in a hot pot. The handles can become hot enough to leave a nasty burn.

Remember to choose age- and time-appropriate recipes. Recipes that are too complex or time-consuming will lead to more frustration than pleasure.

Try baking together. There are numerous safe, kid-friendly activities involved, and the rewards are oh, so sweet.

Cleaning up is part of cooking, so don't let your children forget it. Our kids have kitchen-related chores every day that include emptying the dishwasher, wiping counters, setting the table, washing and spin-drying lettuce, and peeling carrots and potatoes.

such as whole grains and high-fiber fruits and vegetables, are more slowly and efficiently absorbed by our bodies. Simply put, they produce less fat.

Nonetheless, we don't subscribe to a dogmatic dining regime of whole grains, nuts, and raw vegetables. In fact, we eat our share of sweets and white bread—albeit fresh baked and consisting of nothing but flour, salt, and yeast. Red meat is also an integral part of our diet, but in modest amounts—and not every day.

The secret to healthy eating is variety and moderation. Eating right involves selecting real, unprocessed foods that our bodies are designed to digest. As demonstrated throughout this book, the choices are legion.

FAST FOOD CAN BE GOOD, JUNK FOOD NEVER IS

Let's not confuse fast food with junk food. Fast food can be anything that is quickly and easily prepared. As working parents, we don't have the time or energy to spend all day in the kitchen preparing a meal worthy of the world's best restaurants. Baby-sitters were invented for us to enjoy those kinds of meals. What we need at home is a dinner that can be quickly prepared and is good to eat.

Unfortunately, the idea of fast food has been corrupted by a commercial food industry more concerned with the bottom line than with good nutrition. During the last fifty years, food corporations have found that the use of sugar and corn syrup, saturated fats, refined carbohydrates, and artificial flavorings is by far the cheapest way to make bland foods taste and look good. These inexpensive ingredients lead to higher profits, too.

Sugar and corn syrup (which is also sugar) contribute mightily to the caloric overdose responsible, in part, for America's weight problem. In fact, it's shocking to think that many of the so-called reduced-fat foods on supermarket shelves today have traded natural fats for ever-increasing amounts of sugar and high-fructose corn syrup to compensate for lost flavor.

And it's not just in your food. It's in what you drink, too. A can of soda may contain as much as ten teaspoons of sugar, which deliver about 150 calories. On top of that, a Food and Drug Administration (FDA) study published in 1996 indicates that excessive childhood consumption of soft drinks can lead to calcium deficiency. Given the negative impact of soft drinks on our bodies, it's hard to believe that Americans suck down more than fifty gallons per person per year, an astronomical figure that translates to nearly 600 twelve-ounce cans per year per person.

When you order a quarter-pound burger, a forty-two-ounce soda, and a large (seven ounce) portion of fries at your local fast-food restaurant, you will consume about 1,600 calories. That's more than a child's entire daily caloric requirement. And because many of these calories are ingested as sugar or saturated fats, they can easily be transformed into body fat. It leaves little reason to wonder why we—as a nation—battle obesity.

To keep tabs on your sugar intake, check the ingredients listed on cereal boxes, canned goods, potato chips, sodas, and other daily staples in your pantry or refrigerator. The ingredients will be listed in their order of volume. If sugar, corn syrup, and dextrose are the first three ingredients listed, you might want to replace those foods with others offering flavors that come from more legitimate sources.

Does this mean that the Morgans never drink soda or eat at fast-food restaurants? Of course not. Eating well on a daily basis means our bodies can handle the occasional junk-food splurge. That's part of the concept of balance. Eating healthy foods every day means a small amount of saturated fat, sugar, or worse shouldn't pose a significant health issue. The problem occurs when junk food becomes the norm, not the exception.

THE SKINNY ON FAT

The skinny on fat is that no one really seems to understand it. Until recently, common wisdom assumed that a low-fat diet rich in vegetables, fruits, and carbohydrates was the most healthy way to eat. But fat alone does not appear to be the only culprit regulating weight. Most likely, the villain is overeating—especially eating too many sugars with fats—and lack of exercise.

With a balanced diet, we can celebrate moderate amounts of fat in our food. Fat is the ultimate flavor vector; it carries flavors across the palate. That's why your whole-milk caffe latte tastes better than one made with skim milk.

We suggest a logical approach to eating. In the right context, most foods are acceptable, including saturated fats. Butter? We love it, but not in all foods and not all the time. Cheese? Absolutely, but not as the main course every night. It's no accident that the French eat their cheese at the end of a meal, when they're too full to overindulge.

You don't need to be a nutritional expert to adopt a commonsense approach to eating well. Eat your greens, grains, fruits, vegetables,

We all need fats and oils, both of which have essentially the same chemical structure. Fats usually come from animals and are solid at room temperature. Oils often come from vegetables and are liquid at room temperature.

About one-fourth of our caloric intake should come from fats, which supply energy, carry vitamins, and transport flavors. Unfortunately, many people consume twice the daily recommended dosage.

The building blocks of fats are fatty-acid molecules, which are composed of hydrocarbon molecular chains. To visualize this, think of a chain made up of carbon atoms. Each carbon-atom link in this fatty-acid molecule can have up to two hydrogen atoms parked at its side. When all the parking spaces are full, the fat is saturated. When a certain number of spaces are not filled, the fat is either monounsaturated or polyunsaturated.

Animal fats contain a lot of saturated fats. They also can cause a rise in low-density-lipoprotein (LDL) cholesterol in our bodies, which can lead to strokes or heart attacks. Most vegetable oils contain monounsaturated and polyunsaturated fats. They tend to lower the amount of

proteins, and dairy products in a moderate and balanced manner. Snack reasonably on real foods and don't overindulge in sugary drinks and fat-filled desserts. Perhaps most important, steer clear of processed foods booby-trapped with hydrogenated oils and high-caloric sweeteners.

TRANS FATS, THE REALLY BAD STUFF

Even more insidious than excess sugar are trans fats, or partially hydrogenated oils, as they are more commonly listed among ingredients on packaged-food labels. They form a building block for much of the fast-food industry.

Trans fats are manufactured by adding extra hydrogen atoms to monounsaturated or polyunsaturated vegetable oils, which transforms them into saturated oils (or fats) that are solid at room temperature and less susceptible to spoilage. They keep cakes moist, cookies fresh, margarine spreadable, and potato chips crisp, and they extend the shelf life of processed foods.

But they don't necessarily extend human lives. Trans fats can increase the level of artery-clogging cholesterol in our bodies, making it no surprise that their consumption is linked to heart attacks and strokes. They have been connected to other illnesses, too, such as diabetes and cancer. In addition, some researchers are convinced that trans fats are the single most guilty culprit in our nation's current confrontation with child obesity. We believe trans fats play a pervasive role in adult obesity as well.

Amazingly, we have even noticed hydrogenated oils on the ingredient list for at least one flavor of Gatorade, although we don't know why the so-called sports drink needs a shot of trans fat. Take a look at the ingredients listed on the processed foods at your supermarket. You will find that many of them contain this ubiquitous man-made fat.

The worst news may be that the National Academy of Sciences has found there is no safe level for trans fats. Better news is that trans fats are easy to avoid. And you don't have to give up cookies and potato chips either. Just remember to read the ingredient labels on packaged foods, including sandwich breads, mayonnaise, canned goods, pastries and pastry mixes, breakfast cereals, power bars, peanut butter, bean dips, nondairy creamers, tortillas, microwave popcorn, and frozen pizza and other frozen foods. Avoid those items that contain hydrogenated or

LDL cholesterol in the body. They also help maintain levels of "good" high-density lipoproteins (HDL), which can remove excess cholesterol from the body.

Oils high in monounsaturated fats, such as olive oil, do this even better than oils high in polyunsaturated fat, such as corn and soy oils. But watch out for palm and coconut oils. They buck the vegetable oil trend and serve up plenty of saturated fat.

A man-made oil called trans fat may be the most dangerous fat in our diet today. Also known as hydrogenated oil, it is commonly used in processed foods and at fast-food restaurants.

partially hydrogenated oils. Rest assured that there are plenty of viable alternatives that taste equally good if not better. Regard most margarines as questionable, too. They are usually loaded with trans fats.

As a rule, fast-food chains and family-style restaurants also cook with or serve products processed with trans fats. French fries and chicken are routinely fried in the stuff. Grills and griddles are often slathered with them. Condiments can be riddled with them. Trans fats are so pervasive that few of us are able to divorce ourselves from them completely. The less we indulge, the better.

MILK AND DAIRY PRODUCTS

Milk is overrated. Yes, it's good for us, but it's not the Holy Grail it has been made out to be. Homespun tradition and the dairy industry would have us believe that if we don't drink our milk, we'll end up with calcium deficiency, stunted growth, brittle bones, and rotten teeth.

While it's true that milk provides our bodies with much needed calcium and vitamin D, calcium can also be found in cheese, yogurt, eggs, leafy greens, broccoli, cabbage, and blueberries, among other items. Our bodies even produce their own vitamin D from moderate exposure to sunlight.

If your kids love milk, that's terrific. Let them drink it to their hearts' content. Our children, however, are less enthusiastic. Some days they tolerate milk, and some days they don't. But they eat plenty of vegetables, enjoy many kinds of cheeses, and slurp up lots of yogurt.

The key to good nutrition for adults and children alike is a balanced diet relatively free of processed, sugary foods and empty calories. If your children eat a varied diet and play outside on a regular basis, you do not need to argue with them about that daily glass of milk.

Full Fat versus Low Fat
The popularity of low-fat milk is somewhat amusing when we consider how readily we eat a high-fat pastry with a low-fat cappuccino. Low-fat milk with sugar-laden breakfast cereal also provides grist for the humor mill. Yet many children start their day off with this popular combination.

Let's face it, most of the fat in our lives doesn't come from moderate amounts of milk. Whole milk is more flavorful than skim, 1 percent, or 2 percent. Yet through habit, many of us now prefer the low-fat option. From a taste perspective, we recommend guilt-free full-fat milk. The choice is yours.

DRINKING WELL: ALTERNATIVES TO SODA

Soda, America's most popular drink, can rot your teeth, clog your arteries, make you fat, and contribute to calcium loss—a particularly disturbing prospect for growing children. There are better, healthier ways to quench your thirst.

First, try water. At our house, it's the number one drink of choice: A versatile beverage that goes with every meal and in between. For a refreshing alternative, fill a pitcher with water and add a few slices of lemon or lime with several sprigs of fresh mint.

Milk is an excellent choice as well, although not equally appreciated by everyone. Fruit juice is fine, too. But fruit juice, with its high levels of natural sugar, should be consumed in moderation. We often cut it by half, or even more, with sparkling water to make a healthy, sparkling fruit beverage. Smoothies (page 66) made from real fruit and yogurt are also satisfying, especially on hot summer days.

Unsweetened herbal teas, iced or hot, can offer great satisfaction both during and between meals. We like coffee, too, especially espresso, either in the morning or after a meal.

We don't recommend caffeine for children, however, although a few drops to flavor a glass of warm milk should not pose any problems. It seems to work for millions of children in France, Italy, and other countries of Europe.

France also conjures up images of wine. If wine fits into your cultural or dietary regime, then consider moderate wine consumption with meals. Wine has graced family tables throughout the world for thousands of years. From a health perspective, the last decade has witnessed a parade of scientific studies that clearly demonstrate wine—particularly red wine—can reduce the risks of strokes, coronary disease, and cancer. Of course, wine's alcohol content makes it an unsuitable beverage for children. Adults, too, should remember that alcohol is a potentially dangerous substance that needs to be treated with respect and common sense.

What about diet drinks and artificial sweeteners like saccharine or aspartame? Many of these have been tentatively linked to various illnesses such as cancer. Even if these fears turn out to be unfounded, they are hardly comforting.

Vitamins AND MINERALS

Vitamins and minerals are the nutrients required for a healthy body. They can boost the immune system, promote cell growth, improve vision, strengthen bones, and help blood clot, among other activities. More specifically, the vitamins found in leafy greens can heal painful bruises, while those found in olive oil may retard wrinkling as we age. Eating enough whole grains, citrus fruits, carrots, and garlic can even diminish skin damage due to sunburn.

The information included here is not intended to be a comprehensive blueprint for personal nutrition. Collected mainly from the U.S. National Library of Medicine and the National Institutes of Health, the following chart is meant to illustrate common sources of vitamins and key minerals. Clearly, fruits and vegetables are particularly vitamin rich. Plant foods also provide us with energy-producing carbohydrates and with fiber, which improves digestion and may help prevent heart disease. Animal proteins such as meat, fish, and cheese deliver essential vitamins and minerals as well.

We need to consume many different vitamins, which are present in many different foods. That's why it's important to eat a varied diet. Our chart lists basic sources of vitamins and key minerals.

VITAMIN or MINERAL	FUNCTION	SOURCES
A	improves vision, helps immune system, keeps skin healthy	green vegetables, carrots, melons, apricots, milk, eggs, blueberries
B12	facilitates cell growth, makes red blood cells	fish, poultry, beef, dairy products, eggs
B6	builds proteins, helps growth, makes red blood cells	fish, poultry, meats, beans, eggs, vegetable juices, bananas, avocados
B1 (THIAMINE)	encourages a healthy nervous system, increases energy	yeast, whole grains, pasta, rice, citrus, peas, leeks
B3 (NIACIN)	lowers cholesterol	nuts, poultry, eggs
B2 (RIBOFLAVIN)	increases energy	dairy products, avocados, spinach
B5 (PANTOTHENIC ACID)	metabolizes food, promotes hormone synthesis	eggs, fish, dairy products, whole grains, cabbage
BIOTIN	metabolizes proteins and carbohydrates, and promotes hormone synthesis	eggs, fish, dairy products, whole grains, cabbage
B9 (FOLIC ACID)	promotes a healthy heart, normal tissue growth	leafy greens, spinach, beans, citrus fruits, nuts

VITAMIN or MINERAL	FUNCTION	SOURCES
C	helps circulation, gums, teeth, immune system. Aids in absorption of iron and calcium	citrus fruits, bell peppers, tomatoes, broccoli, Brussels sprouts, cabbage, kale, mustard greens, spinach, bok choy, blueberries, almonds, sesame seeds, chiles, asparagus, parsley, lettuce, radishes, cilantro, cucumbers, carrots, celery, chard, mushrooms, green beans, peas, collard greens, beets
D	strengthens bones	dairy products
E	protects tissues, promotes use of vitamin K	olive oil, other vegetable oils, leafy greens, nuts
K	clots blood	green vegetables, cereals
CALCIUM	strengthens bones and teeth, promotes cell growth	milk, cheese, eggs, salmon, tofu (bean curd), spinach, broccoli, whole grains, blueberries, cabbage
IRON	carries oxygen through the blood	red meats, beans, whole grains, raisins, spinach, kale, collard greens, blueberries, eggplant, peas, leeks

Chapter

2

GETTING STARTED

Speed and efficiency are key elements in the quest for kitchen and dining room harmony. At our house, our children's most common refrain is, "I'm hungry. I want to eat now!" Not surprisingly, the sooner we eat, the less likely the chance of juvenile meltdown.

This chapter explains kitchen techniques that will be helpful throughout the book. Also covered are shortcuts and organizational tips to streamline preparation times, along with information on how best to follow recipes, stock your kitchen, and deal with the simultaneous challenges of children and mealtime.

FOLLOWING A RECIPE

The daily demands of parenthood make us partial to straightforward recipes that work well in most modest home kitchens. Some of our recipes have a long list of ingredients. But before you shrug them off as "too complicated," read the method. More often than not, many of the ingredients are simply mixed together at once in a bowl or a pan.

Always start by taking a look at the short introductory note that accompanies each recipe to gauge potential challenges. The ingredients are listed in the order they will be needed. You should assemble them before you begin cooking to make your task faster and easier.

A NOTE ABOUT PREPARATION AND COOKING TIMES

In order to establish a realistic timeframe for recipe preparation, we timed ourselves in action. Your first attempts will probably be slower than your later efforts. Eventually, you'll find your own rhythm, which may be faster than ours.

However, this is no race. Have your ingredients laid out in advance and try to work efficiently. Remember, too, that haste can lead to accidents in the kitchen. With this in mind, preparation times are meant to be guidelines—not goals.

Preparation times and cooking times are kept separate. Cooking time often requires very little actual time spent in the kitchen. After mustering enough energy to get dinner started, we are often able to relax while it cooks. And if certain family needs—such as helping a child with homework—take precedence over relaxation, a simmering stew might offer the perfect window for preprandial study.

We've noticed that our kids can wait longer for dinner in the spring and summer, when daylight hours are extended and they are happy to stay

THE OVEN AS A TIME-SAVER

We indicate the times both for preparation and cooking for each recipe. While preparation time requires our full attention, cooking time often provides an opportunity to focus somewhere else, such as a child's homework or the daily newspaper.

In this context, the oven can be your best friend. It works tirelessly while you go about your business in another part of the house. Roasted chicken and meats and baked desserts are among the most time-efficient recipes in this book, even though you may have to wait longer for the finished product.

If you're prone to forgetfulness, buy a portable timer with a loud "ding" to keep you apprised of what's cooking wherever you are in the house.

outdoors longer to play. That gives us more leeway in the kitchen after work. Fall and winter require earlier supper times, which may influence our choice of recipe.

ESSENTIAL KITCHENWARE

Having the right tools makes the job easier. Our kitchen is far from a designer kitchen. Indeed, it is rather bare-bones. We have found that being stocked with the following tools makes it possible to put together any family dinner.

COOKING TOOLS
GOOD, SHARP KNIVES FOR PARING, SLICING, AND CARVING
KNIFE SHARPENER
WOODEN CARVING BOARDS, SMALL, MEDIUM, AND LARGE
WOODEN SPOONS, IN SEVERAL SIZES
WHISKS, IN SEVERAL SIZES
SPATULA
LADLES AND SLOTTED SPOONS
LARGE STAINLESS-STEEL COLANDER
SMALL SIEVES
CAN OPENER
MEASURING SPOONS
MEASURING CUPS
MIXING BOWLS, SMALL, MEDIUM, AND LARGE
PLASTIC SPATULA FOR NONSTICK BAKING
SIFTER
FOOD PROCESSOR OR BLENDER
ELECTRIC MIXER, HANDHELD OR STANDING
POT HOLDERS
APRONS (IF YOU VALUE CLEAN CLOTHES)
ABSORBENT KITCHEN TOWELS

COOKWARE

LARGE SOUP POT WITH LID, 6 QUARTS

DUTCH OVEN

SMALL SAUCEPAN, 1 QUART

SAUCEPANS WITH LIDS, 3 QUARTS AND UP

SAUTÉ PANS, 8 INCH, 12 INCH, AND 16 INCH, PLUS LIDS

LARGE CAST-IRON SKILLET, PLUS LID

ROASTING PAN

ROASTING RACK

BAKING DISHES, OVAL AND RECTANGULAR

BAKING SHEET AND COOKIE SHEET

BUNDT PAN, 8 INCH AND 9 INCH

CAKE PANS, 9 INCH

LOAF PANS

PIZZA PANS

TEAKETTLE

ITEMS THAT MAKE OUR LIVES EASIER

GOOD GARLIC PRESS

HANDHELD, ROTARY CHEESE GRATER

CITRUS JUICER

MEAT THERMOMETER, TRADITIONAL PROBE OR INSTANT-READ

GLASS BEAKER FOR REMOVING FAT FROM BROTH

MICROWAVE OVENS

We love our microwave oven. But we're a little old-fashioned, and we use it in a limited capacity. We even received a brand-new one as a wedding present, but it remained unopened, and eventually, we gave it away.

In fact, we might never have had a microwave oven had we not inherited the one we currently use. It came with the home we bought in 1999. That's when we belatedly dis-covered microwaves do come in handy. They cannot replace a traditional oven, but they cer-tainly breathe new life into leftovers. And that, for any parent, is enough to merit respect and attention.

Pastas, soups, stews, beans, and myriad other leftovers invariably end up in the microwave for quick breakfasts, lunches, snacks, or the occa-sional dinner. Indeed, at break-fast our kids are far more adventurous than we are. They happily greet the new day with the previous night's dinner, quickly zapped piping hot.

Cheese melts wonderfully in the microwave, too. A tortilla with melted Cheddar cheese and a dollop of salsa makes a fine snack. In fact, almost any cheese melted in this manner is an option—with or without salsa.

We have not pursued microwave cooking with much enthusiasm, however, as we don't believe it enhances the family dining experience. British-educated Spanish historian and Oxford professor Felipe Fernández-Armesto concurred with us in his book *A History of Food*. The prescient professor suggested that microwave ovens had made it unnaturally easy for family members to eat different meals at different times. As a result, families are regressing to "a presocial phase of evolution." We're not that pessimistic, but the family dinner table certainly takes a hit in the professor's scenario!

For those who are more curious about microwave ovens, we suggest you examine any of the many fine books on microwave cooking currently in print. Meanwhile, we continue to revel in our more traditional kitchen techniques. For us, the microwave remains an unsung hero of (mostly) leftovers.

KEEPING YOUR OVEN CLEAN

The inside of your oven constantly collects spattering oils and other greasy residue. With too much buildup, these fats and oils can begin to smoke during cooking. It's something that can ruin a recipe and stink up a kitchen. It can also threaten domestic harmony, which we know from personal experience.

This scenario can be avoided with a biweekly oven scrub. It's a two-minute affair when done regularly—and a nightmare when ignored for weeks or months. Use oven cleaner or soap and water. If using commercial oven cleaners, rinse well before turning the heat on again. The results are worth the effort.

MEALTIME PLANNING

The transition from work to mealtime can be difficult. But a little planning and preparation will smooth out potential wrinkles in your weekday evenings. Know your family's schedule and your kids' biorhythms. In other words, when do the kids go through a meltdown? Is it after soccer? Is it after school? Is it right before dinner? Hunger is often the culprit.

If we know dinner won't be ready when the kids are, we offer them a simple healthy snack—apple or carrot slices, a slice of cheese, or perhaps some nuts—something that will tide them over without filling them up.

A weekly agenda—or at least a list of ideas—can help ease the burden of mealtime planning. We try to take a few minutes at the beginning of each week to put together a series of rough menus that include plenty of variety. Looking at the week's work and school schedules helps us make the choices.

As a parent, you need to think about how much energy is required to prepare a particular meal. At the end of a busy day, try to make dinner as hassle free as possible. But if you get off from work early, or you're home with a sick child, a more adventurous menu may be a good idea.

Kids are messy. They spill, they fight, they drop. It's normal. Each family has its own perspective and acceptable set of table manners. We don't presume to know what's best for everyone. Consider the following four suggestions as guidelines:

- Set standards with your own behavior.
  Your kids will be watching.

- Give your children a reasonable margin for error.
  When the rules are too rigid, no one can enjoy mealtime.

- Give praise when it is deserved.
  It will reinforce desirable behavior.

- Pick your battles. Sometimes they're not worth the
  effort or the outcome.

GROCERY SHOPPING

Shopping for food may be one of the most commonly shared human pastimes on the planet. In the past, food shopping was as much a social activity as a practical one, and today it still is in many parts of the world. Where we live, we take pleasure in interacting with friends, neighbors, purveyors, and our children, too, as we survey the grocery shelves or visit a local farmers' market.

Seasonality dictates our produce selections, while a natural hunger for dietary variety leads to other forms of exploration along the food chain. There's nothing as delicious as a ripe peach in season, and nothing so unpleasant as the cardboard flavors of one that was picked too soon and shipped from far away. Despite the bounty now available year-round from the northern and southern hemispheres, we buy locally whenever possible. It's not only to ensure freshness. We also want to support nearby growers and producers because our dollars make an impact on the local economy. Shopping is about community.

Whenever you shop, try to remain flexible. You may find that what you had in mind for dinner isn't available at the store. But a shop full of good things to eat is guaranteed to give you a good meal. Just be prepared to change gears, mid-aisle.

Our kids love to come to the grocery store with us, mainly to ensure the purchase of their favorite sweet treats. There's no fighting it either; children love sugar. We comply, but in moderation.

A WELL-STOCKED PANTRY

Keeping your pantry stocked with the basics will make daily cooking easier. It will also help on those occasions when you don t have time to go shopping, or you couldn t find what you wanted for dinner at the market. Most of the items listed here are easy to store at room temperature. A few require refrigeration.

CANNED GOODS

Chickpeas

Low-sodium chicken broth

Whole tomatoes

Soup (good for emergency lunches)

Almond butter

Peanut butter

Tahini (sesame-seed paste)

REFRIGERATED

Eggs

Milk

Unsalted butter

Dijon mustard

Tamari or soy sauce

Mayonnaise

OILS AND VINEGAR

Extra-virgin olive oil

Asian sesame oil

Sesame chile oil

Canola oil

Balsamic or
other wine vinegars

DRIED HERBS, SPICES, AND SALT

Bay leaf

Basil

Oregano

Rosemary

Thyme

Cinnamon, sticks and ground

Curry powder

Ground cumin

Ground nutmeg

Ground turmeric

Peppercorns
(don't forget your pepper grinder)

Salt, table and
coarse sea or kosher

PASTA AND RICE

Dried pasta,
in variety of shapes

Rice, brown and white
(basmati, Arborio)

Polenta (cornmeal)

BAKING SUPPLIES

Unbleached all-purpose flour

High-gluten flour

Baking soda

Baking powder

Sugar, granulated and
confectioners'

Chocolate chips

Baking chocolate,
unsweetened and semisweet

DRIED BEANS AND OTHER VEGETABLES

Dried black beans

Dried kidney beans

Lentils

Split peas

Garlic

Onions

Potatoes

SALT

Used in the right proportions, salt enhances flavors. But be careful. Too much salt can dry out meats, overwhelm flavor, and make you thirsty. A high-salt diet can also lead to high blood pressure and other ailments.

So what's the best quantity to use? For some recipes, such as soups, it's easy to give a finite dose for a given amount. At other times, particularly when salt is used as a garnish, personal taste and the intensity of flavor can vary. Sea salt, for example, may have a stronger taste than salt that is mined from the earth. Because of these variables, many recipes call for "salt to taste." It's a good philosophy: When possible, taste first, add a little salt, and taste again. Repeat as necessary.

Kosher salt—and other coarse-textured salts—cling to food better than fine-textured table salt. They draw flavors more efficiently, and can add a pleasing, crunchy element when sprinkled over a dish at the last minute. Also, not all salt is white. There are, for example, gray sea salts from France and pink salts from Hawaii. The colors are a reflection of mineral content.

Given its varying character, salt can make quite an impact in simply prepared foods. A pinch of coarse pink salt on a plate of pasta with olive oil and herbs adds a nice highlight to the dish.

Have fun with salt. It's simple, it's easy, and it tastes good—but in moderation only.

HERBS AND SPICES

Used with restraint, herbs and spices can add great interest to the simplest dishes. Unfortunately, many of us forget to use herbs like thyme or rosemary on a regular basis. We'll pick up a small vial at the grocery store only to leave it sit for months—and sometimes years—on the cupboard shelf. From the perspective of flavor, that's not good. As they linger in the pantry, herbs lose their potency.

Some individual spices, such as ginger, and spice mixtures, such as curry powder, are assertive and can shape the character of a dish. Chiles also leave a strong imprint in a recipe. Among the best known are ancho, cayenne, habanero, jalapeño, and chipotle, the latter a fully ripened, dried, smoked jalapeño. They all have a reputation for being spicy hot, but chiles actually offer a broad array of flavors that range from fruity and plumy to raisiny and cherrylike. Some chiles even evoke tropical tones such as mango, coconut, papaya, coffee, chocolate, and licorice, so it's not surprising that chiles, in small doses, often find favor among children as well as adults.

FREEZING FOODS

Freezing foods, including leftovers, soups, and meats, is a practical way to save money and time. But freezing does not stop evaporation of the liquids in food. It only slows it down. To limit evaporation, wrap or seal freeze-worthy items in plastic or another water-resistant material. Remember that most foods expand when frozen, so fill plastic containers no more than three-fourths full. Do not use glass containers for freezer storage, particularly if freezing liquids. As liquids freeze, they may expand and shatter the glass. Label and date leftovers or meats. Otherwise you might forget exactly what it is you've stashed in your freezer, and when you did it.

Unfortunately, freezing does not improve the quality of food. In fact, when food defrosts, certain cells lose some of their water content, which can affect texture, particularly in meats. Perhaps for this reason, we don't freeze a lot of foods, aside from the notable exceptions listed below.

CHEESE

Normally, we don't buy cheese in large enough quantities to warrant freezing it. And common wisdom states that cheese freezes poorly. But when we have, on occasion, frozen aged cheeses like Parmesan, Gruyère, and raclette—usually after binge buying on a sale we couldn't ignore— they have defrosted surprisingly well.

MEATS AND FISH

Fat does not freeze as well as protein, so fattier meats do not freeze as well as lean ones. But despite the loss of cell water, we've had good luck freezing uncooked meats. Fresh fish also freezes well.

SOUPS, STOCKS, VEGETABLES, AND LEFTOVERS

Soups and stocks are perfect for freezing and will keep for up to three months. Vegetables do well in the freezer, too. Freeze leftovers as soon as they cool to room temperature.

BASIC TECHNIQUES AND RECIPES

Inevitably, we use a handful of recurring techniques in much of our cooking. These basic methods and recipes form a foundation of simple, common building blocks for many of the diverse dishes we enjoy on a daily basis.

MINCING GARLIC

Not only does it add a flavor boost to many dishes, but garlic is also good for you (see page 166). That's why we use it in so many recipes. Without a garlic press, mincing and peeling garlic can be mildly tedious. With an inexpensive garlic press, tough little garlic cloves are quickly rendered into peel-free minced mush.

Garlic presses can be found just about anywhere that kitchenware is sold. We use a Zyliss press, made in Switzerland, although many other good brands are available. Ideally, you should be able to plop an unpeeled garlic clove into the press, squeeze the little hammer that forces it through tiny holes, and discard the skin left behind. With a good press, mincing garlic is a five-second operation.

PEELING AND SEEDING TOMATOES

Cooked tomato skins can be unsightly and unpleasant to chew, particularly in tomato-based sauces. Peeling tomatoes is easy, however. With a paring knife, cut a shallow X in the blossom end of each tomato. Bring a large pot three-fourths full of water to a boil. Add the tomatoes, but be careful not to fill the pot to overflowing. After 30 to 40 seconds, use a slotted spoon to transfer them to a bowl, then let cool for a minute or two. Starting at the X on each tomato, peel off the skin. Do not throw out the water if you are cooking pasta, as the same water can be used.

Many cooks like to remove the seeds from tomatoes because they find them slightly bitter. We have never found them to taste unpleasant, however, so we don't bother. Who has time for that anyway?

Now, if you still insist on seeding your tomatoes, it's not difficult. Just cut the tomatoes in half crosswise and gently squeeze each half to release excess juice and the seeds, using the edge of a knife to scrape off any seeds that stick.

TOASTING SESAME SEEDS AND NUTS

Toasting sesame seeds brings out their aroma and adds a pleasing crunch to these otherwise mild and chewy seeds. Enjoy them tossed in a salad or in a side dish such as Spiced Ginger Sesame Noodles (page 190). Toast nuts, such as walnuts, for similar results.

In a dry sauté pan or skillet over medium heat, toast the seeds or nuts, stirring fairly constantly, until they are fragrant and take on color, 2 to 3 minutes.

Every time we turn around, it seems like there's another potluck scheduled for parents and school-age children. More often than not, these gatherings have an unequal representation: Too many salads and desserts, but not enough pasta or protein.

The best way to ensure a nourishing meal is to bring a dish you know will satisfy you and your children. Also, bring something that can sit safely, uncovered, at room temperature.

Most of the salads in Chapter 6 and many pastas in Chapter 7 will shine at potlucks. Among the possibilities are such items as Couscous Salad with Tomato and Cilantro (page 145), Spiced Ginger Sesame Noodles (page 190), Asian Slaw (page 132), Yellow Rice and Black Bean Salad (page 142), Lentil Salad (page 141), String Bean and Potato Salad (page 133), and Cold Sauce Pasta (page 130). Of course, you'll rarely go wrong with everyone's favorite—dessert (see Chapter 13). It's just not the best main-course option.

We have only one warning regarding potlucks: Make sure you bring your serving dish home. We've lost too many to the potluck demon.

MAYONNAISE

Mayonnaise is versatile, and we use it more often as a dipping sauce than as a sandwich spread. Commercial mayonnaise relies on sugar or honey for flavor, which means that it's often too sweet for the food it accompanies.

Unlike the commercial product, homemade mayonnaise is made with raw eggs. This fact makes the threat of salmonella poisoning a real—if highly unlikely—one, particularly for small children, pregnant women, older individuals, or anyone with a compromised immune system. If you have concerns regarding salmonella, buy a good commercial mayonnaise that relies less on sugar and more on fine ingredients for flavor. That said, our family has enjoyed homemade mayonnaise without incident since our children were born. Use fresh eggs from a reputable source for the best results.

Cold eggs don't emulsify easily, so remember to bring your egg to room temperature prior to making mayonnaise. If you use a food processor or blender, add the oil very slowly in a thin stream. You can begin to add it slightly faster once the mixture begins to thicken. For small batches, whisking by hand is quick and efficient.

You may use olive oil alone, but we find the flavor too strong. We also find that using canola or other vegetable oils, which are used in most commercial mayonnaise, produce a bland result. In our opinion, a blend of olive oil and canola oil is the best option.

---

1 egg yolk, at room temperature
2 teaspoons Dijon mustard
Pinch of salt
½ cup extra-virgin olive oil
⅔ cup canola oil

In a bowl, combine the yolk, mustard, and salt and whisk to blend. Whisk in the oils, a very small amount at a time, until an emulsified sauce forms. Alternatively, in a food processor or blender, pulse the yolk, mustard, and salt to combine. With the machine running, add the oils in a fine, steady stream, processing until an emulsified sauce forms. Taste and adjust the salt if needed. Use immediately, or cover and refrigerate for up to two days.

Makes about 1⅓ cups

AIOLI

Adding minced garlic to mayonnaise is common in France, Spain, and Italy. In France, this mixture is known as aioli, a name that reflects the key ingredient, *ail*, or "garlic" in English. It makes an excellent sauce or dip for many dishes, such as Seafood Aioli (page 244) and Artichoke Aioli (page 147), and is loved by grown-ups and kids. We usually make it with homemade, rather than commercial, mayonnaise, but either will work. A little of this powerful condiment goes a long way.

1 clove garlic, minced
1½ cups mayonnaise, homemade (page 33) or purchased

In a bowl, stir the garlic into the mayonnaise, mixing well.

Makes about 1½ cups

HARD-BOILING EGGS

Sure, hard-boiled eggs are easy to cook, but we're amazed at how many folks get it wrong. The yolk is too runny, or the eggs crack while the white is still liquid, leaving a white trail throughout the boiling water. So here's our foolproof method:

Place the eggs in a saucepan and cover with cold water. Bring the water to a boil, then reduce heat to a slow boil and cook for 10 minutes. (For soft-boiled eggs, cook for 4 minutes after boiling begins.) Drain and rinse with cold water until the eggs are cool enough to handle.

To peel a hard-boiled egg, crack it at the wide end, where there is an air pocket to help you get started.

COOKING DRIED BEANS

Dried beans are among our favorite staples. They pair well with myriad other foods and many styles of cooking. The easiest way to prepare them involves an overnight soak. But if you forget to soak them (as we usually do), you can cook them in a little over 2 hours by bringing them to a boil, letting them soak, and then simmering (see facing page). When using this shortcut, we like to add bay leaf and onion, which enhances flavor with minimal effort, but it's not necessary.

Most presoaked beans will cook in 45 minutes to 1 hour. Chickpeas require more time—2½ to 3 hours—which is why we often buy them canned. If you cook 2 cups dried beans, your yield will be about 5 cups.

**SERVING INDICATIONS—
NOT FOR ADULTS ONLY**

The yield at the end of most recipes is gauged for adult portions. If a recipe serves four, it will most likely serve two adults and three small children easily. Strapping teenage athletes may eat more than the average adult, however. You'll have to gauge your children's appetites and plan accordingly.

THE OVERNIGHT SOAK

2 cups dried beans

8 cups water, plus additional water to cover

2 teaspoons salt

Rinse and pick over the beans to remove any pebbles or misshapen beans. Place in a bowl, add the 8 cups water to cover by 2 inches, and let soak over-night. Drain off the remaining water and discard. Transfer the beans to a large pot, add fresh cold water to cover by 1 to 2 inches, and bring to a boil. Add the salt, reduce the heat to a simmer, and cook, uncovered, until tender, 45 minutes to 1 hour. Drain the beans in a colander.

THE SHORTCUT METHOD

2 cups dried beans

8 cups water, plus additional water to cover

2 teaspoons salt

1 bay leaf (optional)

1 onion, quartered (optional)

Rinse and pick over the beans to remove any pebbles or misshapen beans. In a large pot, combine the water, salt, and bay leaf and onion (if using) and bring to a boil. Add the beans, cover, and boil for 5 minutes. Remove from the heat and let the beans soak, covered, for 1 to 1½ hours. Drain the beans in a colander and discard the onion and bay leaf. Return the beans to the pot, cover with fresh water by 1 to 2 inches, and bring to a boil. Reduce the heat to a simmer and cook, uncovered, until tender, 30 to 45 minutes. Drain the beans in a colander.

ROASTING RED PEPPERS

We use roasted red peppers in many different recipes. You can buy them, packed in a vinegar-laden brine, but they rarely taste as good as the simple, sweet-yet-tangy home-roasted version. Little labor is required here, aside from peeling off the skins once the peppers are roasted.

Enjoy roasted red peppers as an appetizer, on pizza, in salads, and in a sandwich or pasta sauce. The peppers can be stored with their skins on in a plastic container in the refrigerator for a week. If peeled and marinated in extra-virgin olive oil, they will keep longer—up to two weeks.

We offer two methods here: Oven roasting and broiling. Roasting takes longer than broiling, but it requires less attention in the kitchen and leaves a flavorful juice that can be added to pasta sauce. Roasting also leaves the peppers softer. We roast from five to ten peppers at a time.

ROASTING

Preheat the oven to 400°F. Arrange the peppers in a roasting pan or baking dish, and place in the oven. Roast until the tops of the peppers begin to change color from red to black, 20 to 30 minutes. Remove from the oven and let cool.

Peel off the skins and remove the seeds by partially pulling the peppers apart under cold running water, using your fingers to rub the seeds away. You can pull the peppers into quarters or halves for storage. Pat the peppers dry with paper towels. If desired, store in olive oil for added flavor and easy storage in the refrigerator.

BROILING

Preheat the broiler. Arrange the peppers in a roasting pan and slip into the broiler about 3 inches from the heat source. Broil the peppers, turning them as they begin to change color, about every 3 minutes. Repeat until the skin is blistered and blackened on all sides. Remove from the broiler and let cool. Peel, remove the seeds, and store as directed in the roasting method.

A QUICK GRAVY WITH WINE

After you panfry meat or fish, a certain amount of oil or fat remains on the surface of the skillet. Likewise, an oven-roasted chicken deposits fats in the roasting pan. You can balance these oils and fats with a jolt of natural acidity from wine. The alcohol in the wine quickly evaporates as it cooks, leaving a child-appropriate gravy in the pan.

Our children love this sauce spooned over everything from salmon steaks and roast chicken to pork chops and mashed potatoes.

Pan drippings (fish, chicken, pork, lamb, or beef)
2 cups red or white wine
2 to 3 tablespoons unsalted butter

COOKING WITH WINE

Why bother to cook with wine? Because wine's natural acidity balances fats and oils in food and also can highlight flavor.

What about kids and alcohol? That's not an issue. The alcohol in wine evaporates quickly as it cooks. A sauce or stew made with wine will be alcohol-free long before anyone sits down to eat.

Does it matter what kind of wine you use? A white wine will make a sauce that is lighter in color and texture than a red wine. But the subtle drinking qualities sought after in expensive, high-end wines will be for the most part lost in cooking. That's why most chefs don't bother cooking with great wine. We recommend using inexpensive table wine for recipes that call for several cups of wine. You can also use that forgotten, half-full bottle that has been hiding in the back of your

Discard excess fat and oil that have collected in the sauté or roasting pan, leaving no more than a layer of about $\frac{1}{8}$ inch. Place the pan over high heat. Add the wine and stir to scrape up any browned bits from the pan bottom. Cook until the liquid is reduced by half. Reduce the heat to low, add the butter, and stir until it melts. (The more butter, the richer the gravy.) Transfer to a gravyboat, or spoon over individual portions.

Makes about 1 cup

WHIPPED CREAM

We like homemade whipped cream because it's so much richer and more satisfying than what comes out of a pressurized can. It's easy to make, too, and the kids love to lick the spoon. It also spruces up otherwise simple fare. For example, a little whipped cream with fresh fruit is a stunning last-minute dessert.

You can sweeten whipped cream in a number of ways. Most often, we use granulated sugar. But confectioners' sugar is also a good choice; it gives the whipped cream a lighter texture. Or try maple syrup, as we do with Honey Baked Apples and Maple Whipped Cream (page 324).

1 cup heavy cream
2 teaspoons sugar

In a deep bowl, combine the cream and sugar. Beat with an electric mixer or a whisk until the cream becomes stiff and peaks.

Makes 1½ to 2 cups

refrigerator for several weeks. It may be over the hill for drinking, but it's fine for cooking. Don't buy wines labeled "cooking wine" at the supermarket. These are usually salted, a practice originally intended to discourage minors from drinking them. They will not enhance your meal.

What if a recipe calls for wine and you don't have any? Substitute water or stock. The recipe won't be the same, but the result should still taste good.

CHAPTER **3**

Breakfast

Breakfast preferences are personal.

For some people, breakfast is an inspiration to get out of bed in the morning. Others can't be bothered. They'd rather sleep in until the very last minute and grab a piece of toast on the way out the door to school or work.

When we were children, we were advised to stock up on energy with a "nutritious" combination of orange juice, cereal, milk, eggs and bacon, or pancakes. The idea was to ingest copious amounts of vitamin C (to prevent colds and scurvy), vitamin D and calcium (for strong bones), and proteins and carbohydrates to propel us forward to lunch. In theory, it's a good idea. But it's not the only way to start the day.

Had we grown up in France, we probably would have skipped the orange juice—and the bacon and eggs, too. Hot chocolate or café au lait would have been the beverage of choice, accompanied with fresh bread, butter, and jam, or perhaps a croissant. In Japan, we might have drunk tea and dined on rice, pickled vegetables, and fish.

In fact, it really doesn't matter what we eat in the morning, as long as it is **reasonably healthy** and **thoroughly satisfying.** As far as nutrition is concerned, breakfast should be viewed from a daily perspective. No orange juice in the morning? Well, there are many other fruits and vegetables that supply vitamin C (see chart on pages 20–21), and they can be consumed at various times throughout the day. Your children won't drink their milk? Maybe they will later in the afternoon. There are many other good sources of vitamin D and calcium, too, such as yogurt or cheese. Carrots, kale, and green beans, among other vegetables, also contain calcium.

At 7:00 A.M., we look forward to something simple. A cappuccino and a piece of toast or fresh bread with butter are adequate for us. However, our children revel in a more adventurous early morning menu. Their favorite breakfast consists of leftovers from a well-loved meal the night before. Pasta, pork chops, mashed potatoes— even pizza—all work well for the kids. We love their selections, too, because they're easy to heat up in the microwave.

On some days, the kids prefer a less ambitious menu—perhaps a piece of toast and an egg, or toast and hot chocolate. Sometimes they ask for yogurt and a piece of fruit, or hot oatmeal. What's important to us is that they eat something—preferably something healthy and easy to prepare.

On weekends, we are more flexible. Sometimes we cook waffles, for example, and always make too many. We freeze the leftovers for easy toasting on a weekday morning.

EGG Scrambles

Scrambled eggs are among the easiest of all breakfasts. These quick-cooking eggs stand in equally well for lunch or dinner. You can also wrap them in a warm tortilla to make an egg burrito.

We always use very fresh eggs and scramble them in extra-virgin olive oil because fresh, fruity olive oil adds enticing aroma and flavor to this simple dish. However, neutral-tasting canola oil will also work. Many people use butter instead of oil for scrambling eggs. We prefer oil. It's lighter, fresher, and coats the pan with greater ease.

We streamline preparation and cleanup by working directly in the frying pan; there are no mixing bowls. For single servings, use a small sauté pan. Increase pan size as needed when doubling or tripling quantities.

Many optional items can be incorporated into scrambled eggs. (Note that additional ingredients will increase preparation and cooking times, however.) Listed below are more than a dozen possibilities. Choose only one, or select a combination. If using more than a single cheese, use only 1 teaspoon of each, with a maximum of two cheeses per single serving. Serve the eggs with buttered toast or a slice of country bread.

---

2 teaspoons extra-virgin olive oil or canola oil
2 eggs
Salt and freshly ground pepper to taste

OPTIONAL INGREDIENTS:
2 tablespoons freshly grated Parmesan cheese
2 thin slices Gruyère cheese
2 tablespoons crumbled feta cheese
2 tablespoons crumbled fresh goat cheese
2 tablespoons diced bell pepper
2 tablespoons diced tomato
2 tablespoons diced avocado

1 tablespoon thinly sliced green onion, white and green parts
1 tablespoon minced smoked salmon
1 tablespoon crumbled cooked bacon
1 teaspoon minced fresh sage or dill
1 teaspoon minced fresh rosemary
1 teaspoon dried thyme
¼ teaspoon chipotle chile flakes or red pepper flakes

Place the oil in a small sauté pan over high heat. Immediately crack the eggs directly into the pan. (Do not wait for the oil to get hot. That will cause the egg whites to cook before they blend with the yolks.) Using a wooden spoon, a whisk, or a dinner fork, stir the eggs until the whites and yolks are blended. Add 1 or more of the optional ingredients and stir until most of the egg has solidified and the optional ingredients have been incorporated, about 1 minute. Remove from the heat and stir a few more times to complete the cooking. Eggs should be moist, but not runny. Season with salt and pepper and serve at once.

Serves 1

EGG IN THE Hole

This is an old-time egg recipe that our kids always seem to enjoy. As with most of our egg dishes, we prefer to use olive oil. Other vegetable oils, such as canola oil, will do, but they don't offer as much flavor. Butter is an option also. It's your call.

---

1 slice white or whole-wheat bread
2 teaspoons extra-virgin olive oil or canola oil, or 1 tablespoon
    unsalted butter
1 egg
Salt and freshly ground pepper to taste

Using the rim of a drinking glass 2 to 2½ inches in diameter, cut or press out a hole in the center of the bread slice. Use the crust "frame" for the next step and reserve the soft bread "hole."

In a small frying pan, heat the oil or butter over medium heat for about 30 seconds. Place the crust frame in the middle of the pan and fry it until it is partially cooked, 45 to 60 seconds. Reduce the heat to low, flip the bread over, carefully crack the egg, and slip it into the hole. (If you break the yolk, you'll probably have to start over.) Let the egg cook until the bottom is firm and white, about 2 minutes. Flip the toast with the egg now attached, and cook until the egg white is firm on both sides, 30 seconds longer. If there is room in the pan, you can cook the reserved bread "hole" alongside the egg, turning it once until browned, about 30 seconds per side. Alternatively, cook it in the pan after the egg is done. Season the egg with salt and pepper and serve immediately with the bread "hole" on the side.

Serves 1

WEEKDAY French Toast

At least one school morning each week, our kids enter the kitchen with an "attitude." Something's not right. They're tired. They're cranky. And they're not happy about their breakfast options. Fortunately, an offer of French toast usually turns the tide. It's also so easy to make that we lose very little of our limited, precious coffee and newspaper time.

The French call French toast *pain perdu*, or "lost bread." Typically, they use day-old bread, which they consider "lost," or unfit for eating. Rehydrating old bread with egg gives it a second chance.

You can use day-old French bread here, but we generally employ sliced sandwich bread. Also, sometimes we forgo the syrup and instead stir together ½ teaspoon ground cinnamon and 1 teaspoon sugar. We then lightly sprinkle the cinnamon-sugar over each slice of toast.

---

1 egg
¼ cup milk
2 tablespoons canola oil
2 slices white or whole-wheat bread
Unsalted butter and maple syrup for serving

In a bowl, mix the egg and milk together with a fork or whisk. In a skillet, heat the canola oil over medium heat. One at a time, soak each piece of bread on both sides (about 10 seconds per side) in the egg mixture and place in the hot skillet. Cook on the first side until toasty brown, about 2 minutes. Flip and cook on the second side until toasty brown, about 1 minute longer. Serve with a pat or two of butter and maple syrup.

Serves 1 or 2 grumpy children

HONEY RAISIN Granola

PREPARATION TIME: 10 minutes   **COOKING TIME:** 35 minutes

This blend of crunchy grains is backed by just a hint of honey and spice. Packed with healthy fiber, granola is terrific with milk for breakfast, but it also makes a tasty snack in the afternoon. Try it with yogurt, too.

The kids like to help us make this cereal. For holidays, we place it in jars decorated with ribbons and give it as gifts to teachers and friends.

¾ cup raisins
⅓ cup water
4 cups rolled oats
¾ cup unsweetened shredded dried coconut
½ cup sesame seeds
1 teaspoon ground cinnamon
½ teaspoon ground nutmeg
½ cup canola oil
½ cup honey

Preheat the oven to 300°F.

In a small bowl, combine the raisins and water and let soak for 10 minutes.

Meanwhile, in a large bowl, combine the oats, coconut, sesame seeds, cinnamon, and nutmeg. Pour in the canola oil and then, using the same measuring cup, measure the honey and pour it into the bowl. (The coating of oil left in the cup keeps the honey from sticking.)

Mix the raisins and any remaining liquid into the oat mixture. Spread the mixture over a wide, shallow baking pan or baking sheet. Bake, stirring occasionally for even toasting, until the granola is golden brown and the raisins are plump, about 35 minutes.

The granola may still be slightly moist when you remove it from the oven, but it dries out quickly to the proper consistency. Let cool before eating. Store in a jar or tightly sealed plastic bag.

Makes 6 to 8 servings

BREAKFAST CEREALS

We buy very few of the seemingly countless dry cereals that permeate the marketplace. Most of them are insidious boxed breakfast candies that saturate kids' bodies with sugar and hydrogenated oils, or trans fats, now pegged as the single most likely source of obesity in America today.

That said, we have no problem with dry cereals that contain "real" food. Indeed, a small number of nutritious commercial products have been widely available for many years. We are not anti-sugar, but believe it should be consumed only in moderation. Understandably, we shy away from any breakfast cereal with an ingredient list that begins with dextrose, fructose, and corn syrup. Large food companies that produce such cereals are basically churning out a breakfast candy couched as a healthful wake-up meal.

Before you eat out of a box, look at the ingredients. It's the easiest way to make an informed decision about how you want to nourish your children and yourself.

Pancakes, PURE AND SIMPLE

PREPARATION TIME: 10 minutes   **COOKING TIME:** 4 minutes per batch

Many good, natural pancake mixes are on the market today. But this recipe is so quick and simple, you won't need them. Feel free to add fresh fruit, such as blueberries, diced strawberries, or sliced bananas, to the batter. We like them plain, too.

---

1 cup whole-wheat flour
1 cup unbleached all-purpose flour
2 teaspoons baking powder
½ teaspoon baking soda
½ teaspoon salt
2½ cups whole milk
2 eggs
1 cup cut-up fresh fruit of choice (optional)
Canola or other vegetable oil for cooking
Unsalted butter and maple syrup for serving

In a large bowl, stir together the flours, baking powder, baking soda, and salt with a fork. Add the milk and eggs and stir with a wooden spoon or whisk until the batter is smooth. Stir in the fruit, if using.

Heat a large, heavy skillet, griddle, or sauté pan over medium-high heat. Add 1 teaspoon oil and, using a paper towel, distribute it evenly over the pan bottom. You'll need to monitor the pan temperature closely. Try to keep it as hot as possible without smoking.

Ladle small—silver-dollar size—pancakes, or 1 or 2 larger ones, onto the hot oiled surface. When you see bubbles forming on top, after about 2 minutes, flip the pancakes and cook until lightly browned on the second side, about 2 minutes longer. Serve immediately with a pat or two of butter and maple syrup. Or keep multiple batches warm on a platter in a preheated 200°F oven until everyone is ready to eat.

Serves 4 to 6

Stevie Weevie's **W A F F L E S**

PREPARATION TIME: 15 minutes   **COOKING TIME:** 3 minutes per waffle

Stevie Weevie (a.k.a. Steve Goldfinger) has been regaling us with his waffles for years. He often comes to visit on Sunday morning and works his magic with his own waffle iron, which he brings along with the ingredients listed below. These light, toasty waffles may not be great for the waistline, but they satisfy a Sunday morning hunger perfectly.

Unless you've got your own neighborhood Stevie Weevie, you will need to invest in a waffle iron. But if your kids like waffles as much as ours do, the investment is well worth the price. They freeze well, and toasted leftover waffles also make a fine midweek breakfast treat for tired, cranky schoolkids. They make great afternoon snacks, too.

Look for dried orange peel on the spice rack at your local supermarket. It adds a special zest to these yummy waffles. Sliced strawberries or bananas can be served as a topping along with the butter and maple syrup.

---

2 eggs, lightly beaten
3 tablespoons canola or other vegetable oil
1¼ cups plain yogurt
½ cup milk, plus more if needed
¼ teaspoon vanilla extract
½ teaspoon chopped dried orange peel
1½ cups unbleached all-purpose flour
1 tablespoon baking powder
2 teaspoons sugar
¼ teaspoon baking soda
Unsalted butter and maple syrup for serving

Preheat a waffle iron. In a large bowl, mix together the eggs, oil, yogurt, ½ cup milk, vanilla, and dried orange peel with a whisk or a wooden spoon. In a separate bowl, stir together the flour, baking powder, sugar, and baking soda with a fork.

Pour the dry ingredients into the wet ingredients and stir with a whisk or a wooden spoon until the lumps are gone and the batter is smooth and creamy. Add additional milk, if needed, to achieve this consistency.

Ladle the batter onto the center of the hot waffle iron, using just enough to cover the grid without overflowing the rim. (That comes with a little practice.) Close the lid and cook until the waffle lifts easily from the iron with a fork, 2 to 3 minutes, depending on the waffle iron. The center should be moist but not wet, and the outside should be lightly browned. The first waffle tends to stick and may need to be cooked longer than subsequent waffles.

Serve the waffles hot, directly off the waffle iron, with butter and maple syrup.

Makes 6 or 7 round waffles each about 7 inches in diameter; serves 4 to 6

CHAPTER 4

Lunch,

Snacks, **AND** Appe-tizers

Making school lunches at 7:00 A.M. is no picnic. Yet many of us find ourselves doing just that while sipping our morning coffee. It's exhausting, but we aim to please. With a sandwich, or leftovers from the previous night's dinner, fresh fruit, and a carefully chosen sweet—usually cookies made without processed and unhealthy products—our children enjoy their lunches and appear to be thriving.

Snacks provide an important spike in everyone's daily energy level. In a perfect world, we would eat only fresh fruit and healthy homemade items to carry us through the day. Indeed, we do eat a lot of fruit. We keep a bowl filled with whatever fresh fruit is in season. Bananas with nut butters (like peanut or almond) are a staple in our house year-round. Persimmons, pomegranates, pears, and apples are enjoyed in the fall; figs, peaches, melons, and nectarines in the summer; tangerines and grapefruits in the winter. Carrot sticks, bell pepper slices, yogurt, and whole-grain cereals like granola are also high on our list of favorite snacks.

But we also have the same cravings for salt, sugar, and starch that everyone else has. We've said it before: Moderation is the answer. Potato chips, cheese puffs, cookies, ice cream, and cakes all find their way into our tummies—but not every day. Remember that your choice of brand name makes a difference. Buy commercial snacks that are free of trans fats and are made with a limited number of processed ingredients.

The following pages offer a variety of additional suggestions for snacks. Many of these same dishes—Bruschetta (page 58); Feta Cheese with Lemon, Fresh Rosemary, and Olives (page 61); Guacamole (page 57); Hummus (page 54); and Sweet and Spicy Pecans (page 63)—can also be served as appetizers when you entertain at home, making this chapter a particularly versatile one.

Hummus

PREPARATION TIME: 15 minutes

You can easily buy hummus, a seasoned chickpea spread, but it rarely tastes as good as the homemade version. We use this flavorful Middle Eastern staple on sandwiches (page 71) or as a dip for pita bread, tortilla chips, or raw vegetables such as carrots or celery. The addition of cumin and cayenne contributes spice and heat respectively.

As a dip, we like hummus topped off with a dollop of searing-hot *harissa*, a North African condiment available in many specialty food shops. Any spicy Mexican-style salsa can be substituted. The recipe makes enough hummus for two platters: A spicy adult version and a tamer kids' portion without the hot sauce.

---

1 can (15 ounces) chickpeas, rinsed and drained,
 or 2 cups drained home-cooked chickpeas (see page 34)
½ cup extra-virgin olive oil
½ cup water
¼ cup roasted tahini paste
3 tablespoons fresh lemon juice
2 cloves garlic, minced
1½ teaspoons salt
½ teaspoon ground cumin (optional)
⅛ teaspoon cayenne pepper (optional)

FOR SERVING AS A DIP:
1 to 2 tablespoons extra-virgin olive oil
½ cup small black olives
1 tablespoon harissa *or other hot sauce*

In a blender, combine the chickpeas, olive oil, water, tahini, lemon juice, garlic, salt, and the cumin and cayenne, if using. Pulse on low, stopping to stir as needed, until a smooth, thick consistency forms. The mixture can be used immediately or covered and refrigerated for up to 3 days.

To serve as a dip, spread the chickpea mixture in a thin layer on a platter, or spoon it into a bowl. Drizzle with the olive oil and garnish with the olives. Place the *harissa* in a dollop at the center of the platter or bowl.

Makes about 2½ cups

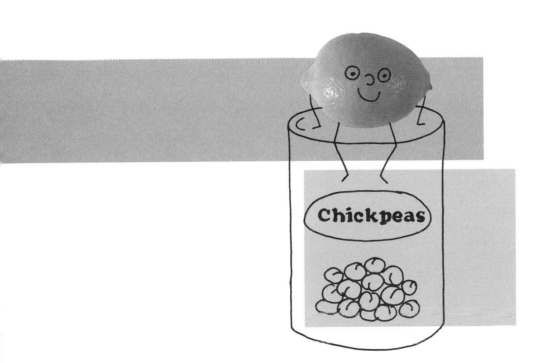

TANGY Olives WITH Herbs

PREPARATION TIME: 2 minutes

At our home in Napa Valley, we grow and cure our own olives. It's a lot easier to buy them, however, and today a wide selection of fine olives is available in most food shops. Steer clear of most canned olives, though, which are usually bland and uninteresting. We recommend brine-cured or salt-cured varieties such as meaty Greek Kalamata or tiny French Niçoise. Eat them as they are or enhance them with the simple recipe below.

We enjoy olives for snacks, as appetizers, in salads, and in cooked dishes. When serving olives with pits, remember to set out a designated "pit bowl."

---

1 cup green or black olives, with or without pits
1 tablespoon extra-virgin olive oil
½ teaspoon fresh lemon juice
¼ teaspoon dried thyme or herbes de Provence
¼ teaspoon red pepper flakes or chipotle chile flakes (optional)

In a small bowl, toss together all the ingredients.

Serves 4

Guacamole

PREPARATION TIME: 5 minutes

This is a simple, versatile avocado dip. We don't make it with chiles or salsa, so it's mild enough for sensitive kids' palates. In fact, our children enjoy preparing this recipe themselves. (The mashing technique speaks to the inner child in us all!) Serve it with tortilla chips as a snack or appetizer, or use it as a sandwich garnish (page 92).

---

2 avocados, halved, pitted, and peeled
1 teaspoon fresh lemon juice
3 tablespoons finely diced red onion
½ clove garlic, minced
½ tomato, finely diced
¼ cup finely chopped fresh cilantro
¼ teaspoon salt
Freshly ground pepper to taste

Using a fork, mash the avocados in a bowl until fairly smooth. (If you like lumps, mash less.) Add the lemon juice and mix well. Add the onion, garlic, tomato, cilantro, and salt, and mix well again. Season with the pepper and serve.

Makes about 2 cups

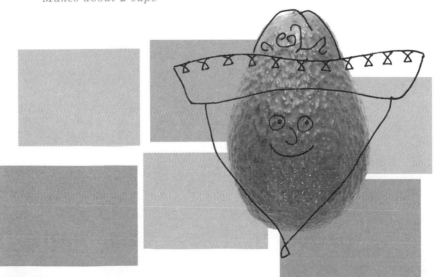

Bruschetta

PREPARATION TIME: 15 minutes

This tasty tomato mixture on country bread is among our children's favorite appetizers. That's because it's so simple to prepare, they can do it on their own. The kids take great pride in offering their bruschetta to dinner guests. Even better, nothing but healthy ingredients are used here. So if the kids decide they want to eat most of the batch on their own, we're okay with that, too. It's also a healthy snack for after school. Keep plenty of napkins on hand for messy eaters.

4 tomatoes, cut into ¼-inch cubes

¼ cup, plus 2 tablespoons extra-virgin olive oil

2 teaspoons dried basil, or ¼ cup coarsely chopped fresh basil

1 teaspoon fresh lemon juice

Coarse sea salt or kosher salt and freshly ground pepper to taste

6 slices country bread, each about ½ inch thick,
   toasted or grilled until golden brown

2 cloves garlic, halved

1 teaspoon freshly grated Parmesan cheese (optional)

In a small bowl, combine the tomatoes, the ¼ cup olive oil, basil, lemon juice, salt, and pepper and stir to mix. Set aside.

Brush one side of each bread slice with the remaining 2 tablespoons olive oil. Then rub the oil-topped sides with the garlic. Top each slice with the tomato-basil mixture and garnish with the Parmesan, if using. Serve at once.

Serves 4 to 6

Marinated ROASTED Red Peppers

PREPARATION TIME: 5 minutes

COOKING TIME: 10 or 30 minutes, depending on method

Serve this deliciously spare appetizer with a wedge of crusty country bread on the side. The peppers can be combined with the olive oil and seasonings, tightly covered, and refrigerated for up to 2 weeks before serving.

---

6 to 8 red bell peppers
½ cup extra-virgin olive oil
2 garlic cloves, minced
¼ teaspoon coarse sea salt or kosher salt, plus salt to taste
Freshly ground pepper to taste

Roast or broil, peel, and seed the peppers as directed on page 35, then quarter them lengthwise. Pour the olive oil into a bowl. Stir in the garlic and ¼ teaspoon salt. Place the roasted peppers in the bowl and toss gently, until they are evenly coated with the oil. Divide among individual plates and season with the additional salt and with pepper.

Serves 4 or 5

Ricotta Cheese Spread
WITH Fresh Mint

PREPARATION TIME: 5 minutes

This recipe offers a tantalizing juxtaposition of light, creamy cheese and fresh mint. Gloriously simple and elegant.

---

1 cup ricotta cheese
2 tablespoons extra-virgin olive oil
1 tablespoon finely minced fresh mint
Coarse sea salt or kosher salt and freshly ground pepper to taste
Crackers or pita bread wedges for serving

Mound the ricotta on a large flat plate and drizzle with the olive oil. Garnish with the mint and season with salt and pepper. For the best flavor, bring to room temperature (about 30 minutes) before serving with crackers or pita bread.

Serves 4 to 6

Feta Cheese WITH LEMON, FRESH Rosemary, AND Olives

PREPARATION TIME: 10 minutes

Feta is that briny, crumbly white cheese stocked in delicatessens across the nation. Traditionally made from either sheep's or goat's milk, feta has a natural tanginess that is complemented by the flavors present in olives and many herbs. Here, a finish of citrus zest and rosemary results in a dish that is as pleasing to the eye as it is to the palate. You can substitute a fresh goat cheese for the feta, if desired.

3 tablespoons extra-virgin olive oil
1 tablespoon fresh lemon juice
Pinch of coarse sea salt or kosher salt
½ teaspoon freshly ground pepper
8-ounce chunk or wedge feta cheese
1 tablespoon coarsely chopped fresh rosemary, plus 1 sprig (optional)
Zest of 1 lemon, finely chopped
⅓ cup pitted black olives
Baguette or country bread slices or crackers for serving

In a bowl, stir together the olive oil, lemon juice, salt, and pepper. Place the cheese on a serving plate and pour the oil mixture on top of it. Garnish with the chopped rosemary, lemon zest, olives, and with the rosemary sprig, if using. Serve with crusty bread slices.

Serves 4 to 6

ROASTED Halloween **Pumpkin** SEEDS

PREPARATION TIME: Depends on how long you spend carving your pumpkins

COOKING TIME: 40 minutes

This is as much an activity as it is a snack. In the fall, our daughters love munching crunchy, salty pumpkin seeds. So we harvest and roast the seeds from our Halloween pumpkins and pack them in lunches or use them for after-school treats.

---

2 pumpkins, about 5 pounds each
1 tablespoon extra-virgin olive oil or canola oil
½ teaspoon salt

Preheat the oven to 300°F.

Cut the stem-end off of each pumpkin, and have your children remove the seeds with their hands or a spoon.

Place the seeds in a colander and rinse well under running cold water. Remove any remaining pumpkin pulp. Coat the surface of a roasting pan with the olive oil, and spread the seeds out on the pan. Stir them to coat lightly with the oil. Add the salt and stir again.

Place in the oven and bake for 20 minutes. Stir the seeds to prevent them from sticking and continue to bake until golden, about 20 minutes longer. If they are not ready after 40 minutes, stir again and continue to bake for a few minutes longer, watching carefully to prevent burning. Remove from the oven and stir the seeds one more time. Taste and add more salt if desired. Let cool completely before eating. Store in a tightly covered jar at room temperature for up to 7 days.

Makes 2 to 3 cups

SWEET AND SPICY Pecans

PREPARATION TIME: 5 minutes   **COOKING TIME:** 15 minutes

A handful of these tangy, rich nuts makes a great walking snack as you head out on an errand. Spicy pecans also work well in salads, with cheese, or as a simple predinner treat when friends are visiting.

---

2 tablespoons unsalted butter
2 teaspoons brown sugar
1 tablespoon maple sugar
¼ teaspoon cayenne pepper
½ teaspoon ground cinnamon
Pinch of salt
2 cups pecan halves

Preheat the oven to 325°F.

In a small saucepan, melt the butter over low heat. Stir in the brown sugar, maple sugar, cayenne, cinnamon, and salt, mixing well. Stir in the pecans until they are evenly coated with the butter mixture.

Spread the pecans on a baking sheet or cookie sheet. Bake until toasty brown, about 15 minutes, stirring the pecans every 5 minutes to keep them from sticking or burning. Remove from the oven and let cool completely before eating. Store in a tightly covered jar at room temperature for up to 7 days.

Makes 2 cups

POOPSIE'S CREAMY Corn Cakes

PREPARATION TIME: 20 minutes   **COOKING TIME:** 30 minutes

Our friend Karen Hatten, who is nicknamed Poopsie, served these marvelous corn cakes one night and won us over immediately. We eat them with soups, salads, chili, as snacks, or as a breakfast treat.

---

1 tablespoon canola or other vegetable oil
1 cup cornmeal
1½ cups unbleached all-purpose flour
⅔ cup sugar
1 tablespoon baking powder
½ teaspoon salt
2 eggs
1½ cups whole milk
½ cup (1 stick) unsalted butter, melted
1 onion, diced
2 jalapeño chiles, seeded and finely chopped
1 clove garlic, minced
1½ cups freshly grated Cheddar cheese
1 can (15 ounces) creamed corn

Preheat the oven to 375°F. Lightly brush 18 muffin-pan cups with the oil.

In a large bowl, stir together the cornmeal, flour, sugar, baking powder, and salt. In a medium bowl, stir together the eggs, milk, and melted butter. In a third, small bowl, stir together the onion, jalapeños, and garlic. Using a wooden spoon, stir the egg mixture into the flour mix. Then stir in the onion mixture, the cheese, and the creamed corn.

Ladle the batter into the muffin cups, filling each cup about three-fourths full. Bake until a toothpick inserted into the center of a corn cake comes out dry, about 30 minutes. Remove from the oven and let cool on a rack for 5 minutes. Turn out and serve warm or at room temperature.

Makes 18 corn cakes

POWER BARS AND HIGH-ENERGY DRINKS

The occasional candy bar or soda won't kill you. Neither will today's so-called power, protein, or diet bars and high-energy drinks. But if you consume them regularly, don't expect health benefits. Most are packed with vitamins and minerals, but they may also contain significant amounts of sugar and fat-producing, artery-clogging saturated or hydrogenated oils. In addition, investigations have shown that the ingredients listed on many power bar wrappers are not always accurate. Enjoy your favorites for their flavors, not their purported health claims.

Cinnamon **APPLE**SAUCE

PREPARATION TIME: 10 minutes   **COOKING TIME:** 10 minutes

Our children enjoy this smooth-textured, tangy applesauce as a snack, and we all like it for dessert, doused with a bit of cream. Kids can help prepare it, too, but make sure they use a vegetable peeler, not a knife, to peel the apples, or you may wind up with cut fingers.

1½ cups water
2 tablespoons fresh lemon juice
1 cup sugar
4 pounds tart green apples such as Granny Smith (7 or 8 apples),
*   peeled, cored, and cut into 2-inch chunks*
1 teaspoon ground cinnamon

In a large pot or saucepan, combine the water, lemon juice, and sugar. As you peel, core, and chop the apples, drop them into the pot. When all of them are in the pot, cover and bring to a boil, stirring occasionally to dissolve the sugar. Reduce the heat to low and cook, stirring occasionally, until the apple chunks are reduced to a smooth sauce, about 10 minutes.

Remove from the heat, stir in the cinnamon, and let cool. Serve immediately, or cover and refrigerate for up to 3 days.

Serves 4 to 6

Fruit AND Yogurt SMOOTHIES

PREPARATION TIME: 5 minutes

Once upon a time, milk shakes were considered an acceptable snack. We still love them, but we don't recommend them on a daily basis. Fortunately, richly textured smoothies, made with yogurt and fresh fruit, serve up both a similar level of satisfaction and some wholesome nutrition. Not only do they make great snacks, but they also work well for breakfast.

The sweetness level will vary depending on whether or not you use sweetened yogurt. In our family, Jodie and the girls lean toward whole-milk vanilla yogurt, which has sugar in it. Jeff prefers unsweetened yogurt, though he may cheat occasionally and add a teaspoon of maple syrup or honey to the blend.

As a default, we use vanilla yogurt in these recipes. You can use just about any combination of fresh fruits, and you may also vary the type of fruit juice. Remember that the banana is what keeps the drink thick, like a milk shake.

Some of our favorite smoothies include those shown here. The instructions are easy: combine all ingredients in a blender and blend until they are smooth but still thick.

BANANA STRAWBERRY SMOOTHIE

1 banana, peeled and cut into 3 equal pieces
5 large fresh or frozen strawberries, stems removed and
halved lengthwise if fresh
1 cup vanilla yogurt
1 cup apple juice
1 cup crushed ice

RAZZLEBERRY SMOOTHIE

1 banana, peeled and cut into 3 equal pieces
½ cup fresh or frozen blueberries
½ cup fresh or frozen raspberries
1 cup vanilla yogurt
1 cup apple juice
1 cup crushed ice

PEACH SMOOTHIE

1 banana, peeled and cut into 3 equal pieces
½ cup fresh or frozen raspberries
2 peaches, skin on, pitted and cut into chunks
1 cup vanilla yogurt
1 cup whole milk
1 cup crushed ice

Each recipe makes two 16-ounce servings or four 8-ounce servings

SANDWICHES

We'd be lost without sandwiches, which are often the centerpiece of our midday meal. But just because sandwiches are commonly eaten doesn't mean that they have to be commonplace.

Good sandwiches range from the simple to the sublime. A little unsalted butter and salty ham framed by a crusty baguette may do the trick one day, while a more adventurous blend of tangy goat cheese, smoked salmon, and fresh dill will deliver satisfaction on another.

When we have the luxury of enjoying lunch at home, we take advantage of our stove top to make grilled cheese and other hot sandwiches. Accompanied with a bowl of leftover soup (almost always better the second day), lunch doesn't get much better (see Chapter 5).

Some children may have unusual—and particular—sandwich preferences. For example, a friend's son loves mustard sandwiches—simply mustard with bread. And, as most parents know, children sometimes insist on eating the same sandwich every day for weeks at a time. So we give it to them. What we hate to see is an uneaten sandwich in a lunchbox at the end of the day. That means the child has either gone hungry or scrounged cookies from friends at lunch.

You may find that your child's particular tastes require substitutions in certain sandwich recipes. For example, our children love the Brie cheese in Brie and Grated Carrot on Raisin Bread (page 74). Yours may prefer cream cheese, however. Our experience suggests that childrens' evolving palates inspire ongoing flexibility in the kitchen.

CONDIMENTS

The sandwich condiment that seals in flavor and moisture is of primary importance. Mayonnaise is an easy and practical choice. If you don't use a homemade mayonnaise, look for a commercial brand that does not rely on sugar for flavor. Unsalted butter is versatile, too. It's a flavor vector; it transports the flavors in your sandwich to your taste buds.

However, breaking away from traditional spreads can be liberating. Olive oil can be a fine option at times. So, too, can nut butters, like those made from cashews and almonds, both of which offer a refreshing alternative to peanut butter. Remember to steer away from commercial nut butters that are factory sweetened and pumped up with artery-clogging, fat-producing hydrogenated oils, qualities quickly revealed when you read the jar labels.

Other sandwich condiments we love include Curried Mayonnaise (page 75), Lemon Tarragon Mayonnaise (page 77), commercial mango chutney, whole-grain mustard, and caper berries.

What about ketchup? We rarely use it—except possibly with hamburgers. It's too sweet and muscles out most other flavors.

BREADS

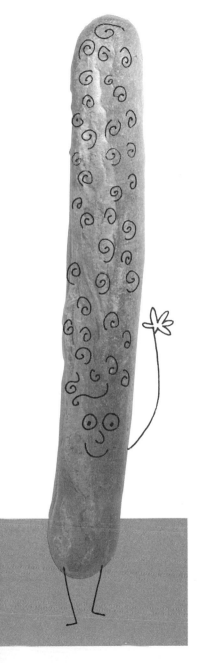

Bread is the other critical factor in a successful sandwich. Generally, our kids prefer packaged, commercial sandwich breads. Unfortunately, many commercial brands are loaded with hydrogenated oils and too much sugar. Look for bread that primarily contains flour, water, yeast, and salt. Even many so-called health-food breads are packed with multiple sweeteners that render them more akin to cake. Read the ingredients on the package and look for "real" breads that you and your children enjoy eating.

We grown-ups prefer fresh-baked country breads and rolls with crunchy crusts and soft, chewy centers. The best ones are made with a significant portion of high-gluten flour, which gives them texture and weight. Many such breads are found around the country, turned out by artisanal bakeries. Most are sold in a simple, paper wrapping. Avoid storing them in plastic bags in the refrigerator, or they will quickly reduce to soggy, chewy parodies of themselves. Leave these fresh-baked breads overnight in the paper bag they came in. Stored in this manner, a well-made bread will maintain its freshness from sundown through lunch the following day. It's not supposed to last much longer.

Whole-wheat versus white bread? With its added fiber and other nutritional properties, whole-wheat bread is better for your health. But if your diet is otherwise balanced, we don't consider this much of a selling point. It's those insidious hydrogenated oils and sugars in many commercial breads—both whole-wheat and white—that compromise health. Enjoy your sandwiches on breads made from real, wholesome ingredients.

Remember that little things can make a big difference. A sprinkling of coarse salt will heighten flavor. Likewise, a touch of cilantro, a leaf or two of basil, a sliced fig, a hint of curry powder, or a crusty roll can transform an otherwise banal lunch into a special midday meal.

Avocado, Parmesan, AND SLICED Onion

PREPARATION TIME: 5 minutes

Sometimes we gaze into the refrigerator at lunchtime and wonder despairingly where all the food has gone. But there's usually a chunk of tangy, nutty Parmesan cheese tucked away in a corner, and maybe a stray avocado. Add a slice or two of onion, some mayonnaise, and two pieces of bread, and you have a pretty decent lunch after all.

---

1 teaspoon mayonnaise

2 slices country bread

2 or 3 thin slices Parmesan cheese

1 or 2 thin slices onion

2 slices or spoonfuls ripe avocado

Spread the mayonnaise on 1 slice of bread. Lay down the Parmesan cheese, onion, and avocado. Close the sandwich with the remaining bread slice and cut in half.

Makes 1 sandwich

OUR FAVORITE SANDWICH BREADS

Bread makes the difference. It gives a sandwich character and acts as a framework for flavor. You wouldn't mount a favorite painting in a frame you didn't like, and you shouldn't frame a fine sandwich with mediocre bread. Bakery-fresh country breads are our first choice, but some packaged, commercial breads are also good. The following are among our family's favorite breads:

PUGLIESE: an oblong, crusty white or whole-wheat loaf

BAGUETTE: a French classic, long and narrow, usually white

FOCACCIA: a dimpled, light-textured bread, often made with savory toppings such as onion, cheese, or tomato

HUMMUS-AND-SALAD-STUFFED Pita

PREPARATION TIME: 5 minutes

Our kids love eating Middle Eastern pita bread because of its round shape. Here it is paired with another Middle Eastern specialty, hummus. The latter is easy to make at home, but good commercial hummus is available in many supermarkets. The sprouts provide a nutty, crunchy contrast to the smooth purée, and the sesame chile oil adds some spice. Look for the oil in the Asian foods section or among the cooking oils at your local supermarket. If you don't have pita in the house, use whatever bread you do have and make this sandwich between two traditional slices.

---

1 pita bread round
¼ cup hummus, homemade (page 54) or purchased
½ teaspoon sesame chile oil (optional)
2 slices tomato
6 thin slices cucumber
1 green onion, white part only, thinly sliced
A handful of sunflower or alfalfa sprouts

Cut off the top quarter of the pita bread. Carefully insert it into the bottom of the larger, hollow pocket for added strength. The pita tears easily, so work slowly to open the pocket. Spread the hummus inside the pocket. If using, drizzle the sesame chile oil over the hummus. Insert the tomato, cucumber, and green onion slices, and top them with the sprouts.

Makes 1 sandwich

CIABATTA ROLLS: more of a small loaf than a roll, about 8 inches long, with a light, delicate crust

PITA BREAD: a round, flat, white or whole-wheat Middle Eastern bread that can be opened into a pocket

SOURDOUGH: tangy, bright-textured bread made with a sourdough culture rather than yeast

TORTILLA: Mexican flat bread made with wheat or corn flour

Prosciutto AND SWEET BUTTER ON A Baguette

PREPARATION TIME: 3 minutes

Forget about ham and cheese. Prosciutto, a sweet-and-salty dry-cured Italian ham, is so flavorful on its own, it needs nothing more than a touch of butter as a sandwich foil. Thinly sliced Italian *sopressata* (a spiced dry sausage) or a dry-cured French sausage, usually labeled simply *saucisson,* can be substituted. Either one is more distinctive and flavorful than typically bland American versions, and is worth seeking out in better markets.

In fact, you may substitute any thinly sliced cold cut for the prosciutto. The meat should never be thickly layered, as it so often is in typical "deli-style" sandwiches in the United States. It's the crusty, fresh bread and sweet (unsalted) butter that provide substance here. Think of the meat as a garnish.

Is it any wonder that these spare meat sandwiches on buttered breads are so popular throughout the Mediterranean countries? The flavors are so pure and seductive. Grown-ups will enjoy this sandwich with a few olives on the side.

½ baguette (6 to 8 inches long)
½ to 1 tablespoon unsalted butter
2 ounces (about 4 slices) prosciutto, thinly sliced

Split the baguette in half lengthwise and spread butter to taste evenly across one of the bread halves. Loosely drape the prosciutto slices over the butter. Close the sandwich with the top half of the baguette.

Makes 1 sandwich

A TIP FOR SOFTENING DAY-OLD BAGUETTES

If your day-old French baguette or Pugliese loaf is too hard, preheat the oven to 200°F. Moisten your hands with water and rub them over the bread several times. Place the loaf in the oven for 5 to 7 minutes. It will soften for easy slicing.

Prosciutto, Fresh Fig, GOAT CHEESE, AND Rosemary

PREPARATION TIME: 5 minutes

This sandwich offers a lively juxtaposition of distinctive flavors. The ingredients may seem somewhat exotic at first, but they are readily available at most fine food shops. Look for a mild, easy-to-spread goat cheese, and use it in an amount that suits your taste.

1 teaspoon extra-virgin olive oil
2 slices country bread
Fresh goat cheese to taste (about 1 tablespoon)
½ teaspoon minced fresh rosemary
1 fresh fig, sliced lengthwise
2 thin slices prosciutto or other dry-cured ham

Spread the olive oil on 1 slice of bread. Add a thin layer of goat cheese and sprinkle the rosemary on the cheese. Top with the fig and prosciutto slices. Close the sandwich with the remaining bread slice and cut in half.

Makes 1 sandwich

Brie AND GRATED Carrot ON Raisin BREAD

PREPARATION TIME: 5 minutes

You can substitute any mild, soft cheese, such as Camembert, for the Brie. We like the mild sweetness of raisin bread, and the way it pairs with carrots and creamy, soft cheese. However, feel free to experiment with other breads as well. Olive bread, for example, is another excellent choice.

½ teaspoon extra-virgin olive oil
2 slices raisin bread
2 or 3 slices ripe Brie cheese
2 tablespoons grated carrot

Spread the olive oil on 1 slice of bread. Top with the cheese and sprinkle the grated carrot evenly over the cheese. Close the sandwich with the remaining bread slice and cut in half.

Makes 1 sandwich

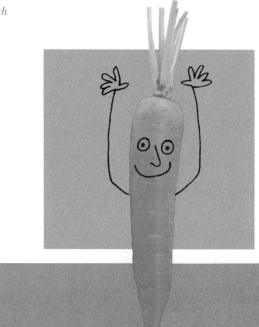

CURRIED Egg Salad

PREPARATION TIME: 10 minutes

A touch of curry and fresh cilantro add high notes to this old standard. Fittingly, egg salad relies heavily on mayonnaise, which is also made from eggs. Since we don't always have time to make our own mayonnaise, we seek out alternative high-quality commercial brands, usually made with canola oil, that don't rely on sweetness for flavor. This recipe yields a mild curry taste. If your home spice rack doesn't hold curry powder, it is easily found in most supermarkets. Sprouts, used as garnish, offer a crunchy contrast in texture.

CURRIED MAYONNAISE:

¼ cup mayonnaise, homemade (page 33) or purchased
1 tablespoon Dijon mustard
1½ teaspoons curry powder

6 hard-boiled eggs (see page 34), peeled and sliced
1 celery stalk, diced (about ⅓ cup)
2 tablespoons minced red onion
2 tablespoons minced fresh cilantro
Salt and freshly ground pepper to taste
1 or 2 tomatoes, sliced
A handful of alfalfa sprouts

To make the Curried Mayonnaise, in a small bowl, combine the mayonnaise, mustard, and curry powder and mix well.

In another bowl, using a fork, mix together the eggs, celery, and onion, gently breaking up the egg slices. Stir in the mayonnaise and then the cilantro. Season with salt and pepper. When making the sandwiches, garnish them with the tomato slices and alfalfa sprouts.

Makes enough for 4 sandwiches

Goat Cheese, CUCUMBER, Tomato, AND Lettuce ON FOCACCIA

PREPARATION TIME: 5 minutes

These simple and pure flavors team up admirably on focaccia. Plain or herb-flavored focaccia will both work. Soft ciabatta rolls make a nice framework for this sandwich as well.

---

1 teaspoon extra-virgin olive oil
2 pieces focaccia, each about 4 inches square and ½ inch thick
1 to 2 tablespoons fresh goat cheese
½ teaspoon dried thyme
6 to 8 thin slices cucumber
Pinch of salt
2 thin slices tomato
A handful of lettuce leaves, baby greens, or arugula

Spread the olive oil on 1 piece of focaccia. Spread on the goat cheese, adding it to taste. Sprinkle the thyme over the cheese. Layer the cucumber slices over the cheese, and season with the salt. Top with the tomato slices and the lettuce. Close the sandwich with the remaining focaccia piece, press together firmly, and cut in half.

Makes 1 sandwich

Salmon Salad SANDWICH
WITH **LEMON-TARRAGON** Mayonnaise

PREPARATION TIME: 15 minutes

This is the perfect recipe for using up leftover cooked salmon steaks or fillets. (You can also make this with canned salmon.) Bright-tasting, lemony mayonnaise offers a fine foil to the rich, meaty fish.

LEMON-TARRAGON MAYONNAISE:

⅓ cup mayonnaise, homemade (page 33) or purchased
Zest of 1 lemon, finely chopped
1½ teaspoons dried tarragon
1 teaspoon Dijon mustard

2 cups cooked salmon chunks, picked over for bones
3 green onions, white part only, chopped
¼ teaspoon salt
8 pieces focaccia, each about 4 inches square and ½ inch thick
Salad greens for garnish

To make the Lemon-Tarragon Mayonnaise, in a small bowl, combine the mayonnaise, lemon zest, tarragon, and mustard and mix well.

In another bowl, combine the salmon, mayonnaise, green onions, and salt. Using a fork, blend the ingredients together. Divide the salmon salad among 4 of the focaccia pieces. Garnish with the greens. Close the sandwiches with the remaining focaccia pieces and cut each in half.

Makes 4 sandwiches

Smoked Salmon TORTILLA
WITH FRESH GOAT CHEESE, DILL, AND Capers

PREPARATION TIME: 5 minutes

This rolled tortilla sandwich is not only easy to prepare, but also extremely portable, making it well suited to a working lunch. Many commercial tortillas contain guar gum, which both increases shelf life and gives normally soft tortillas an unpleasant, chewy, gummy texture. Read package labels carefully to avoid this ingredient.

⅓ cup crumbled fresh goat cheese

4 burrito-sized flour tortillas (about 10 inches in diameter)

¼ pound smoked salmon, thinly sliced

3 fresh dill sprigs, chopped

1 tablespoon capers (optional)

Divide the goat cheese equally among the tortillas, spreading it evenly over the surface. Lay the smoked salmon slices on the goat cheese, then distribute the dill and the capers (if using). Roll up each tortilla into a cylinder. Cut each cylinder in half, or into 3-inch-long pieces, for easy eating and to expose the eye-catching pinwheel pattern of the cheese and salmon.

Makes 4 wraps; serves 2

SMOKED Turkey, Tomato, AND FRESH Basil

PREPARATION TIME: 5 minutes

Fresh basil, with its sweet, almost licorice-like flavors, transports this sandwich far from the ordinary. We often use basil as a refreshing alternative to lettuce or baby salad greens.

---

1 teaspoon mayonnaise, homemade (page 33) or purchased
2 slices country bread
2 ounces smoked turkey, thinly sliced (3 to 4 slices)
2 thin slices tomato
4 fresh basil leaves

Spread the mayonnaise on 1 slice of bread. Layer the turkey, tomato, and basil on top. Close the sandwich with the remaining bread slice and cut in half.

Makes 1 sandwich

Chicken WITH ROASTED Red Pepper, Basil, AND AIOLI

PREPARATION TIME: 5 minutes

Here is a great way to use leftover roast chicken (page 256). We love the flavors of chicken and roasted red peppers, which we always keep on hand. To be honest, we rarely make aioli expressly for this sandwich. Instead, we use leftover aioli from a previous dinner. So add an extra 10 minutes to the preparation time here if you're planning to make aioli on the spot. Or use commercial mayonnaise, with or without minced garlic, for more immediate gratification.

1 teaspoon aioli (page 34)
2 slices country bread
¼ roasted red bell pepper, peeled and seeded (see page 35)
About 2 ounces cooked chicken meat
4 fresh basil leaves

Spread the aioli on 1 slice of bread. Top with the bell pepper, then the chicken, and add the basil leaves. Close the sandwich with the remaining bread slice and cut in half.

Makes 1 sandwich

Curried Chicken SALAD
WITH Green Apple

PREPARATION TIME: 10 minutes

How often have you forgotten about that leftover chicken carcass in the refrigerator, only to find it weeks later, spoiled? If you're not making chicken stock, this is the perfect solution for leftover roast chicken (page 256). Just pull off all the remaining meat and use it for the next day's lunch sandwich. A tart apple and some mango chutney (available in many supermarkets) add bright flavors to the sandwich.

¼ cup Curried Mayonnaise (page 75)
1 tablespoon minced onion
2 cups diced cooked chicken
½ tart green apple such as Granny Smith, unpeeled, cored, and diced
2 tablespoons mango chutney (optional)
Baby salad greens or arugula for garnish

In a bowl, using a fork, stir together the mayonnaise, onion, chicken, and apple until well mixed, then stir in the chutney, if using. When making the sandwiches, garnish them with the greens.

Makes enough for 4 sandwiches

COUNTRY PATÉ WITH Cornichons
AND SLICED ONION

PREPARATION TIME: 5 minutes

This is a study in contrast. Rich, robust paté is offset by tiny, tangy French cornichons and the mild bite of onion. Mustard adds extra zing, although it's not required. We also enjoy this sandwich open faced.

---

1 teaspoon whole-grain or Dijon mustard (optional)
2 slices sourdough or country bread
1 or 2 thin slices full-bodied paté such as pâté de compagne
   or duck liver mousse pâté
2 small cornichons, halved lengthwise
2 thin slices onion

If using, spread the mustard on 1 slice of bread. Layer the pâté, cornichons, and onion on top. Close the sandwich with the remaining bread slice and cut in half.

Makes 1 sandwich

Sausage, ONIONS, AND Roasted Red Pepper

PREPARATION TIME: 5 minutes   **COOKING TIME:** 12 minutes

This robust hot sandwich requires a bit more labor than most sandwiches described here, but the flavors are worth the effort. We parboil the sausage to reduce cooking time and keep it moist.

---

1 sweet or hot Italian sausage
1 tablespoon extra-virgin olive oil
½ onion, sliced
1 roasted red bell pepper, peeled and seeded (see page 35),
   then cut lengthwise into narrow strips
½ teaspoon dried thyme
⅛ teaspoon red pepper flakes (optional)
1 Italian-style sourdough roll or other complementary roll
1 teaspoon whole-grain or Dijon mustard

Using a fork, poke a series of holes in the opposite sides of the sausage. Pour water to a depth of 1 inch into a small saucepan and bring to a boil over high heat. Place the sausage in the pan, cover, reduce the heat to medium, and simmer until cooked through, about 5 minutes. Remove the sausage from the pan and discard the water. Cut the sausage in half lengthwise.

Dry the pan, add the olive oil, and heat over medium heat. Add the onion and sauté until translucent, about 2 minutes. Stir in the roasted red pepper strips, thyme, and the pepper flakes, if using. Cook for 1 minute longer, then push the onion and bell pepper to one side of the pan. Add the sausage halves to the exposed pan surface and cook, turning as needed, until lightly browned, about 2 minutes per side. Remove from the heat.

Halve the roll lengthwise and remove some of the soft interior to make room for the sausage and peppers. Spread the mustard on the bottom of the roll and top with the onion, pepper strips, and sausage. Close the sandwich and cut in half.

Makes 1 robust sandwich

Sopressata, ROASTED RED PEPPER, MOZZARELLA, AND Cilantro

PREPARATION TIME: 5 minutes

Sopressata, a cured Italian sausage flavored with lemon and spices, then aged for at least forty days, is available in many delicatessens. Fresh cilantro heightens the flavors of the other sandwich ingredients.

¼ teaspoon extra-virgin olive oil

2 slices country bread

2 ounces (3 or 4 slices) sopressata or any salami, thinly sliced

½ roasted red bell pepper, peeled and seeded (see page 35)

1 slice fresh mozzarella cheese

2 tablespoons chopped fresh cilantro

Brush the olive oil on 1 slice of bread. Layer the *sopressata*, bell pepper, and mozzarella on top. Garnish with the cilantro. Close the sandwich with the remaining bread slice and cut in half.

Makes 1 sandwich

Notes

GRILLED SANDWICHES

A hot grilled sandwich always puts a bright face on lunch. When we were children, we reveled in the joy of grilled "American cheese" on rye bread. Our kids love this simple pleasure, too, especially on weekends, and also during vacations when we have access to a stove top. (They like grilled cheese for breakfast, too.)

But today, with so many other fine cheeses on the market, we rarely use the bland, yellow dairy product known as American cheese. Try a New York or Wisconsin Cheddar if, for nostalgia's sake, you must have that orange-colored stuff in your sandwich. (Some very fine orange-hued English Cheddars are available as well. Their color comes from natural carotene in the grass eaten by dairy cattle. By contrast, most American Cheddars are artificially colored with a benign natural coloring.)

Most cheeses will grill well, as long as they are not too crumbly. We often use French or Swiss Gruyère, which has a vaguely nutty flavor and melts evenly. Softer cheeses such as Brie and mozzarella melt nicely, too. And while a simple grilled cheese sandwich can be heavenly, the addition of a few other ingredients can lead to greater enjoyment with little extra effort. Do not use too many ingredients, or too much of any one ingredient, or the cheese will overflow onto the hot skillet and burn. It's possible to avoid a messy grill by using one of a variety of electric sandwich presses currently on the market. We've had great success with the Cuisinart sandwich grill.

Because many fillings include cheese or meat with high fat content, grilling sandwiches requires only a little oil to prevent the bread from sticking. Extra-virgin olive oil is our choice because it also adds flavor and nuance—far more than neutral oils such as canola or safflower. Although 1 tablespoon is plenty, you may want to use more or less oil, depending on your preference. To our taste, butter isn't much of an option here. It's too heavy and certainly less healthy.

GRILLED Ham WITH Mozzarella, ROASTED Red Pepper, AND Basil

Substantial and colorful, this sandwich is loaded with mouthwatering flavors. Enjoy it with a few black olives on the side.

---

4 thin slices imported Black Forest ham or other ham of choice
4 slices sandwich bread
2 slices fresh mozzarella cheese
½ roasted red bell pepper, peeled, seeded, and halved (see page 35)
4 fresh basil leaves
1 tablespoon extra-virgin olive oil

Divide the ham slices evenly between 2 slices of the bread. Place 1 mozzarella slice on top of each ham portion, then top each with a piece of the bell pepper and 2 basil leaves. Close the sandwiches with the remaining bread slices and press firmly together with your hands.

In a large, heavy skillet or griddle, heat the olive oil over medium-high heat. Place the sandwiches on the hot skillet, add a weight (see sidebar), and cook until golden brown on the bottom, 3 to 4 minutes. Remove the weight, flip the sandwiches with a spatula, and replace the weight. Cook until the second side is golden brown, 2 to 3 minutes longer, reducing the heat if the pan begins to smoke. Cut each sandwich in half and serve at once.

Makes 2 sandwiches

TECHNIQUES FOR A PERFECT GRILLED SANDWICH

A grilled sandwich needs to be pressed from the top while it's cooking. That way, the heat is evenly distributed throughout, and the sandwich holds together more tightly. You can buy a griddle press, which is just a flat piece of iron with a handle on it. We bought a griddle press not long ago and returned home only to discover that it didn't fit into our favorite cast-iron skillet, so we continue to use our time-honored technology: A teakettle filled with water. A second skillet can also effectively serve as a weight. If you don't have a griddle press, teakettle, or other heavy object handy, simply press down regularly on your sandwiches with a spatula. It's not practical, but it works. High-tech parents may also purchase a neat and effective electric sandwich press.

GRILLED Gruyère AND Tomato

PREPARATION TIME: 3 minutes   **COOKING TIME:** 7 minutes

This is basically a grilled pizza sandwich made with nutty, rich Gruyère cheese, which is made primarily in France and Switzerland. Other firm-textured, aged cheeses will work here as well.

4 to 6 slices Gruyère cheese
4 slices country bread
2 to 4 slices tomato
½ teaspoon dried thyme
2 tablespoons extra-virgin olive oil

Divide the cheese between 2 slices of the bread. Top with the tomato slices and sprinkle with the thyme. Close the sandwiches with the remaining bread slices and press firmly together with your hands.

In a large, heavy skillet or griddle, heat the olive oil over medium-high heat. Place the sandwiches on the hot skillet, add a weight (see sidebar, page 87), and cook until golden brown on the bottom, 3 to 4 minutes. Remove the weight, flip the sandwiches with a spatula, and replace the weight. Cook until the second side is golden brown, 2 to 3 minutes longer, reducing the heat if the pan begins to smoke. Cut each sandwich in half and serve at once.

Makes 2 sandwiches

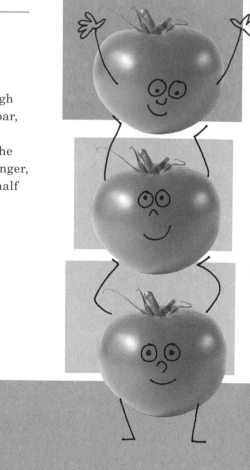

GRILLED Ham with Italian Fontina, TOMATO, and Mustard

PREPARATION TIME: 8 minutes   **COOKING TIME:** 7 minutes

Mild, creamy Italian Fontina cheese has a slightly sweet quality that pairs well with salty ham. The tomato adds moisture and a little bite, as does the mustard.

¼ teaspoon whole-grain or Dijon mustard
4 slices sandwich or country bread
4 thin slices dry-cured or cooked ham of choice
2 slices Italian Fontina or other soft, mild cheese
2 large slices tomato, each about ⅛ inch thick
1 tablespoon extra-virgin olive oil

Spread equal amounts of the mustard on 2 slices of the bread. Divide the ham between the mustard-topped bread slices. Place 1 slice of Fontina on top of each ham portion. The cheese slices should be large enough to cover most of the sandwich. Place 1 tomato slice on each cheese slice. Close the sandwiches with the remaining bread slices and press firmly together with your hands.

In a large, heavy skillet or griddle, heat the olive oil over medium-high heat. Place the sandwiches on the hot skillet, add a weight (see sidebar, page 87), and cook until golden brown on the bottom, 3 to 4 minutes. Remove the weight, flip the sandwiches with a spatula, and replace the weight. Cook until the second side is golden brown, 2 to 3 minutes longer, reducing the heat if the pan begins to smoke. Cut each sandwich in half and serve at once.

Makes 2 sandwiches

GRILLED FRESH Mozzarella, TOMATO, AND Arugula

PREPARATION TIME: 3 minutes   **COOKING TIME:** 7 minutes

Mild mozzarella cheese contrasts nicely with the peppery character of arugula and the tang of a tomato vinaigrette. Vary the amounts of tomato, cheese, and arugula to fit your taste and the size of your sandwich, which may also be enjoyed without grilling.

---

2 tablespoons extra-virgin olive oil
½ teaspoon balsamic vinegar
Pinch of salt
2 to 4 slices tomato
2 to 4 slices fresh mozzarella cheese
4 slices sourdough or sandwich bread
4 to 6 arugula leaves

In a bowl, mix 1 tablespoon of the olive oil with the vinegar and salt. Add the tomato slices, toss gently, and set aside. Divide the mozzarella between 2 of the bread slices. Top with the tomato slices and then the arugula. Close the sandwiches with the remaining bread slices and press firmly together with your hands.

In a large, heavy skillet or griddle, heat the remaining olive oil over medium-high heat. Place the sandwiches on the hot skillet, add a weight (see sidebar, page 87), and cook until golden brown on the bottom, 3 to 4 minutes. Remove the weight, flip the sandwiches with a spatula, and replace the weight. Cook until the second side is golden brown, 2 to 3 minutes longer, reducing the heat if the pan begins to smoke. Cut each sandwich in half and serve at once.

Makes 2 sandwiches

GRILLED Raclette AND Onion

PREPARATION TIME: 3 minutes   **COOKING TIME:** 7 minutes

Raclette is a pungent, firm, buttery cheese made in the French and Swiss Alps. The French version is often less expensive than the Swiss, although they are equally delicious. The French verb *racler* means "to scrape." Typically, the cheese is heated in front of a hot fireplace. As it melts, a portion is scraped off onto a plate and enjoyed with potatoes, onions, and cornichons (small French pickles). You can also make this sandwich with another good melting cheese.

---

4 slices raclette cheese

4 slices rye or other sandwich bread

2 to 4 thin slices onion

3 cornichons, halved lengthwise (optional)

½ teaspoon dried thyme

1 tablespoon extra-virgin olive oil

Divide the cheese between 2 slices of the bread. Top with the onion slices, cornichon halves (if using), and the thyme. Close the sandwiches with the remaining bread slices and press firmly together with your hands.

In a large, heavy skillet or griddle, heat the olive oil over medium-high heat. Place the sandwiches on the hot skillet, add a weight (see sidebar, page 87), and cook until golden brown on the bottom, 3 to 4 minutes. Remove the weight, flip the sandwiches with a spatula, and replace the weight. Cook until the second side is golden brown, 2 to 3 minutes longer, reducing the heat if the pan begins to smoke. Cut each sandwich in half and serve at once.

Makes 2 sandwiches

Tortilla Flats WITH FRESH Salsa
AND GUACAMOLE

PREPARATION TIME: 20 minutes   **COOKING TIME:** 3 minutes

These crispy, stuffed corn tortillas are Mexican-inspired grilled cheese sandwiches. They can be eaten with a knife and fork or cut in half and held by hand. Hot tortillas with melted cheese alone make a fine snack or breakfast, but stuffed with additional ingredients and garnished with salsa and guacamole, they make a satisfying and easy lunch or dinner. The preparation time here reflects both the making of the salsa and the guacamole. To save time, use purchased fresh salsa.

We use corn, instead of flour, tortillas. Panfried corn tortillas carry more flavor and have a crunchier texture. Look for them made with only corn flour, lime, and water for the best result. (If possible, avoid buying tortillas—corn or flour—that contain guar gum. It gives them an unpleasant, chewy, sticky character.)

SALSA (OPTIONAL):

> ½ or 1 jalapeño chile
> 1 cup water
> ⅓ cup diced red onion
> 1 clove garlic, minced
> ½ cup finely chopped fresh cilantro
> 4 cups chopped tomato (about 6 tomatoes)
> 2 tablespoons fresh lime juice
> 1 teaspoon salt

FOR THE BASIC SANDWICH:

> 2 tablespoons extra-virgin olive oil
> 2 corn tortillas
> 4 slices Cheddar or Jack cheese

OPTIONAL INGREDIENTS:

Chopped fresh cilantro

Slices or spoonfuls of ripe avocado

Tomato slices

Sliced or chopped onion, raw or sautéed

Sliced ham

Guacamole (page 57)

If you are making, rather than purchasing, the salsa, in a small saucepan, combine the jalapeño (using the lesser amount for a milder result) and water, bring to a boil, and boil for 5 minutes. Drain and rinse in cold water. Remove the seeds and stem, then chop coarsely. Place the chile and all the remaining ingredients in a blender and pulse 4 to 6 times to blend; do not purée, or the texture will be lost. You should have about 4 cups salsa.

To make the basic sandwich, in a small, heavy skillet or sauté pan, heat the olive oil over medium-high heat. Place 1 tortilla in the oil. Place 3 cheese slices on the tortilla, then top with 1 or more optional ingredients. (Avoid using too many items. If the sandwich is more than $\frac{1}{4}$ to $\frac{1}{2}$ inch thick, it will not cook evenly or hold together.) Cover with the remaining slice of cheese and the second tortilla. Press down briefly with a spatula and cook until fairly crisp on the underside, about 1 minute. Using the spatula, gently flip the sandwich and cook, occasionally pressing down on the sandwich, until the cheese is melted, another 45 seconds. If the cheese is not thoroughly melted, reduce the heat to medium and cook for 30 seconds longer, flipping again once or twice. Serve immediately with the salsa and the guacamole, if using, either as a topping or on the side. Serve at once.

Makes 1 sandwich

S O U

chapter
5

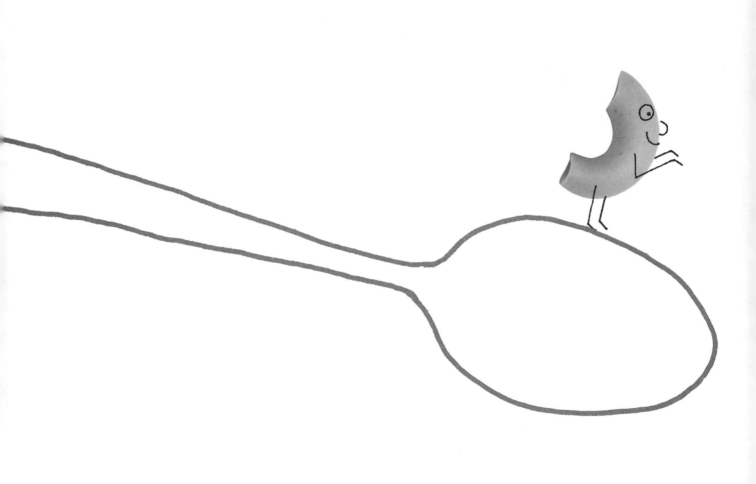

Great for lunch and supper, soups are inexpensive and easy to prepare. Although many people think of soup as a first course, we often enjoy ours as the centerpiece of a meal. We might start off with a simple salad, then serve the soup with crusty country bread on the side. The meal is topped off with a little cheese or dessert. It's a straightforward and satisfying three-course endeavor. You can pair leftover soup with any of the sandwiches featured on pages 70 – 93. Perhaps the best thing about soup is that it usually tastes even better when it is reheated. Most soups can also be frozen for up to three months, which is handy on those evenings when you want a good dinner but do not have the time to cook.

FRESH Corn AND Tomato SOUP

PREPARATION TIME: 15 minutes   **COOKING TIME:** 30 minutes

This recipe was given to us by our Mexican friend Martha Vierra, who has raised three children, works full time, and still finds joy in the kitchen. A creamy, smooth base contrasts nicely with the crunchy corn kernels. If you're cautious regarding spice, start by using half the recommended amount of jalapeño pepper.

---

8 fresh plum tomatoes or 1 can (28 ounces) plum tomatoes
4 ears corn
½ cup, plus 4 teaspoons sour cream
2 tablespoons extra-virgin olive oil
½ cup minced onion
1 clove garlic, minced
1 small jalapeño chile, seeded and minced
1 teaspoon salt
1½ cups chicken stock (page 105) or canned low-sodium chicken broth
Freshly ground pepper to taste
1 to 2 tablespoons chopped fresh cilantro

If using fresh tomatoes, peel them (see page 32) and chop coarsely. If using canned tomatoes, drain them and chop coarsely.

Shuck the corn, then cut off the kernels from the cobs and reserve the kernels. In a blender or food processor, combine the tomatoes and ½ cup sour cream and process until a liquid forms. Set aside.

In a large soup pot, heat the olive oil over medium heat. Add the onion, garlic, and jalapeño and sauté until tender, 3 to 4 minutes. Add the tomato–sour cream liquid and salt, reduce the heat to low, and simmer for 5 minutes. Add the corn and stir in the chicken stock. Cover and simmer for 20 minutes.

Season the soup with pepper. Ladle into soup bowls and garnish each serving with 1 teaspoon sour cream and a sprinkling of cilantro.

Serves 4

HEARTY Lentil
AND Vegetable SOUP

PREPARATION TIME: 15 minutes   **COOKING TIME:** 40 minutes

Lentils are inexpensive, nutritious, richly textured, and downright delicious. Our kids love this soup with its tasty kale, parsnips, carrots, and tomatoes. The addition of wine is optional, but it adds a bit of brightness and quickly loses its alcohol to evaporation while cooking. Enjoy this soup accompanied with crusty country bread.

---

8 cups water
2½ teaspoons salt
1 cup green lentils, picked over and rinsed
3 carrots, peeled and coarsely chopped
2 parsnips, peeled and coarsely chopped
2 celery stalks, chopped
2 cups chopped kale
4 plum tomatoes, coarsely chopped
1 teaspoon dried thyme
1 teaspoon dried oregano
½ teaspoon ground cumin
1 cup red wine (optional)
¼ cup freshly grated Parmesan cheese
Freshly ground pepper to taste

In a large pot, combine the water and salt and bring to a boil over high heat. Add the lentils, cover, reduce the heat to low, and simmer until tender, about 20 minutes. Add all the vegetables, herbs, cumin, and the wine, if using. Raise the heat to high, bring to a boil, cover, reduce the heat to low, and simmer until the vegetables are tender, about 20 minutes.

Ladle into soup bowls and garnish each serving with Parmesan cheese and a grinding of pepper. Serve at once.

Serves 4 to 6

Curry AND Ginger Miso SOUP
WITH Udon

PREPARATION TIME: 10 minutes   **COOKING TIME:** 15 minutes

Miso soup, the "chicken soup" of Japan, translates easily to an American kitchen. Many supermarkets now carry soy-based miso paste, in a variety of colors and flavors, in the dairy section. Udon, Japanese wheat noodles, are also widely available, cook quickly, and add heartiness to the soup.

3½ quarts water
5 tablespoons red miso paste
1 tablespoon grated fresh ginger, or ½ teaspoon ground ginger
1 teaspoon curry powder
½ teaspoon ground cumin
1 clove garlic, minced
2 carrots, peeled and diced
3 cups tiny broccoli florets
½ pound firm tofu, cut into 1-inch cubes
½ pound dried udon
4 green onions, green and white parts, thinly sliced
½ cup bean sprouts
Red pepper flakes or chipotle chile flakes for garnish (optional)

In a soup pot, bring 1½ quarts (6 cups) of the water to a boil over medium-high heat. Whisk in the miso paste. Add the ginger, curry, cumin, and garlic and mix well, whisking until the paste is totally dissolved. Add the carrots, broccoli, and tofu. Cover, reduce the heat to low, and simmer 10 minutes.

While the soup is cooking, in a separate pan, bring the remaining 2 quarts water to a boil over high heat. Add the noodles and, when they begin to boil, adjust the heat to medium and cook until tender, about 4 minutes. Drain in a colander.

To serve, divide the noodles evenly among soup bowls. Ladle the broth, vegetables, and tofu over the noodles. Garnish with the green onions, bean sprouts, and the pepper flakes, if using. Serve immediately.

Serves 4

EASY Onion SOUP

PREPARATION TIME: 15 minutes   **COOKING TIME:** 30 minutes

This variation on the old French standard is a fine last-minute recipe.
Most kids will overcome their aversion to onions when they see plenty of
goopy, melted cheese on top of the bowl. We generally use chicken stock
or broth, but vegetable or beef broth will work equally well.

---

3 tablespoons extra-virgin olive oil
2 large cloves garlic, minced
4 large onions, thinly sliced into rings and rings cut in half
2 teaspoons dried thyme
1 bay leaf
1 teaspoon salt, plus salt to taste
¼ teaspoon freshly ground pepper, plus pepper to taste
6 cups chicken stock (page 105) or low-sodium canned chicken broth
4 slices country bread, each about ½ inch thick, lightly toasted
1 cup freshly grated Gruyère or other mild, firm cheese

In a soup pot, heat the olive oil over medium-high heat. Add the garlic
and onions and sauté, stirring to coat them well with the oil, for about 2
minutes. Stir in the thyme, bay leaf, 1 teaspoon salt, ¼ teaspoon pepper
and reduce the heat to low. Cover and simmer until the onions are
tender, about 20 minutes.

Meanwhile, in a separate pot, bring the stock to a boil. When the onions
are tender, add the boiling stock to the onion pot. Simmer for 5 minutes
to blend the flavors, then remove and discard the bay leaf. Season with
the additional salt and pepper.

Preheat the broiler. Ladle the soup into individual flameproof bowls on a
baking sheet. Place 1 slice of toast on top of each portion, and top each
slice with ¼ cup of the Gruyère cheese. Place the bowls under the broiler
for 1 minute to melt the cheese. Serve immediately.

Serves 4

Potato, LEEK, AND Fennel SOUP

PREPARATION TIME: 15 minutes   **COOKING TIME:** 45 minutes

Creamy, yet delicate, this soup features traditional favorites from the
produce department.

---

1 tablespoon extra-virgin olive oil
2 slices bacon, cut into matchsticks
2 leeks, white part only, sliced
3 pounds potatoes, peeled and diced
1 fennel bulb, leaves and stems removed, then diced
2 teaspoons salt, plus salt to taste
5 cups chicken stock (page 105) or canned low-sodium chicken broth
1 cup heavy cream
Freshly ground pepper to taste

In a soup pot, heat the olive oil over medium-high heat. Add the bacon
and fry until crisp, about 4 minutes. Add the leeks and potatoes and
sauté, stirring, until the vegetables are well coated with the oils, about
3 minutes. Add the fennel and cook for 2 more minutes. Sprinkle in the
2 teaspoons salt and stir well. Pour in the stock, bring to a boil, cover,
reduce the heat to low, and cook until the vegetables are tender, about
30 minutes.

In small batches, in a blender, briefly pulse the soup to form a coarse
purée. As each batch is processed, pour it into a large bowl. When all the
soup has been puréed, return it to the pot over medium heat, bring to a
simmer, and cook for 5 more minutes to heat through. Stir in the cream
and heat to serving temperature.

Season the soup with the additional salt and with pepper. Ladle into
soup bowls and serve at once.

Serves 6 to 8

ROASTED **Red Pepper** SOUP

PREPARATION TIME: 25 to 45 minutes, depending on method for roasting peppers   **COOKING TIME:** 30 minutes

The unique sweet and tart flavors typical of red bell peppers shine in this soup. If you already have the roasted peppers on hand, the preparation time is reduced to 15 minutes. Do kids like red pepper soup? At our house it's classic: one does and the other doesn't. The dissenting palate invariably finds a substitute, or passes and waits for the main course.

---

2 tablespoons extra-virgin olive oil
1 onion, diced
7 roasted red bell peppers, peeled and seeded (see page 35)
2 teaspoons salt, plus salt to taste
3 cups chicken stock (page 105) or canned low-sodium chicken broth
¾ cup heavy cream
Freshly ground pepper to taste

In a large soup pot, heat the olive oil over medium heat. Add the onion and sauté until translucent, about 3 minutes. Add the bell peppers and the 2 teaspoons salt and continue cooking, stirring occasionally, for about 3 minutes. Add the stock, raise the heat to high, and bring to a boil. Cover, reduce the heat to low, and simmer for 15 minutes to blend the flavors.

In small batches, in a blender, process the soup until smooth. As each batch is processed, pour it into a large bowl. When all the soup has been puréed, return it to the pot over medium heat. Pour in the cream, bring to a simmer, and cook for 5 minutes to heat to serving temperature.

Season the soup with the additional salt and with pepper. Ladle into bowls and serve at once.

Serves 6

Split Pea SOUP

Nearly everyone knows this old-fashioned soup, but it still brings a fresh smile at mealtime. Creamy smooth, with chewy chunks of smoked ham, this split pea soup makes a winning first course. It also makes a good centerpiece with country bread and cheese or a grilled sandwich (pages 86 to 93) on the side. Leftovers work well for kids' lunches.

---

5 cups water

5 cups chicken stock (facing page) or canned low-sodium chicken broth

2 teaspoons salt, plus salt to taste

2 cups split peas, picked over and rinsed

3 ham hocks (about 1 pound total weight)

2 bay leaves

2 tablespoons extra-virgin olive oil

1 large white onion, diced

2 cloves garlic, finely chopped or minced

3 carrots, peeled and diced

3 celery stalks, diced

Freshly ground pepper to taste

In a large soup pot, combine the water, stock, and 2 teaspoons salt and bring to a boil over high heat. Add the split peas, ham hocks, and bay leaves. Cover, reduce the heat to low, and cook, stirring occasionally until the peas take on a puréed texture, about 50 minutes.

Remove and discard the bay leaves. Remove the ham hocks and, when cool enough to handle, cut the meat off the bones with a knife. Discard the bones and return the meat to the pot.

In a sauté pan, heat the olive oil over medium heat. Add the onion and garlic and sauté, stirring occasionally, for 2 minutes. Stir in the carrots and celery and sauté, stirring occasionally, until softened, about 3 minutes longer. Add the vegetables to the soup, cover, and simmer until the vegetables are tender and the soup has a smooth, thick consistency, about 30 minutes longer.

About 15 minutes before the soup is done, check its consistency. If it's too thick, add additional water or stock. If it's too thin, simmer uncovered until it thickens.

Season the soup with the additional salt and with pepper. Ladle into bowls and serve at once.

Serves 4 to 6

■ ● ■ ■ ■ ● ■ ■ ■ ■ ● ■ ■ ■ ● ■ ■ ■ ■ ● ■ ■ ■ ■ ● ■ ■ ■ ● ■ ■ ■ ■ ● ■ ■ ■ ● ● ■ ■ ■ ■ ● ■ ■ ■ ■ ● ●

CHICKEN STOCK

Chicken stock isn't quite soup. But it provides an easy, flavorful foundation for many of the soups offered in this book. It is also used in other dishes from beans to risottos to stews. You can use leftover chicken and chicken bones from roast chicken or raw chicken parts.

When we have time, we make chicken stock, but we admit that more often than not we don't. Instead, we usually buy canned chicken broth made from free-range chickens. It is comparable to canned low-sodium chicken broth, which we also use with equally fine results.

---

3 to 4 pounds cooked chicken carcass or raw chicken parts such as
*   backs, wings, and necks*
1 onion, coarsely chopped
1 large carrot, peeled and coarsely chopped
4 cloves garlic
½ teaspoon dried thyme
1 bay leaf
1 teaspoon salt
3 quarts water

In a large pot, combine all the ingredients and bring to a boil. Reduce the heat to low and cook, uncovered, for 1½ hours, skimming off any foam that collects on the surface. Remove from the heat and strain through a fine-mesh sieve into a clean container.

Discard the solids and let the stock cool. Cover and refrigerate until the fat congeals on the surface, then lift off the fat and discard. Use the stock immediately, or re-cover and refrigerate for up to 3 days or freeze for up to 3 months.

Makes about 2½ quarts

White Bean soup
with Kale

PREPARATION TIME: 15 minutes, plus soaking time for beans

COOKING TIME: $1^1/_2$ hours

Hearty and rich, this smooth-textured, creamy soup makes a fine centerpiece for a meal. Although we often substitute canned beans for dried beans, in this case we find that dried beans are best.

---

2 tablespoons extra-virgin olive oil

3 slices bacon, cut into matchsticks

1 onion, diced

3 cloves garlic, minced

1 celery stalk, chopped

1 carrot, peeled and diced

1 tablespoon dried rosemary

½ teaspoon salt, plus salt to taste

1½ cups dried white beans, soaked overnight or quick-soaked
(see page 35) and drained

6 cups chicken stock (page 105) or canned low-sodium chicken broth

2 cups firmly packed chopped kale

Freshly ground pepper to taste

In a large soup pot, heat the olive oil over medium-high heat. Add the bacon and fry until it begins to brown, about 4 minutes. Add the onion and garlic and sauté for 2 minutes. Add the celery, carrot, rosemary, and ½ teaspoon of the salt and continue cooking, stirring occasionally, for 5 more minutes. Add the beans and mix well. Add the stock and bring to a boil. Cover, reduce the heat to low, and simmer until the beans are tender, about 1 hour.

In a blender or food processor, purée half of the soup and return it to the pot. Add the kale and simmer until tender, about 10 minutes. Season with the additional salt and with pepper. Ladle into bowls and serve at once.

Serves 4 to 6

Black Bean soup
with GREEN and RED Peppers

PREPARATION TIME: 15 minutes   **COOKING TIME:** 25 minutes

Perfect for fall or winter evenings, this bean soup delivers just a hint of spice. Crunchy green onions add texture. To keep things quick and simple, we use canned black beans, which do the job nicely.

---

2 tablespoons extra-virgin olive oil
1 onion, diced
3 cloves garlic, minced
1 teaspoon ground cumin
1½ teaspoons salt
⅛ teaspoon cayenne pepper
1 green bell pepper, seeded and diced
1 red bell pepper, seeded and diced
3 cans (15 ounces each) black beans, rinsed and drained
4 cups chicken stock (page 105) or canned low-sodium chicken broth
4 green onions, white part only, thinly sliced
6 tablespoons sour cream

In a soup pot, heat the olive oil over medium-high heat. Add the onion and sauté for 2 minutes. Add the garlic, cumin, salt, and cayenne and mix well. Add the green and red bell peppers and sauté, for 3 more minutes. Add the black beans, stir well, and pour in the stock. Bring to a boil, cover, reduce the heat to low, and simmer until the bell peppers are soft and the beans begin to break down, about 15 minutes.

In small batches, in a blender, process the soup until it is fairly smooth but still retains small pieces of bean. As each batch is processed, pour it into a large bowl. When all of the soup has been puréed, return it to the pot over medium heat and simmer, uncovered, for 5 minutes to heat to serving temperature.

Ladle the soup into bowls. Garnish with the green onions and sour cream. Serve at once.

Serves 6

Minestrone SOUP

PREPARATION TIME: 20 minutes   **COOKING TIME:** 1 hour

With its multi-textured vegetables, beans, and squiggly noodles, this soup is appealing both to children and adults. Don't panic, however, when you see all the recipe ingredients. Most of them are just chopped vegetables. You can use dried beans here (see page 34), but we're usually too tired, lazy, or rushed when making this soup. That's when we reach for the canned cannellini beans.

1½ pound elbow macaroni
1 tablespoon extra-virgin olive oil
3 slices bacon, cut into matchsticks
1 leek, white part only, diced
3 cloves garlic, minced
1 teaspoon dried thyme
1 teaspoon dried oregano
1½ teaspoons salt
2 carrots, peeled and diced
2 celery stalks, chopped
1 medium-sized white potato, finely diced
1 zucchini, diced
2 cups finely chopped kale
1 can (14 ounces) whole tomatoes, drained and coarsely chopped
6 cups chicken stock (page 105) or canned low-sodium chicken broth
Parmesan cheese rind, about 2 inches square, plus freshly grated
*   Parmesan cheese to taste*
2 cans (15 ounces each) cannellini (white kidney) beans,
*   drained and rinsed*
½ cup finely chopped fresh basil
Freshly ground pepper to taste

Before you begin making the soup, or while it is cooking, you can cook the macaroni. It does not need to be hot when the soup is served. In a large pot of boiling water, cook the macaroni according to the package directions until al dente. Drain and rinse to prevent sticking, then set aside.

In a large soup pot, heat the olive oil over medium-high heat. Add the bacon and fry until crisp, about 4 minutes. Add the leek and garlic and sauté for 2 more minutes. Reduce the heat to low, add the thyme, oregano, and 1 teaspoon of the salt, and stir well. Mix in the carrots, celery, potato, zucchini, and kale and sauté, stirring occasionally, for 3 more minutes. Stir in the tomatoes and add the stock, the remaining ½ teaspoon salt, and the Parmesan rind. Cover and simmer until the vegetables are tender, about 30 minutes.

Put the beans in a bowl and partially mash with a fork or a potato masher. Add ½ cup of the broth from the soup pot and stir until the beans are a lumpy paste. Then mix the bean paste into the soup pot, cover, and simmer for 10 minutes. Stir in the basil.

Place ½ cup noodles in the bottom of each bowl. Ladle the hot soup over the noodles and garnish with the Parmesan cheese and the pepper. Serve at once.

Serves 6 to 8

NICKI'S **Salmon** Chowder

PREPARATION TIME: 15 minutes   **COOKING TIME:** 50 minutes

Our neighbor Nicki works full time, has two children, and still manages
to invite us over for dinner now and then. One evening she served us this
delicious soup, which makes a wonderful first course or main course.
Although the broth is delicate, it is loaded with plenty of rich, savory
salmon chunks and a broad, colorful array of vegetables. The kids in the
neighborhood enjoy this chowder for lunch, snacks, and dinner, too.

For this recipe, we buy salmon cut from the tail end of the fish because
it harbors fewer tiny pin bones. Look for the clam juice near the canned
tuna in the supermarket.

---

2 tablespoons extra-virgin olive oil

1 onion, diced

2 cloves garlic, minced

½ jalapeño chile, seeded and finely chopped

3 white potatoes, coarsely diced

2 leeks, white part only, cut into ¼-inch-thick rounds

1 can (28 ounces) whole tomatoes, drained and chopped

4 bottles (8 ounces each) clam juice

2 teaspoons salt, plus salt to taste

1½ cups dry white wine

1 pound salmon fillets or steaks, skin and bones removed and
   cut into 1-inch chunks

2 ears white corn, shucked and kernels removed

6 white button mushrooms, trimmed and sliced

1 cup half-and-half

½ cup finely chopped fresh cilantro

Freshly ground pepper to taste

In a large soup pot, heat the olive oil over medium heat. Add the onion,
garlic, and jalapeño and sauté for 3 minutes. Stir in the potatoes and
leeks and continue to cook for another 2 minutes. Add the tomatoes, clam
juice, 2 teaspoons of the salt, and wine, raise the heat to high and bring

to a boil. Cover, reduce the heat to low, and simmer until the potatoes are half cooked, about 10 minutes.

Add the salmon chunks, cover, and continue to simmer for 10 more minutes. Stir in the corn and mushrooms, re-cover, and simmer for another 10 minutes. Add the half-and-half and simmer, uncovered, for 5 minutes to heat through and blend the flavors.

Stir in the cilantro and season with the additional salt and with pepper. Ladle into bowls and serve at once.

Serves 6

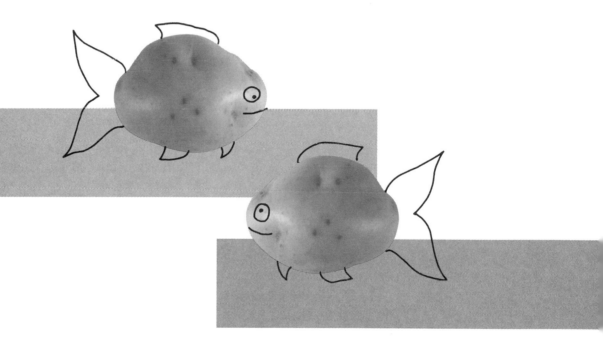

SECOND-DAY
Chicken SOUP

PREPARATION TIME: 15 minutes   **COOKING TIME:** $1^1/_2$ hours

Leftover roast chicken is our ongoing inspiration for making this simple, budget-friendly soup. Just remember to wrap the chicken carcass well to prevent it from drying out. It will keep in the refrigerator for a few days until you find a moment to recycle it as soup. A big-time winner with kids of all ages, this soup helps us make two meals from one chicken.

BROTH:

2 quarts water

1 tablespoon salt

1 onion, quartered

1 chicken carcass from roasted 3- to 4-pound chicken (page 256),
* plus any leftover chicken meat*

3 carrots, peeled and diced

2 red potatoes, peeled and finely diced

1 teaspoon dried thyme

1 clove garlic, minced

3 celery stalks, chopped

2 zucchini, diced

Salt and freshly ground pepper to taste

1 to 2 cups cooked white or brown rice (page 206) or pasta (page 175)

4 to 6 teaspoons finely chopped fresh dill

To make the broth, in a large soup pot, combine the water and salt and bring to a boil over high heat. Add the onion and the chicken carcass—if necessary, break it in half to fit it into the pot—cover, reduce the heat to medium, and simmer for 45 minutes. Uncover and simmer for 15 more minutes.

Using a slotted spoon, remove the chicken carcass and all the bones from the broth. Set the carcass aside until cool enough to handle. Add the carrots and potatoes to the broth and reduce the heat to low. Add the thyme, garlic, and celery.

Pull off any meat from the chicken carcass and bones, discard the bones and skin, and return the meat to the soup pot. Continue to simmer for 15 minutes. Add the zucchini and simmer until all the vegetables are tender, about 5 more minutes. Season with salt and pepper.

Place ¼ to ½ cup cooked rice or pasta in each bowl. (Do not put the rice or noodles directly into the soup pot. Both will eventually soak up the broth.) Ladle the soup into the bowls. Garnish each serving with 1 teaspoon dill.

Serves 4 to 6

HEARTY Beef AND Barley SOUP

PREPARATION TIME: 20 minutes   **COOKING TIME:** 1½ hours

This substantial soup is a meal in itself. It's made with short ribs—or stew meat on a bone. Prior to serving, the bones are discarded, but they leave behind long-lasting flavor. Great as a leftover, this soup is among our children's favorite winter lunches.

---

3 tablespoons extra-virgin olive oil

1 onion, diced

2 cloves garlic, minced

15 white button mushrooms, trimmed and quartered

2 pounds beef short ribs

¾ cup pearl barley

1½ teaspoons dried thyme

1 bay leaf

8 cups chicken stock (page 105) or canned low-sodium chicken broth

½ cup red wine (optional)

1½ teaspoons salt, plus salt to taste

3 carrots, peeled and diced

3 celery stalks, diced

1 parsnip, peeled and diced

Freshly ground pepper to taste

In a large soup pot, heat 2 tablespoons of the olive oil over medium-high heat. Add the onion and garlic and sauté for 2 minutes. Add the mushrooms and sauté for 3 more minutes. Transfer the onion-mushroom mixture to a bowl and reserve. Add the remaining 1 tablespoon of olive oil and the short ribs to the pot and brown for 2 minutes on each side. Pour off the excess fat from the pot. Stir in the barley and thyme and add the bay leaf, stock, wine (if using), and 1½ teaspoons of the salt. Bring to a boil, cover, reduce the heat to low, and simmer until the barley is soft and the soup is thick, about 1 hour.

Remove the short ribs and set them aside. Add the carrots, celery, parsnip, and reserved onion-mushroom mixture to the soup. Reduce the heat to low. Using a knife and fork, remove the meat from the ribs and shred it into small, thin strips. Return the meat to the pot and discard the bones. Cover and simmer until the vegetables are tender, about 20 more minutes.

Season the soup with salt and pepper. Ladle into soup bowls and serve at once.

Serves 6

PICKY EATERS

Foods may taste different to kids than they do to adults, and it's probably because youthful, evolving taste buds are actually more sensitive than grown-up ones. Children also often have a healthy suspicion of anything new at the table. What can parents do when it seems as though their children will eat almost nothing?

We have found that accommodation, rather than confrontation, is usually the best solution. It is, unfortunately, far too easy to become entrenched in a daily parent-child battle over food. Power struggles arise on many fronts, but we try to keep mealtime reserved as an opportunity to resolve them.

SETTING THE TONE
Eventually most children develop a well-rounded palate, particularly if they grow up exposed to a balanced diet. Our first responsibility as parents is to set a healthy standard and put nutritious meals on the family table. Ultimately, it's our children's responsibility to eat them. Don't expect kids to like everything you like. But in due time, and with repeated exposure to various foods, children will accept most of what you put on the table.

WHAT KIDS REALLY NEED FOR NOURISHMENT
Meanwhile, you can take comfort in knowing that your children don't necessarily require as much healthy food as you might imagine. A ten-year-old child's normal appetite can be less than one-fourth of that of an adult. Try to encourage your children to eat a small, varied amount of the kinds of foods listed in the chart on pages 20 and 21.

ONE-TRACK EATING
Yet sometimes a child becomes so comfortable with a particular food, he or she will eat seemingly little else. If one of our daughters decides she wants a turkey sandwich for lunch every day,

we give it to her. It's easy enough to do, and we don't want her to go hungry during the day. Most kids go through phases, and that includes food phases. Eventually she'll tire of turkey.

However, some children remain in the one-track, limited-food phase longer than others. We know a world-famous chef who can't convince his ten-year-old son to dine on much besides hamburgers, chicken breasts, potatoes, and ketchup. It was once a source of great frustration for our friend, who has spent many meals arguing with his son. But he has since learned to be more accepting of the youth's current preferences. The boy is growing up healthy, while father and son have a vastly improved relationship.

At our house, we aren't as accommodating with our daughters. There is a "two-bite" rule in effect that requires a second taste of any questionable food item. If, after these two tastes, the child still cannot stomach it, we adopt a wait-and-see attitude. Oddly enough, this week's poison may become next week's passion.

WHAT'S REASONABLE
There are issues of fairness. When we try out a brand-new dish on the whole family, we usually have a back-up offering in the wings to prevent someone from going hungry. It may be simple pasta with cheese or even leftovers. The point is to make new foods a source of excitement rather than dread.

HOT STUFF
Spicy foods can be challenging for young, sensitive palates. We love tangy-edged spices, but our daughters are less enamored with them. Too much spice turns them off. But over time, we have slowly introduced mild amounts of peppery ingredients into many of the foods we regularly enjoy as a family. And the girls have grown used to them. In recipes that include hot spices, we often mark them as optional, or to be used in varying amounts. Ultimately, the more adventurous your children become at mealtime, the better you all will eat.

LOOKS MAKE A DIFFERENCE
Kids taste with their eyes, and a pleasing—or poor—presentation may turn the tide of acceptance of a new dish. When possible, we arrange foods artfully on the plate or in patterns. For example, orange wedges or apple and pear slices can be formed into stars. For a main course, we avoid crowding or piling up too many items. A simple, uncluttered presentation is more palatable and allows kids to pick and choose at will easily, and to avoid undesirable elements.

BRIBERY
Some parents use dessert as bait or bribery. In the long run, this technique will cause more harm than good by setting up unhealthy relationships all around—between parents and children, and for children toward food. Yet we think it's important to understand that a balanced meal consists of more than sweets. In our house, we don't dangle the dessert carrot. But those who haven't eaten a reasonable amount of the main course won't be filling up with sugary sweet, empty calories afterward.

Notes

From the
GARDEN

CHAPTER
6

PLANT POWER!

Contrary to popular assumption among the younger set, **GREENS ARE NOT A CHILD'S WORST ENEMY.** The same applies to non-leafy vegetables. There are so many varieties available today, and so many ways of preparing them, that virtually all families can embrace a roster of healthy edible plants.

Grown-ups and children alike will wince when confronted with a plate of bland, boiled vegetables, or commercial salad dressing atop a flavorless mass of iceberg lettuce. Yet the produce portion of a meal can be as interesting as the protein portion. At our dinner table, the children complain when we forgo the salad. That's a far cry from our memories of growing up! Rich in vitamins and minerals, vegetables and fruits are a critical element in maintaining a balanced, nutritious diet. The vegetable component sometimes seems easiest for our children to swallow in soups (see Chapter 5). But whether in liquid or solid form, vegetables form a cornerstone of our diet. With a modest effort, you can accord them the same status as every other element on the dining table.

OUR **House Salad** AND **VINAIGRETTE**

PREPARATION TIME FOR VINAIGRETTE: 2 minutes
FOR SALAD: 3 minutes

When we were children, we considered salad on par with medicine–distasteful but necessary. Looking back, those feelings don't surprise us. Tasteless iceberg lettuce was the "green" du jour. And it was smothered with a commercial vinaigrette dressing that reeked of sugar, vinegar, and cheap vegetable oil.

Today, our whole family enjoys a green salad as a daily preface to the main course at dinner. We still do not like commercial salad dressings, however, so we make our own every night from scratch. It takes only about a minute—maybe two. Our kids—and many of their friends who often join us for dinner—regularly request this salad, so we know we are doing something right. We also know that we are delivering not only good flavor, but also sound nutrition. Once our daughters have eaten their green salads, we don't fret about whether or not they've eaten their string beans, too.

Make sure you use enough mustard in the vinaigrette. It acts as an emulsifier, holding the ingredients together. We use a light-bodied Dijon mustard. Dried thyme is also a key ingredient, as it offers a refreshing, bright taste.

Also, it's important to dry your greens thoroughly after washing them. Water droplets inhibit an even coating of the vinaigrette and dilute flavor. We dry our greens with a lettuce spinner, which can be purchased in most shops that carry kitchenware. Alternatively, you can wrap wet greens in a dish towel and vigorously shake them dry. If using the dish towel method, remember to do it outside, or in the shower. Otherwise your greens will be dry, but your kitchen will be wet!

We make our salad dressing with extra-virgin olive oil, but other oils will also do. Walnut and hazelnut oils, among others, add their own special nutty character. Canola and safflower oils are neutral tasting, but may be more to your liking.

One last tip: It's difficult to toss a salad in a small serving dish or plate because half the greens can wind up on the table or the floor. We suggest tossing salad in a large wooden or ceramic bowl immediately prior to serving. (If you toss too far in advance, the leaves become soggy.) Make your dressing in the bottom of the salad bowl whenever it's convenient, then add the greens and toss at the last minute.

HOUSE VINAIGRETTE:

> *3 tablespoons extra-virgin olive oil*
> *1 tablespoon balsamic or red wine vinegar*
> *1 teaspoon Dijon mustard*
> *½ teaspoon dried thyme*
> *1 small clove garlic, minced*
> *Pinch of salt (optional)*
> *Freshly ground pepper to taste*

HOUSE SALAD:

> *4 to 6 very thin slices onion (optional)*
> *1 head butter or other lettuce, leaves separated, or 8 to 10 ounces*
>   *mixed baby salad greens, rinsed and dried*
> *1 or 2 tomatoes, quartered (optional)*
> *10 to 15 olives (optional)*
> *1 avocado, halved and pitted, then flesh spooned out*
>   *or peeled and diced (optional)*

To make the vinaigrette, place all ingredients in a large salad bowl. With a wooden spoon, stir until evenly blended.

If using the onion, place the slices in the vinaigrette to coat thoroughly. Immediately prior to serving, add the greens and any of the optional ingredients. Toss until the greens and other ingredients are evenly coated with the vinaigrette. Serve at once.

Serves 4 to 6

Caesar SALAD

PREPARATION TIME: 10 minutes   **BAKING TIME:** 15 minutes

The Caesar is a much-loved salad, and our household is among its fans. The kids love the crunchy, little homemade croutons, but to save time, you can also buy perfectly fine croutons at the store.

Traditional Caesar salad requires a raw egg yolk, which gives texture and flavor and acts as an emulsifying agent. There is, however, a real (if unlikely) chance of salmonella poisoning from raw eggs. Salmonella is particularly dangerous for small children, older individuals, pregnant women, or anyone with a compromised immune system. To minimize risk, find a reliable source of organic or free-range eggs.

CROUTONS:

1 tablespoon unsalted butter
1 tablespoon extra-virgin olive oil
4 cups diced day-old baguette or country bread

DRESSING:

¼ cup extra-virgin olive oil
1 tablespoon Dijon mustard
1 egg yolk
½ teaspoon salt
1 tablespoon Worcestershire sauce
1 clove garlic, minced
1 tablespoon fresh lemon juice
¼ teaspoon anchovy paste

1 head romaine lettuce, leaves separated and cut crosswise
    into 2-inch-long pieces
¼ cup freshly grated Parmesan cheese
Freshly ground pepper to taste

To make the croutons, preheat the oven to 350°F. In a skillet or sauté pan, melt the butter with the olive oil over low heat. Add the bread and stir until all the pieces are evenly coated with the butter and oil. Spread the croutons on a baking sheet and bake in the oven until golden brown, about 15 minutes. Remove from the oven and let cool to room temperature before using.

To make the dressing, in a small bowl, whisk together the olive oil, mustard, egg yolk, and salt. Add the Worcestershire sauce, garlic, lemon juice, and anchovy paste and continue to whisk until smooth and thick. Cover and refrigerate until needed, or for up to 12 hours.

In a large bowl, combine the lettuce and croutons. Drizzle the dressing over the top and toss to coat evenly. Garnish with the Parmesan cheese and pepper. Serve at once.

Serves 4 to 6

Chickpea SALAD

PREPARATION TIME: 10 minutes

Although you can cook dried chickpeas—also known as garbanzo beans—for this salad, we generally make it with canned. It saves loads of time and does not sacrifice flavor.

---

2 cups drained home-cooked chickpeas (see page 34) or
  1 can (15 ounces) chickpeas, drained and rinsed
½ cup pitted Kalamata or other black olives
⅓ cup finely chopped red onion
½ cup finely chopped red bell pepper
⅓ cup minced fresh cilantro
½ teaspoon salt
1 tablespoon fresh lemon juice
2 tablespoons extra-virgin olive oil
Freshly ground pepper to taste

In a large bowl, combine the chickpeas, olives, onion, bell pepper, and cilantro. Sprinkle with the salt and mix well.

In a small bowl, stir together the lemon juice and olive oil. Pour the oil mixture into the chickpea mixture and toss thoroughly. Grind pepper over the top and serve.

Serves 4

Cucumber **Raita** SALAD

PREPARATION TIME: 10 minutes

This Indian-inspired dish features cool, crunchy cucumber; creamy yogurt; and a hint of mint. It's refreshing on the palate and a perfect side dish for most Indian menus. Try it with Indian Spiced Potatoes with Mixed Green Vegetables and Tangy Tomato Sauce (page 154). Additionally, for a quick low-calorie lunch, try the raita as a centerpiece flanked with a few cherry tomatoes and sliced, raw vegetables such as green bell peppers and carrots. Kids who like yogurt will enjoy this refreshing salad.

---

1 clove garlic, minced
1½ cups plain yogurt
2 teaspoons ground cumin
1 cucumber, peeled and sliced or coarsely chopped
2 tablespoons coarsely chopped fresh mint
Salt and freshly ground pepper to taste (optional)

In a bowl, using a whisk or wooden spoon, mix together the garlic, yogurt, and cumin. Gently stir in the cucumber and mint. Season with the salt and pepper, if using.

Serves 4

WHITE **Fennel** Salad

PREPARATION TIME: 10 minutes

Fennel used to be considered exotic in America, but now it is found nearly everywhere. The large, pale green bulbs are almost white on the inside and have a celery-like texture. But the flavor is quite different, serving up a delicate anise or vaguely licorice-like taste.

This salad is fresh and light. It's also very white; all the sliced ingredients are different shades of the same pale color scheme. The fennel flavor readily complements crunchy celery and spicy radish. Parmesan cheese adds pizzazz to this easy opener for any meal.

---

1 fennel bulb, leaves and stems removed, then sliced crosswise into thin rounds
6 small radishes, thinly sliced
2 celery stalks, thinly sliced
10 to 12 thin slices Parmesan cheese, each 1 to 2 inches square
¼ cup extra-virgin olive oil
Juice of ½ lemon
Salt and freshly ground pepper to taste

On a large serving plate, arrange the fennel slices to cover the surface evenly. Distribute the radish and celery slices over the fennel. Do the same with the Parmesan cheese slices. Drizzle with the olive oil and lemon juice. Season with salt and pepper.

Serves 4

SALAD GREENS

The word *green* is only a partial descriptor for today's many multihued lettuces. We can choose from any number of shades of red, orange, white, and purple. Nevertheless, green remains a consistent theme among the varied shoots, sprouts, and leaves in produce stores and supermarkets today. Why buy the same lettuce every day when you can easily diversify your grazing possibilities?

Small-leaved, young lettuces and fresh herbs generally offer the greatest concentration of flavors, which makes them ideal for blending as mixed greens. Other lettuces, such as Bibb or romaine, are milder. They may be more acceptable to picky palates. Look for any of the following leafy greens to include in your next salad.

ARUGULA: Small, peppery, notched, dark green leaves that the English call rocket. Not advised for sensitive kid palates.

BABY SPINACH: Small green leaves that are mildly sweet and almost chewy.

LEMON Avocado SALAD

BASIL: Pungent and assertive, green leaves that are best mixed with lettuces. Remove stems before using.

BELGIAN ENDIVE: Thick, crisp white leaves that end in yellow, green, or red tips; almost mineral-like in flavor. Good alone or mixed with other greens.

BUTTER (OR BOSTON) LETTUCE: Small, pale green, loose-leaved head lettuce; mild and refreshing, it is our favorite all-purpose salad lettuce.

FRISÉE: Like it sounds, with frizzled, light green leaves; tart on the palate.

MÂCHE: Small, oval, light green leaves with a delicate, fresh sweetness. Although it is French (pronounced mah-sh), it is not very exotic, but rather a delightfully mild, delicious salad option. Also known as corn salad and lamb's lettuce.

(continued)

PREPARATION TIME: 5 minutes

Here is a straightforward little dish that is almost too good to be true. Just four ingredients—and one is salt! Make sure you use ripe avocados. They should yield to a gentle finger pressure, but not feel mushy. If an avocado is not ripe enough, the pit will be difficult to remove. Coarse salt, such as kosher salt or coarse sea salt, adds a welcome dimension on the palate.

Our daughters have always loved avocados. Sometimes they eat the onion slices in this dish, and sometimes they don't, preferring to push them to the side.

---

1 large or 2 medium avocados
½ onion, thinly sliced into rounds
Juice of ½ lemon
Coarse sea salt or kosher salt to taste

Cut the avocado(s) in half and remove the large pit. Lay the halves, cut-sides down, on a cutting board, and cut lengthwise into slices ¼ to ½ inch thick. Peel the skin off each slice, and lay the skinned slices on a serving plate.

Garnish the avocado with the onion slices and drizzle with the lemon juice. Season with the salt.

Serves 2 to 4

MEDITERRANEAN SALAD WITH Tomatoes, Green Peppers, OLIVES, Feta Cheese, AND CUMIN

PREPARATION TIME: 15 minutes

Summertime, with its garden bounty, is the perfect time to enjoy this colorful, flavor-packed salad. If you have your own garden, let your children pick the tomatoes and peppers. Enjoy with crusty country bread on the side.

¼ cup extra-virgin olive oil

2 tablespoons tahini (sesame-seed paste)

1 tablespoon ground cumin

½ onion, finely chopped

2 green bell peppers, seeded and cut into ¼-inch dice

4 tomatoes, cut into ¼-inch dice, or 1 pint cherry tomatoes, halved

½ cup olives, with or without pits

¼ pound feta cheese, crumbled or diced

In a large salad or serving bowl, stir together the olive oil, tahini, and cumin. Stir in the onion. Add the bell peppers and tomatoes, and toss to coat evenly with the sauce. Add the olives and feta and toss again.

Serves 4

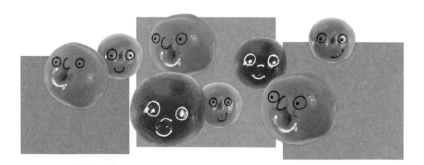

(Salad Greens continued)

PARSLEY: Small flat or curly green leaves; its assertive, grassy mineral flavor will add lift to a blend of other greens.

RADICCHIO: Chewy red and white leaves with a pleasantly peppery taste; usually mixed with other greens. Kids will probably rebel against radicchio's inherent bitterness.

ROMAINE: Long, crisp green or reddish leaves; best when eaten young and tender.

WATERCRESS: Small, dark green leaves with a refreshing, spicy, menthol edge.

SPICED Carrot AND Raisin SALAD

PREPARATION TIME: 10 minutes   **COOKING TIME:** 6 minutes

Easy-to-prepare and loaded with color, this Moroccan-inspired salad serves up a riotous blend of cumin, mint, and citrus flavors that act as the frame for a centerpiece of sweet carrots and raisins.

2 cups water
1 teaspoon whole cloves
5 carrots, peeled and thinly sliced
¼ cup raisins
1¼ teaspoons ground cumin
½ teaspoon paprika
¼ teaspoon salt
⅛ teaspoon cayenne pepper
1 tablespoon fresh lemon juice
2 tablespoons extra-virgin olive oil
2 tablespoons minced fresh mint

In a saucepan, bring the water to a boil over high heat. Add the cloves, and cook for 30 seconds. Add the carrots and cook for 4 minutes. Add the raisins and cook for 1 more minute.

Drain the carrots and raisins in a colander and rinse under cold water. Discard the cloves. Pat the carrots and raisins dry with a paper towel. Place them in a large bowl and sprinkle with the cumin, paprika, salt, and cayenne.

In a small bowl, mix together the lemon juice and olive oil. Pour the oil mixture over the carrots and raisins and toss to coat well. Add the mint and toss again.

Serves 4

ASIAN Slaw

PREPARATION TIME: 20 minutes

We especially love this tangy, refreshing slaw, a fine blend of Asian flavors and textures, as a side dish for grilled meats and fish. Look for Asian sesame oil and fish sauce in Asian food shops and some supermarkets.

---

1 head green cabbage, thinly sliced and then cut crosswise
    into 3-inch-long ribbons
1 cucumber, peeled and cut into thin strips
2 carrots, peeled and coarsely grated
3 green onions, white and green parts, thinly sliced

SAUCE:

2 tablespoons tamari or soy sauce
2 tablespoons rice vinegar
¼ cup Asian sesame oil
Juice of 1 lime
1 tablespoon Asian fish sauce
1 clove garlic, minced
1 tablespoon grated fresh ginger
Pinch of cayenne pepper

⅓ cup chopped fresh cilantro
3 tablespoons sesame seeds, toasted (see page 32)

In a large bowl, combine the cabbage, cucumber, carrots, and green onions and mix well. Set aside.

To make the sauce, in a small bowl, stir together the tamari, vinegar, sesame oil, lime juice, fish sauce, garlic, ginger, and cayenne. Pour the sauce over the chopped vegetables and toss to mix thoroughly, then mix in the cilantro. Garnish with the sesame seeds and serve.

Serves 6

WHAT IS SO GREAT ABOUT OLIVE OIL?

We use extra-virgin olive oil for many of our culinary needs. It offers a fresh, fruity edge that is lacking in most other commonly used vegetable oils, such as canola or safflower. Nonetheless, if you want to substitute a milder oil for the olive oil suggested in our recipes, do so.

Flavor is not the only benefit that comes from a good olive oil. The health benefits are also noteworthy. Olive oil is a monounsaturated oil that can actually lower cholesterol in your body. In addition, it is loaded with vitamin E, which is thought to strengthen the skin's cell walls and thus slow down the wrinkling process as we age. Nutritional attributes notwithstanding, we love olive oil because it's so flavorful and versatile, whether used as a garnish, in salads, or in cooking.

Olive oil does have a lower smoke point (the temperature at which an oil breaks down and begins to smoke) than oils like canola or peanut oil, however. For

String Bean AND Potato SALAD

PREPARATION TIME: 15 minutes   **COOKING TIME:** 15 minutes

You can serve this hearty salad as a first course, or as a main course with bread and cheese on the side. It's also a favorite at potlucks. If you cannot find wax beans, which look the same as green string beans but are pale yellow, increase the amount of the green beans to 1 pound.

2 pounds red potatoes, unpeeled, cut into 1-inch cubes
½ pound green string beans, trimmed and halved
½ pound yellow wax beans, trimmed and halved
⅓ cup extra-virgin olive oil
1 tablespoon balsamic vinegar
1 tablespoon Dijon mustard
1 teaspoon dried thyme
1 clove garlic, minced
Pinch of coarse sea salt or kosher salt, plus salt to taste
3 tablespoons diced red onion
Freshly ground pepper to taste

Place a steamer basket in a large saucepan set over 1 inch of water or fill the pan three-fourths full of water. Steam the potatoes or boil them in water for 10 minutes. Add the beans and continue to cook until the potatoes are soft enough to be easily pierced with a fork and the beans are tender-crisp, about 5 more minutes. Whether steamed or boiled, transfer them both to a colander and rinse with cold water to cool them and to set the color of the beans. Set aside.

In a small bowl, whisk together the olive oil, vinegar, mustard, thyme, garlic, and pinch of salt. Stir in the onion.

In a large salad bowl, combine the potatoes and beans. Pour the oil mixture over the potatoes and beans and toss gently but thoroughly until they are well coated with the dressing. Taste and adjust the seasoning with the additional salt and with pepper. Serve warm or at room temperature.

Serves 6 as a first course or 4 as a main course

---

that reason, we don't recommend it for deep-frying. But it's perfectly suited for sautéing vegetables, cooking omelets, frying eggs, and a multitude of other purposes. In fact, you will find olive oil among the most commonly used ingredients in this book.

High-quality olive oils are made throughout the Mediterranean and in California. Prices can range dramatically along with quality, which is generally gauged by low acidity. Extra-virgin olive oils are among the best, and virgin olive oils are also quite good, although they are considered of slightly lesser quality. Both extra-virgin and virgin olive oils are usually made with mechanical presses that do not rely on chemical extraction of the oil from the whole olive. They also tend to serve up the brightest fruit flavors.

In general, many inexpensive extra-virgin olive oils lack the intensity found in the so-called high-end boutique products.

(continued)

MIXED Green Salad with Pear, SWEET and SPICY PECANS, and Goat Cheese

PREPARATION TIME: 15 minutes

We love to use firm, round Asian pears. They tend to be crisper than Bosc pears, which can be used here as well, as can firm, tart apples. Try other types of nuts, too, such as toasted walnuts (see page 32), which can be prepared more quickly than the pecans.

VINAIGRETTE:

⅓ cup extra-virgin olive oil

2 tablespoons balsamic vinegar

½ teaspoon dried thyme

1 tablespoon minced red onion

6 to 8 ounces mixed baby salad greens

½ cup Sweet and Spicy Pecans (page 63)

*4 slices fresh goat cheese, each about ¼ inch thick
   and 1 inch in diameter*

*1 pear such as Asian or Bosc, unpeeled, halved, cored,
   and thinly sliced lengthwise*

Freshly ground pepper to taste

To make the vinaigrette, in a large salad bowl, using a wooden spoon, stir together the oil, vinegar, thyme, and onion until blended.

Add the greens and pecans to the salad bowl and toss with the vinaigrette until evenly coated.

Divide the salad among 4 plates. Place 1 slice of the goat cheese on top of each mound of greens, and surround each cheese slice with 4 to 6 pear slices. Grind pepper over each serving and serve immediately.

Serves 4

(Olive Oil continued)

These cheaper oils, which are usually a blend of bulk oils from Italy, Spain, and North Africa, can still be very good, however. They are fine for cooking and sometimes in salad dressings, where vinegar, mustard, and herbs define flavor, too. But as a garnish or even as a dipping oil for bread, you might want to consider a more expensive, assertive oil. Unfortunately, price is no guarantee of quality. Trust your own taste and experiment with various brands and regions to discover your favorites.

WHEN PURE IS "NOT"
The designation "pure" olive oil is a misleading food-industry perversion. Pure normally implies the highest quality, but, in this case, it means just the opposite. Pure olive oils are not labeled virgin or extra-virgin because they are of lesser quality. They are highly processed

Tomato, MOZZARELLA, AND Basil SALAD

PREPARATION TIME: 5 minutes

When ripe, juicy tomatoes are in season, this salad always hits a home run at our house. Kosher or coarse sea salt adds a refreshing, crunchy aspect to the dish.

---

4 large tomatoes, sliced ¼ inch thick
Coarse sea salt or kosher salt and freshly ground pepper to taste
2 fresh mozzarella cheese balls, about ½ pound each,
    sliced ¼ inch thick
⅓ cup fresh basil leaves
3 tablespoons extra-virgin olive oil
1 teaspoon balsamic or red wine vinegar

On a large serving platter, arrange the tomato slices to cover the surface evenly. Sprinkle with the salt and pepper. Lay the mozzarella slices over the tomato slices. Distribute the basil leaves evenly over the tomatoes and cheese.

In a small bowl, whisk together the olive oil and vinegar. Drizzle over the top of the salad.

Serves 4 or 5

and chemically extracted from a second or even third pressing. So-called light olive oils are even worse. Inferior oils such as these are but a pale shadow of how a rich, fruity olive oil should taste.

STORAGE

If possible, store olive oil in a cool, dark place. It keeps well in the refrigerator, but tends to become cloudy and even partially solid. This is normal and taste is not affected. But it's not practical for many cooking procedures. As a result, we keep olive oil at room temperature on the lower shelves of the pantry closet.

SALADE Niçoise

PREPARATION TIME: 20 minutes   **COOKING TIME:** 15 minutes, or 25 minutes if using fresh tuna

When can a salad stand in for a full meal? Obviously that depends on how hungry you are. But this salad, inspired by the one so often eaten in the French Riviera town of Nice, serves up enough substance to satisfy the heartiest appetites. We often enjoy it on a warm afternoon for lunch, particularly when friends are visiting.

If you've got the time and energy to cook it, seared tuna makes a wonderful addition to this salad. But don't worry about authenticity. In Nice, canned tuna is traditional. In addition, many children prefer canned tuna to fresh tuna. It's what they are used to.

¾ pound fresh ahi tuna fillet, about ½ inch thick,
   or 1 can (6 ounces) tuna packed in olive oil or water
1 teaspoon coarse sea salt or kosher salt, if using fresh tuna,
   plus salt to taste
1 tablespoon extra-virgin olive oil, if using fresh tuna
2 pounds red or white new potatoes, quartered
1 pound green string beans, trimmed and cut into 4-inch lengths
¼ pound lettuce or mixed salad greens, torn into bite-sized pieces
½ large red onion, thinly sliced
¼ cup Niçoise or other small black olives
Double recipe house vinaigrette (page 122)
4 hard-boiled eggs (see page 34), peeled and halved lengthwise
2 large tomatoes, cut into wedges
Freshly ground pepper to taste

If using fresh tuna, sprinkle each side with ½ teaspoon of the salt. Coat a sauté pan with the olive oil and set over medium-high heat. When it is hot, place the tuna in the pan and cook, turning once, just until it begins to flake when tested with a fork, 3 to 4 minutes on each side. Remove the tuna from the pan and set aside. When cool enough to handle, cut into slices 2 inches long by 1 inch wide.

VINEGAR

It's amazing how useful "spoiled wine" can be. That's essentially what many vinegars are—formerly sound wines that have been converted, in part, to acetic acid.

Italy's famed balsamic vinegar has become a staple for many Americans. We are no exception, using it daily in salad dressing. Our choice is any moderately priced balsamic vinegar that carries only a hint of sweetness. To this end, it works far better than the thick, rich (and very expensive) high-end balsamic vinegars that are intended for use as a condiment, rather than in a vinaigrette.

Other red wine and sherry vinegars lend their own character to salad dressings, while lemon juice or cider vinegar can also provide the necessary edge. We keep several different types of vinegar on hand for variety. Store your vinegars at room temperature or in the refrigerator.

If using canned tuna, drain it well and break it into 1- to 2-inch chunks.

Place a steamer basket in a large saucepan set over 1 inch of water or fill the pan three-fourths full of water. Steam the potatoes or boil them in water for 10 minutes. Add the green beans and continue to cook until the potatoes are soft enough to be easily pierced with a fork and the beans are tender-crisp, about 5 more minutes. Whether steamed or boiled, transfer them both to a colander and rinse with cold water to cool them and to set the color of the beans. Set aside.

In a large salad bowl, combine the lettuce, potatoes, green beans, onion, and olives. Pour the vinaigrette—about $\frac{2}{3}$ cup—over the lettuce and other ingredients and toss gently to coat thoroughly. (Do not toss with the tuna, egg, and tomatoes, or you will have a very messy salad.) Place the tuna chunks on top of the mixture at the center. Set the egg and tomato wedges, alternating them, in a circle around the tuna. Season with the additional salt and with pepper and serve.

Serves 4

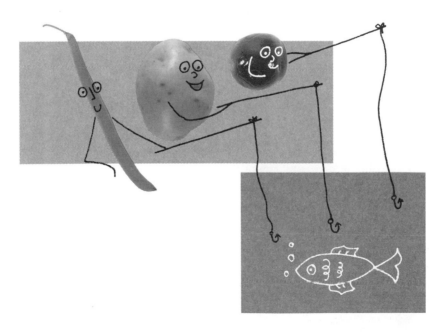

SPICED Beet SALAD

PREPARATION TIME: 15 minutes   **COOKING TIME:** 1 hour

Here, an exotic blend of spices that includes cumin and curry flavors beets in a new way. Our kids love beets, and this salad is a favorite.

---

12 beets, preferably a mix of red and golden
1 large navel orange
2 tablespoons diced red onion

SAUCE:
¼ cup extra-virgin olive oil
1 tablespoon balsamic vinegar
½ teaspoon curry powder
½ teaspoon ground cumin
⅛ teaspoon salt
Pinch of cayenne pepper

Preheat the oven to 350°F.

If the beet greens are intact, cut them off, leaving 2 inches of the stems. (You can rinse the beet greens and steam them like spinach.) Using aluminum foil, wrap the beets in groups of 3, leaving the top of the foil packets slightly open. Place the packets directly on the oven rack and bake the beets until tender, 45 minutes to 1 hour.

Remove the beets from the oven, open the packets, and let the beets cool until you can handle them. Meanwhile, peel the orange, separate the segments, dice them, and place them in a large bowl. Add the onion. When the beets can be handled, peel or rub off the skins, and cut the beets into ½- to 1-inch cubes. Place them in the bowl with the orange and onion.

To make the sauce, in a small bowl, whisk together the olive oil, vinegar, curry powder, cumin, salt, and cayenne. Pour the sauce over the beet mixture and toss to coat thoroughly. Serve warm or at room temperature.

Serves 4 to 6

CUCUMBER, Tomato, AND Avocado SALAD

PREPARATION TIME: 10 minutes

We generally eat some version of a green salad at dinnertime. But this simple alternative—without any leafy greens—serves up different bright, clean flavors for a change of pace. We serve it as a first course before dinner. But sometimes our kids ask for it—believe it or not—as an afternoon snack.

---

1 cucumber, peeled, halved, and thinly sliced

1 large tomato, cut into wedges

15 Kalamata or other black olives, with or without pits

1 avocado, halved and pitted, then flesh scooped out
   or peeled and diced

3 tablespoons finely chopped red onion

3 tablespoons extra-virgin olive oil

1 tablespoon fresh lemon juice

¼ teaspoon salt

1 tablespoon dried basil

Freshly ground pepper to taste

In a large bowl, combine all the ingredients. Toss gently but thoroughly, and serve.

Serves 4

White Bean SALAD WITH
SUN-DRIED Tomatoes AND Arugula

PREPARATION TIME: 10 minutes   **COOKING TIME:** 5 minutes

We use canned beans for this salad in order to keep the preparation time short. (Home-cooked dried beans require more forethought; see page 34.) As such, it's a practical dish for after work or for a potluck.

⅓ cup extra-virgin olive oil
½ onion, diced
3 cloves garlic, minced
2 tablespoons minced fresh rosemary
2 cans (15 ounces each) navy or white kidney beans,
*   rinsed and drained*
⅓ cup pitted Kalamata or other black olives
½ cup sun-dried tomatoes packed in olive oil, drained
*   and cut into narrow strips*
2½ cups firmly packed arugula leaves
Salt and freshly ground pepper to taste

In a large sauté pan or skillet, heat the olive oil over medium heat. Add the onion and sauté until translucent, about 3 minutes. Add the garlic and rosemary, stir well, and sauté for 45 seconds.

Remove from the heat and mix in the beans, olives, sun-dried tomatoes, and arugula. (If you prefer the arugula to be more wilted, keep the heat on and stir all ingredients for another 45 seconds.) Season with salt and pepper. Transfer to a serving bowl and serve warm or at room temperature.

Serves 6 to 8

GARDENING FOR GROWN-UPS AND KIDS

For both parents and kids, gardening is good for the spirit and the body. Growing vegetables helps children establish a special and direct relationship with the earth and leads them to understand better how we get our food. It's a concept that's hard to convey from a supermarket aisle.

Tending a garden is also a good way to introduce new vegetables to your children. If they've gone to the trouble to grow something, they will be more disposed to enjoy eating it. We've noticed as well that both boys and girls are fascinated with mud and dirt. Gardening presents a practical and productive way for them to satisfy this natural affinity while developing a rapport with nature. Finally, time in the garden teaches children the virtue of patience—a plant grows from a seed slowly—and creates a special moment for parents to share with their children.

Even apartment dwellers can garden with pots and other containers. While quantities might be limited, variety is

Lentil SALAD

You can taste fragrant hints of the Middle East in this lightly spiced—yet kid friendly—lentil salad. Serve it as a first course, garnished with freshly cut tomato wedges, or enjoy it as a side dish.

---

3 cups chicken stock (page 105), canned low-sodium chicken broth, or water
1 cup green lentils, picked over and rinsed
½ cup finely diced red bell pepper
½ cup peeled and finely diced carrot
3 tablespoons finely chopped fresh cilantro
2 tablespoons minced red onion
¼ cup extra-virgin olive oil
2 tablespoons fresh lemon juice
½ teaspoon ground cumin
½ teaspoon curry powder
¼ teaspoon salt
Tomato wedges for garnish (optional)

In a 2- to 3-quart saucepan, bring the stock to a boil over high heat. Add the lentils, cover, reduce the heat to a steady simmer, and cook until the liquid is completely absorbed and the lentils are tender, about 20 minutes. (If the liquid disappears and the lentils are still crunchy, add another ¼ cup liquid and simmer until it is absorbed.) Remove from the heat and let cool to room temperature.

To assemble the salad, in a large bowl, combine the cooked lentils, bell pepper, carrot, cilantro, and onion. Then, in a smaller bowl, whisk together the olive oil, lemon juice, cumin, curry powder, and salt. Pour the oil mixture over the lentil mixture and mix thoroughly. Garnish with the tomato wedges, if using, and serve.

Serves 4

---

still an option. Whether you're using containers, raised beds, or a large garden plot, there are numerous vegetables and herbs that are easy to grow, fun to harvest, and healthy to eat. Try lettuce, basil, zucchini, tomatoes, carrots, broccoli, peas, pumpkins, melons, and cucumbers, keeping in mind that the last three will require room to spread.

GARDENING TIPS

Make sure tasks are age appropriate. Young children don't have advanced motor skills, so it's better for them to dig a hole than to separate seedlings.

Small people require child-sized tools, so check out local nurseries and hardware stores for tools that fit tiny hands.

Make sure any flowers you plant for kitchen use are nontoxic. Edible ones include marigolds, nasturtiums, pansies, and Johnny-jump-ups, which we use as salad garnish and sometimes to decorate cakes, too.

Yellow Rice AND Black Bean SALAD

PREPARATION TIME: 15 minutes   **COOKING TIME:** 18 minutes

This creamy-textured blend of rice and beans offers crunchy contrast
on the palate thanks to the use of colorful red and green bell peppers.
The curry component is mild, while the cilantro garnish adds a fresh
finish. If you have planned ahead, substitute 4 cups drained home-cooked
black beans (see page 34) for the canned beans. Pack this hearty salad
for a picnic or potluck.

---

3 tablespoons, plus ¾ cup extra-virgin olive oil

1 onion, diced

4 cloves garlic, minced

½ teaspoon chipotle chile flakes or red pepper flakes

2 cups long-grain white rice

1 teaspoon ground turmeric

4 cups chicken stock (page 105), canned low-sodium chicken broth,
  or water

2 cans (15 ounces each) black beans, drained and rinsed

1 green bell pepper, seeded and diced

1 red bell pepper, seeded and diced

5 green onions, white part only, sliced

⅓ cup coarsely chopped fresh cilantro

Juice of 2 limes

Juice of 1 lemon

1 teaspoon curry powder

½ teaspoon salt

In a large, deep-sided skillet or 3-quart saucepan, heat the 3 tablespoons
olive oil over medium-high heat. Add the onion and garlic and sauté until
the onion begins to turn translucent, 2 to 3 minutes. Add the chile flakes
and mix well. Stir in the rice and add the turmeric, mixing well. Add the
stock, raise the heat to high, cover, and bring to a boil. Reduce the heat
to low and cook until all the liquid is absorbed, about 15 minutes.
Remove from the heat and let cool to room temperature.

In a large serving bowl, combine the rice mixture, beans, bell peppers, green onions, and cilantro. In a separate bowl, whisk together the remaining ¾ cup olive oil, the lime and lemon juices, curry powder, and salt. Pour the oil mixture into the rice and bean mixture and mix well. Serve at room temperature or chilled.

Serves 8 to 10

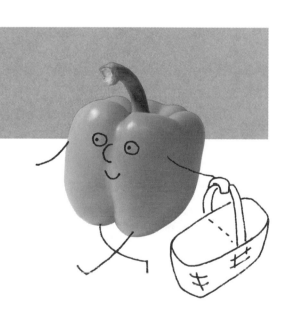

LEMON Bulgur SALAD
WITH SUMMER Vegetables

PREPARATION TIME: 10 minutes   **COOKING TIME:** 15 minutes

This refreshing summer salad builds on bulgur, a delicate cracked wheat that makes a fine alternative to rice or pasta. To have chilled bulgur available for this or another cold salad, cook the bulgur up to 2 days in advance and refrigerate until needed.

2 cups water
1 teaspoon salt
1 cup bulgur wheat
2 tablespoons extra-virgin olive oil
1 teaspoon fresh lemon juice
½ clove garlic, minced
1 tomato, diced
½ cucumber, peeled and diced
4 green onions, white part only, thinly sliced
20 Kalamata olives, preferably pitted
⅓ cup minced fresh mint
⅓ cup minced fresh parsley
Freshly ground pepper to taste

In a saucepan, combine the water and ½ teaspoon of the salt and bring to a boil over high heat. Add the bulgur, cover, reduce the heat to low, and cook until all the water is absorbed and the bulgur is tender, about 15 minutes. Uncover and let cool to taste (see headnote).

While the bulgur is cooking or cooling, in a small bowl, stir together the olive oil, lemon juice, and garlic and set aside.

In a large bowl, combine the tomato, cucumber, green onions, olives, mint, parsley, and bulgur. Pour in the oil mixture and stir to mix well. Season with the remaining ½ teaspoon salt and with pepper and mix again. Serve warm or at room temperature.

Serves 4

Couscous SALAD
WITH Tomato AND Cilantro

PREPARATION TIME: 5 minutes   **COOKING TIME:** 10 minutes

Quick-cooking, delicate couscous grains deftly support the bold flavors of fresh cilantro and juicy cherry tomatoes. A touch each of cumin and cayenne adds a subtle, exotic edge that will not offend most youthful palates.

---

2 cups water

2 tablespoons, plus ¼ cup extra-virgin olive oil

1⅛ teaspoons salt

2 cups instant couscous

2 tablespoons balsamic vinegar

1 small clove garlic, minced

1 teaspoon ground cumin

2 pinches of cayenne pepper

1¼ cups cherry tomatoes, halved

½ cup chopped fresh cilantro

4 tablespoons diced red onion

To cook the couscous, in a saucepan, combine the water, the 2 tablespoons olive oil, and 1 teaspoon of the salt and bring to a boil over high heat. Remove from the heat and, using a fork, stir in the couscous. Cover and let stand until the water is absorbed and the couscous is tender, 5 to 10 minutes. Uncover and fluff the couscous with the fork. Set the pan aside.

To make the dressing, in a small bowl, stir together the remaining ¼ cup olive oil, the vinegar, garlic, cumin, cayenne, and the remaining ⅛ teaspoon salt.

Transfer the couscous to a large bowl and fluff again with a fork to loosen the grains. Gently stir in the tomatoes, cilantro, and onion. Pour the vinaigrette over the couscous mixture and again stir gently to mix. Serve warm or at room temperature.

Serves 4 to 6

Asparagus WITH OLIVE OIL AND Parmesan

PREPARATION: 10 minutes   **COOKING TIME:** 5 minutes

This recipe is so basic—and so delicious. Crumbly Parmesan cheese—not grated, but shaved—offsets the silky smooth asparagus shoots. Coarse salt adds tangy texture as well. Serve as a first course or side dish.

---

1 pound asparagus

3 tablespoons extra-virgin olive oil

2 pinches of coarse sea salt or kosher salt

6 to 8 thinly shaved slices Parmesan cheese, each about 1 inch square

Freshly ground pepper to taste

Trim off the tough end from each asparagus spear—usually 1 to 2 inches. Fill a large sauté pan with water to a depth of 1 inch and bring to a boil over high heat. Lay the asparagus in the water, cover, and cook until tender, 3 to 5 minutes. Drain in a colander and rinse immediately with very cold water to retain the color and stop the cooking.

Pat the asparagus dry with a paper towel and lay them on a serving platter. Drizzle with the olive oil, sprinkle with the salt, and garnish with the shaved Parmesan. Season with pepper.

Serves 4

Artichokes WITH **AIOLI**

PREPARATION TIME: 10 minutes   **COOKING TIME:** 40 minutes

This concept is so easy we'd hardly call it a recipe. You'll have to make the aioli, of course, but that takes only a few minutes. And yes, you have to wait for the artichokes to steam, but while they cook, you are free to do something else. Serve the artichokes as a first course or side dish for any meal, plain or fancy. Enjoy the meaty part of the leaves, the hearts, and the bottoms, dipping them all into the aioli.

4 medium to large artichokes
1 cup aioli (page 34)

Working with 1 artichoke at a time, and using a sharp knife, trim off ¼ inch from the base of the stem, then trim about ½ inch off the top of the leaves to remove the prickly tips. Place the artichokes, stem-side up, on a steamer basket in a saucepan over boiling water, cover, and cook until tender, about 40 minutes. Check the pan occasionally to make sure enough water remains, adding more water, about ½ cup at a time, as needed. To test for doneness, pull off an outer leaf from the base and eat the flesh at the thick, inner edge of the leaf. It should be soft and easy to chew.

Serve the artichokes, accompanying them with the aioli in a communal bowl or as a dollop on each plate.

Serves 4

BRAISED **SPICED** Tofu

PREPARATION TIME: 10 minutes   **COOKING TIME:** 8 minutes

Light and delicate, this dish makes a wonderful first course or side dish. The cumin seeds and aniseeds add an exotic, crunchy twist and the fresh ginger contributes flair to the silky-textured tofu.

If you've never eaten tofu—or don't think you will like it—this recipe will help you understand why it's so popular in Asia, and in Asian communities around the world. At our family table, both children and adults find favor with this distinctly refined, yet assertive dish.

---

2 tablespoons canola, corn, or other vegetable oil
½ teaspoon cumin seeds
½ teaspoon aniseeds
½ teaspoon grated fresh ginger
1 clove garlic, minced
¼ cup thinly sliced green onion, white part only
1 pound firm tofu, cut into 1-inch cubes
½ teaspoon salt, plus salt to taste
½ cup water
2 teaspoons fresh lemon juice
Freshly ground pepper to taste

In a large sauté pan, warm the oil over medium heat. Add the cumin and aniseeds and stir until fragrant, 30 to 45 seconds. Add the ginger, garlic, and green onion and sauté for 2 minutes.

Add the tofu, the ½ teaspoon salt, and the water, mix gently, and simmer until most of the liquid has evaporated, about 5 minutes. Remove from the heat and gently stir in the lemon juice, being careful not to break up the tofu. Season to taste with the addtional salt and with pepper.

Transfer to a serving dish and serve at once.

Serves 4 to 6

Broccoli WITH Lemon OIL

PREPARATION TIME: 5 minutes   **COOKING TIME:** 7 minutes

What can we do to dress up terminally boring broccoli? Actually, the possibilities are countless, and that's the beauty of a mild-tasting vegetable. It can handle many different flavor treatments.

Nonetheless, plain broccoli seems to have quite a few fans among our children's contemporaries, so we don't mess with it much. This subtle and somewhat crunchy variation on the broccoli theme satisfies grown-up palates, while remaining acceptable to younger ones, too.

---

4 cups broccoli florets
4 tablespoons extra-virgin olive oil
¼ lemon
Large pinch of coarse sea salt or kosher salt
Freshly ground pepper to taste

Fill a large sauce pan three-fourths full of water, or fit it with a steamer basket set over 1 inch of water. Boil the broccoli in water or steam it; boiling will take 4 to 5 minutes while steaming will take 6 to 7 minutes. If boiling, drain in a colander. Place the broccoli in a serving bowl.

Drizzle the olive oil over the hot broccoli, then squeeze the lemon over it. Add the salt and pepper and toss gently to coat evenly with the oil and lemon juice. Serve at once.

Serves 4 to 6

FRIED Green Tomatoes with AIOLI

PREPARATION TIME: 15 minutes   **COOKING TIME:** 15 minutes

If you have a vegetable garden, this is a way to use up end-of-season tomatoes that never ripened, which we always have a lot of on our vines. Otherwise, ask your grocer about how best to find green tomatoes. You can also buy Zebra Stripe tomatoes, a variety that sports a green flesh and has a touch more acidity than red tomatoes. Failing those two options, you can use red tomatoes. They will work just fine, although they will not have the same tangy flavor.

The critical technique here is double dipping in cornmeal prior to frying. It's the best way to coat the tomatoes evenly with a crunchy exterior to offset their soft center. We enjoy fried green tomatoes as an appetizer or side dish. Serve them in batches as they are cooked, or keep them warm in a 200°F oven until all are ready to eat. Enjoy them with your fingers or a fork.

---

1 cup cornmeal
1 teaspoon salt
⅓ cup freshly grated Parmesan cheese
1 teaspoon dried basil
⅛ teaspoon cayenne pepper (optional)
2 eggs
1 tablespoon milk
1 cup unbleached all-purpose flour
Canola oil for deep-frying
8 green tomatoes, cut into ¼-inch-thick slices
1 to 2 cups aioli (page 34)

In a bowl, stir together the cornmeal, salt, Parmesan, basil, and the cayenne, if using. Set aside. In a second bowl, whisk or beat the eggs with the milk until blended. Place the flour in a third bowl.

Pour the oil to a depth of about 2 inches into a heavy, deep skillet or sauté pan. Heat the oil over medium-high heat until it begins to bubble.

Reduce the heat to medium so that the oil maintains an even temperature without smoking.

One at a time, dredge the tomato slices in the flour, dip them in the egg mixture, and then dredge them in the cornmeal mixture. Dip them again in the egg, and then dredge them once more in the cornmeal mixture. Slip the slices into the hot oil. Fill the pan but do not crowd the slices. Plan on several batches to fry all the tomato slices.

Keep the tomato slices submerged in the oil by occasionally pressing down on them with a wooden spoon or chopsticks so that both sides cook at once. Fry until golden brown, about 3 minutes. Using a slotted spoon or chopsticks, transfer the slices to paper towels, then serve immediately with the aioli for dipping.

Serves 4 to 6

FRIED **Plantains**

PREPARATION TIME: 5 minutes   **COOKING TIME:** 10 minutes

Although they look somewhat like bananas, plantains are larger and not as sweet. They're also firmer, so they cook without falling apart. We often use them as a side dish in place of potatoes, but they pair marvelously with beans and rice and with eggs, too. Try fried eggs with plantains on the side for breakfast, lunch, or dinner. Make it a two-course meal by starting with Lemon Avocado Salad (page 129).

When shopping for ripe plantains, look for skins that are dark yellow to mottled brown. They look almost rotten. Inside, however, the flesh will range from pale yellow to slightly pink.

---

1 cup canola oil or safflower oil
3 ripe plantains, peeled and cut into ½-inch-thick slices
Coarse sea salt or kosher salt to taste
1 tablespoon chopped fresh cilantro (optional)
Chipotle chile flakes or red pepper flakes to taste (optional)

In a large, deep skillet or sauté pan, heat the oil over medium-high heat. Place the plantain slices in the hot oil and cook until golden brown on both sides, about 10 minutes. Flip the slices occasionally so they brown evenly.

Using a slotted spoon, transfer the plantains to paper towels to drain. Sprinkle lightly with salt and garnish with the cilantro, if using. If you desire a little heat, sprinkle with the chile flakes. Serve immediately.

Serves 4

String Beans
WITH Tomato AND Garlic

PREPARATION TIME: 5 minutes   **COOKING TIME:** 10 minutes

These tasty beans are often featured at our house as a first course in place of salad. They work well as a side dish, too. To save time, we pinch off only the stem of each bean. There's no need to remove the pointy tip.

3 tablespoons extra-virgin olive oil
4 large cloves garlic, minced
1 pound string beans, trimmed
2 tomatoes, coarsely chopped
3 tablespoons water
Salt and freshly ground pepper to taste

In a large sauté pan, heat the olive oil over medium heat. Add the garlic and sauté until fragrant but not browned, about 30 seconds. Add the beans and toss them so that they are evenly coated with the garlic and oil. Stir in the tomatoes.

Add the water, reduce the heat to low, cover, and simmer, stirring occasionally, until the beans are tender, about 10 minutes. If the liquid evaporates, add more water, 1 or 2 tablespoons at a time, to keep the beans moist and prevent burning.

Season the beans with salt and pepper, transfer to a serving plate, and serve at once.

Serves 4

INDIAN SPICED Potatoes WITH
MIXED Green Vegetables AND TANGY Tomato Sauce

PREPARATION TIME: 15 minutes   **COOKING TIME:** 35 minutes

Preparing certain foods in the Indian tradition can be quite easy. But if you don't already have a small cache of spices in your pantry, you will need to invest in a few items, such as turmeric, cumin, and coriander, all of which are available in your grocery store's herb and spice section. Used moderately, these ingredients give a refreshing lift to a meal.

Do kids like them? Ours do, but we must admit they required several attempts before they became accustomed to the exotic spices.

This dish is a fairly heady vegetarian blend. If you use the cayenne pepper, be prepared for heat. Serve with plain rice (page 206) to soak up the light-textured tomato broth. Carnivores may enjoy Chicken Kabobs Marinated in Yogurt and Spices (page 264) on the side as well.

---

2 tablespoons canola oil or corn oil

1 tablespoon grated fresh ginger

1 clove garlic, minced

1 tablespoon ground coriander

1 teaspoon ground cumin

½ teaspoon ground turmeric

¼ teaspoon cayenne pepper (optional)

2 red or white potatoes, peeled and finely diced

2 tomatoes, diced

1 cup cut-up string beans (1- to 2-inch lengths)

1 cup coarsely chopped kale leaves

1 cup fresh or frozen shelled peas

2 cups water

1 teaspoon salt

¼ cup chopped fresh cilantro

2 teaspoons fresh lemon juice

In a large, deep skillet or sauté pan, heat the oil over medium heat. Add the ginger, garlic, coriander, cumin, turmeric, and the cayenne (if using), and sauté until fragrant, about 10 seconds. Add the potatoes, tomatoes, string beans, kale, peas, water, and salt, raise the heat to high, and bring to a boil. Reduce the heat to low, cover, and simmer until tender, about 25 minutes.

Using a fork, crush some of the potatoes to thicken the sauce. If a thicker consistency is desired, simmer uncovered for another 5 to 10 minutes.

Remove from the heat and mix in the cilantro and lemon juice. Transfer to a serving dish and serve at once.

Serves 6

SAUTÉED Kale
WITH Garlic AND Olive Oil

PREPARATION TIME: 5 minutes   **COOKING TIME:** 10 minutes

On its own, kale can be rather drab. But sautéing it with a little olive oil and garlic releases plenty of lively flavor and softens the chewy texture to a smooth silkiness. Easy preparation and the low cost of ingredients have made this side dish very popular at our house. Instead of kale, try other leafy greens, such as Swiss chard or bok choy.

3 tablespoons extra-virgin olive oil
3 cloves garlic, minced
1 pound kale, coarsely chopped
3 tablespoons water
Salt and freshly ground pepper to taste

In a large sauté pan or Dutch oven, heat the olive oil over medium-high heat. Add the garlic and stir lightly until it is evenly coated with oil, about 30 seconds. Add the kale and toss gently, coating all the leaves with oil.

Add the water and gently stir the kale again. Cover and simmer, stirring occasionally, until the leaves are tender, 6 to 8 minutes. If the water evaporates before the kale is tender, and the leaves start to sear, add another 1 or 2 tablespoons water. Season with salt and pepper, transfer to a serving dish, and serve.

Serves 4 or 5

Wilted Spinach
WITH Bacon AND Mushroom DRESSING

PREPARATION TIME: 10 minutes   **COOKING TIME:** 15 minutes

Even if your kids won't usually eat spinach, they may like it prepared this way. Everything seems to taste better with bacon, and highly nutritious spinach is no exception. We must confess, however, that mushrooms can be problematic. One of our daughters likes them, but the other picks them out before she'll eat this dish, which works well as an appetizer or a side dish.

¼ pound bacon, diced
½ pound (8 to 10) mushrooms, trimmed and sliced
1 clove garlic, minced
¼ cup extra-virgin olive oil
1 tablespoon balsamic vinegar
2 tablespoons Dijon mustard
1 tablespoon Worcestershire sauce
¾ pound spinach
4 thin, round slices red onion
Salt and freshly ground pepper to taste

In a Dutch oven or deep sauté pan, fry the bacon over medium heat until crisp, about 5 minutes. Add the mushrooms and sauté until they soften, about 5 minutes. If necessary, add a few tablespoons water to the pan to prevent the bacon from burning. Reduce the heat to low, stir in the garlic, and sauté for another 3 minutes.

Reduce the heat to very low and whisk in the olive oil, vinegar, mustard, and Worcestershire sauce. Remove from the heat. Add the spinach to the pan and toss until all the leaves are evenly coated with the dressing. The spinach will wilt in contact with the warm dressing.

Add the onion and toss again. Season with salt and pepper and serve at once.

Serves 4

SUMMER VEGETABLE Ragout

PREPARATION TIME: 15 minutes   **COOKING TIME:** 20 minutes

With its bright colors and tangy texture, this vibrant stew serves up pure, fresh flavors from a summer garden (or a supermarket produce section). Serve it with polenta (page 209) or mix it with rigatoni or ziti.

---

3 tablespoons extra-virgin olive oil
3 cloves garlic, minced
1 small onion, diced
1 cup sliced mushrooms
2 cups sliced zucchini (¼-inch-thick rounds)
1 green bell pepper, seeded and diced
1 red bell pepper, seeded and diced
1 orange bell pepper, seeded and diced
2 teaspoons dried thyme
2 teaspoons dried oregano
½ cup white wine
4 tomatoes, diced
½ teaspoon salt
Freshly ground pepper to taste
Freshly grated Parmesan cheese for garnish (optional)

In a Dutch oven or large sauté pan, heat the olive oil over medium heat. Add the garlic and onion and sauté until the onion is translucent, about 3 minutes. Add the mushrooms and sauté until soft, about 2 minutes. Add the zucchini and cook, stirring occasionally, until tender, about 3 minutes. Add the bell peppers and herbs and cook, stirring, for 1 minute.

Pour in the wine, raise the heat to high, and bring to a boil. Cover, reduce the heat to low, and simmer for 3 to 4 minutes. Add the tomatoes, re-cover, and simmer until soft, about 5 more minutes. Add the salt and pepper. If there is too much liquid, simmer for a few more minutes uncovered.

Serve the ragout on individual plates with Parmesan, if using.

Serves 4 to 6

CARAMELIZED Onions

PREPARATION TIME: 10 minutes   **COOKING TIME:** 40 minutes

While these silky and sweet onions require a little patience in the pan, they
don't require much attention. Just an occasional stir to keep them from
burning. As a side dish, caramelized onions can add real zip to a number of
recipes such as Panfried Pork Chops (page 284), Pork Roast (page 290), or
even as a second side dish along with mashed potatoes (page 164).

---

3 tablespoons extra-virgin olive oil
5 large yellow or white onions, thinly sliced
1 teaspoon sugar
1 tablespoon balsamic vinegar
½ teaspoon salt

In a large sauté pan, heat the olive oil over medium-high heat. Add the
onions and, using a wooden spoon, separate the slices and coat them with
the oil. Cover, reduce the heat to low, and cook, stirring occasionally,
until the onions have wilted, about 15 minutes.

Sprinkle the sugar over the onions and stir well. Add the balsamic
vinegar and stir again. Finally, add the salt and stir again. Cook
uncovered, stirring occasionally, until the onions are soft and light
brown, 20 to 25 minutes. Transfer the onions to a serving dish and serve
at once.

Serves 4 to 6

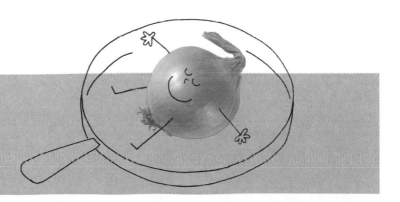

White Beans with Tomatoes, FRESH ROSEMARY, and Parmesan CHEESE

PREPARATION TIME: 10 minutes   **COOKING TIME:** 30 minutes

Using canned beans will significantly cut down on your cooking time here. However, dried beans require relatively little labor—you just soak and boil them. What you lose in time, you may gain in texture. Home-cooked dried beans have a bit more substance and flavor to them than their canned counterparts. But both versions are satisfying, so we make whatever our time dictates. The cooking and preparation times reflect the use of canned beans. If you use dried beans, you will need 4 cups drained home-cooked beans (see page 34).

These beans make a wonderful foil for many meats and meaty fish like tuna or halibut. You can also enjoy them with an omelet, burgers, or simply on their own, accompanied with a green vegetable such as kale, spinach, or string beans.

---

3 tablespoons extra-virgin olive oil

6 cloves garlic, minced

¼ teaspoon chipotle chile flakes or red pepper flakes

4 fresh rosemary sprigs, each about 5 inches long

½ cup red wine

2 pounds fresh tomatoes, coarsely chopped,
   or 1 can (28 ounces) plum tomatoes, drained and coarsely chopped

2 cans (15 ounces each) navy or white kidney beans,
   drained and rinsed

½ teaspoon salt

6 thin, round slices red onion, separated into rings

6 thinly shaved slices Parmesan cheese, each about 2 inches square

---

In a Dutch oven or other large pot, heat the olive oil over high heat. Add the garlic, chile flakes, and rosemary and sauté until fragrant, about 1 minute. Reduce the heat to medium, add the wine, stir well, and simmer for 3 to 4 minutes. Stir in the tomatoes and simmer, uncovered, until soft, about 10 more minutes. Stir in the beans and salt, cover, reduce the heat to low, and simmer for 15 more minutes.

Remove and discard the rosemary sprigs. Pour the beans and their liquid into a large serving bowl. Garnish with the red onion and Parmesan cheese slices and serve at once.

Serves 4 to 6

ROASTED ROSEMARY Potato Crisps

PREPARATION TIME: 10 minutes   **COOKING TIME:** 30 minutes

You'll never crave French fries again after tasting these crispy, thin potato wafers, which admirably deliver on both good taste and good health. True to form, our children insist on dipping them in ketchup. We grown-ups prefer them plain or with Dijon mustard.

As the potatoes bake, the mouthwatering smell of roasting rosemary and olive oil permeates the kitchen. A perfect side dish, try these crisps with salmon steaks, omelets, lamb, chicken, or pork.

---

5 tablespoons extra-virgin olive oil
6 large red potatoes, about 3 pounds total weight
1 tablespoon dried rosemary
Salt and freshly ground pepper to taste

Preheat the oven to 400°F. Coat the bottom of a large rectangular roasting pan with 2 tablespoons of the olive oil.

Wash the potatoes, but leave the skins intact. Cut into ⅛-inch-thick rounds. Arrange the potato slices in slightly overlapping rows to cover the bottom of the pan. (This is a kitchen activity that appeals to our children.) Drizzle the remaining 3 tablespoons olive oil over the top, then sprinkle with the rosemary. Season with salt and pepper.

Bake the potatoes until tender and golden brown, about 30 minutes. Serve piping hot.

Serves 4

CREAMY Potato Gratin

PREPARATION TIME: 15 minutes   **COOKING TIME:** 50 minutes

This creamy, rich dish makes a fine accompaniment for many main courses, from seafood to poultry to pork to beef. It reminds us of the heartwarming fare you find in a no-frills bistro in France on a chilly autumn afternoon. Topped with golden and toasty Parmesan and Gruyère cheeses, these potatoes taste even better when reheated in the microwave for lunch the next day.

If the potato skins are scrubbed clean, the potatoes do not need to be peeled. However, it is important to slice the potatoes thinly or they'll take forever to cook. You can slice them by hand with a large, sharp knife, but a food processor is a lot faster and more precise. You can also use a mandoline, an adjustable-blade vegetable slicer used by many chefs and serious home cooks.

---

1 tablespoon unsalted butter

2 cups heavy cream

½ teaspoon salt

¼ teaspoon freshly ground pepper

¼ teaspoon ground nutmeg

3 pounds white potatoes, unpeeled and thinly sliced

¼ cup freshly grated Parmesan cheese

¼ cup freshly grated Gruyère cheese

Preheat the oven to 350°F. Grease a baking dish about 8 inches square with the butter.

In a bowl, whisk together the cream, salt, pepper, and nutmeg. Using about one-fourth of the potato slices, spread a ¼-inch-thick layer of the potato slices onto the bottom of the prepared baking dish. Cover the potatoes with ½ cup of the cream mixture. Repeat, creating 3 additional layers of potato slices and cream. Sprinkle the 2 cheeses evenly over the top.

Bake the potatoes until tender and the top is bubbly and golden brown, 45 to 50 minutes. Remove from the oven and let cool for 5 minutes to allow the gratin to firm up before serving.

Serves 6 to 8

Mashed **Potatoes**
WITH (OR WITHOUT) **Parmesan Cheese**

PREPARATION TIME: 10 minutes   **COOKING TIME:** 20 minutes

You can use white or red potatoes here. We leave the skins on, not only because it's easier, but also because we like it. That's why we recommend a thin-skinned "new" potato over a thick-skinned baking potato. Extra-virgin olive oil and freshly grated Parmesan cheese give these smooth spuds an edge over the usual fare. But if you're making mashed potatoes to accompany a rich dish like Coq au Vin (page 262), keep things simple and forgo the cheese.

---

3 pounds new potatoes or other thin-skinned potatoes such as
*   Yukon Gold*
1 cup extra-virgin olive oil, plus extra oil for drizzling
1 teaspoon salt, plus salt to taste
1 cup freshly grated Parmesan cheese (optional)
2 tablespoons unsalted butter
Freshly ground pepper to taste

Wash the potatoes, but leave the skins intact. Cut the potatoes into quarters or eighths, depending on their size. In a large saucepan fitted with a steamer basket over 1 inch of water or three-fourths full of water, steam the potatoes or boil them in water until they are tender, about 20 minutes. Drain the potatoes in a colander if boiling them, or remove them from the steamer and empty the water from the steamer pan. Return the potatoes to the pan. (Using the pan again keeps the potatoes warm and shortens cleanup time.)

Using a hand masher, mash the potatoes while adding the olive oil, ¼ to ½ cup at a time, continuing to mash until the potatoes are fairly smooth. Some lumps are inevitable. (If you don't have a hand masher, use a large serving fork.)

Using a wooden spoon, stir in the salt, Parmesan cheese (if using), butter, and any remaining olive oil. The potatoes will become smoother but remain dense, not runny. Season with the additional salt. Serve individual portions garnished with a grind of pepper.

Serves 6

CREAMED Corn WITH Bacon

PREPARATION TIME: 15 minutes   **COOKING TIME:** 40 minutes

Obviously, this is no low-fat vegetable dish. But it tastes so good, we don't think about counting calories! Try it as a side dish for pork, steak, chicken, burgers, or any number of other culinary centerpieces. The cayenne is optional if your kids have ultrasensitive palates. Children with braces will especially appreciate creamed corn as a fine alternative to hard-to-eat corn on the cob.

---

3 slices bacon, cut into ¼-inch dice
2 tablespoons unsalted butter
½ onion, diced
6 ears corn, kernels removed (about 4 cups)
¼ teaspoon salt, plus salt to taste
⅛ teaspoon cayenne pepper (optional)
1½ cups heavy cream
¼ cup whole milk
Freshly ground pepper to taste

In a small sauté pan, fry the bacon over medium heat until crisp, about 5 minutes. Remove from the pan with a slotted spoon and reserve.

In a large skillet, melt the butter over medium heat. Add the onion and sauté until translucent, 3 to 4 minutes. Stir in the cooked bacon bits, then gently stir in the corn, the ¼ teaspoon salt, and the cayenne, if using. Add the cream and milk and bring to a gentle boil, stirring to prevent burning. Reduce the heat to low and simmer, uncovered, until the corn takes on a creamy texture, about 30 minutes.

Season with the additional salt and with pepper. Transfer to a serving dish and serve at once.

Serves 4 to 6

BRAISED Red Cabbage
WITH Apple AND Bacon

PREPARATION TIME: 15 minutes   **COOKING TIME:** 45 minutes

With its spice and cider vinegar edge, this bright-flavored dish is a wake-up call for the palate. It's great alongside turkey breast (page 270) or pork loin (page 285), or perhaps with mashed potatoes (page 164) on the side as well. Look for juniper berries on the spice shelf at your local grocery store. A few berries go a long way, and you can eat or discard them. We like their subtle floral notes and slightly crunchy texture.

A note of caution: This is fragrant, heady stuff, and the kids may balk at its assertiveness. Keep the two-bite rule (see page 116) in mind, and they might grow to love it anyway.

---

5 slices bacon cut into matchsticks
1 onion, diced
1 head red cabbage, shredded
⅓ cup cider vinegar
3 juniper berries
1½ teaspoons whole cloves
1½ teaspoons coarse sea salt or kosher salt
¼ teaspoon freshly ground pepper
1 Granny Smith or other tart apple, peeled, halved, cored, and grated

---

In a deep, large skillet, cook the bacon and onion over high heat until the bacon is crisp, about 5 minutes. Add the cabbage, vinegar, juniper berries, cloves, salt, and pepper. Stir well, reduce the heat to medium, and simmer, uncovered, stirring every 5 to 10 minutes, until the cabbage is thoroughly wilted, about 30 minutes. If the cabbage becomes dry, add ¼ to ½ cup water and continue to simmer.

Stir in the apple and simmer for 5 more minutes. Pick out and discard the juniper berries and as many cloves as you can easily locate. Transfer the cabbage mixture to a serving dish and serve at once.

Serves 4 to 6

GARLIC AND ONIONS— PUNGENT BUT HEALTHY

It is no wonder that garlic and onions have long been touted as natural cure-alls throughout the world. Both belong to the *Allium* genus, the members of which are loaded with good-health-inducing substances known as allyl sulfides. These sulfur-based compounds may not cure everything, but they do reduce the risk of heart disease by lowering cholesterol. Allyl sulfides also give garlic and onions their distinctively pungent aromas, which discourage some people from including them in their daily diet.

Those who don't—especially men—might reconsider. In a study released in 2002 by the National Cancer Institute, garlic and onions are shown to be linked to a decreased incidence of prostate cancer. Eat them raw—minced or chopped—for maximum nutritional benefits. Cooked, they pack less curative powers—and less aromatic punch as well!

Eggplant STEAKS
WITH Tomato AND Mozzarella CHEESE

PREPARATION TIME: 5 minutes   **COOKING TIME:** 10 minutes

This is a takeoff on eggplant Parmesan. But it's a lot easier to make, less messy to eat, and purer in flavor. The eggplant steaks are the meat of your meal. Enjoy them with Asian Slaw (page 132) or Really Simple Pasta with Olive Oil, Thyme, and Parmesan (page 176) on the side.

---

1 large eggplant, unpeeled
Salt and freshly ground pepper to taste
8 to 12 teaspoons extra-virgin olive oil,
    plus extra oil for drizzling (optional)
2 teaspoons dried thyme
1 large tomato, thinly sliced (4 to 6 slices)
1 fresh mozzarella cheese ball, about ½ pound, cut into ¼-inch-thick
    slices (4 to 6 slices)
¼ cup coarsely chopped fresh basil

Preheat the broiler or prepare a fire in a grill.

Slice the eggplant crosswise into 4 to 6 slices each ½ inch thick. Generously sprinkle both sides of each eggplant slice with salt and pepper. Drizzle approximately 1 teaspoon of the olive oil on both sides of each eggplant slice. Sprinkle both sides of each slice with a pinch or two of the thyme.

Arrange the slices on a broiler pan and slip under the broiler, or arrange them on a grill rack over the fire. Cook until browned on the first side, about 5 minutes. Flip each slice and cook until tender, about 3 more minutes. On top of each slice of eggplant, place a slice of tomato and then top it with a slice of mozzarella. If using a grill, cover it at this point. Broil or grill until the cheese begins to melt, 1 to 2 minutes.

Transfer to individual plates and serve immediately, garnished with the basil and a drizzle of the olive oil, if desired.

Serves 4

STUFFED Red AND Green Peppers
WITH LAMB AND PORK

PREPARATION TIME: 20 minutes   **COOKING TIME:** 40 minutes

These hearty meat-and-rice-stuffed peppers are an ideal way to use up leftover rice.

In the interest of color, we like to use red and green bell peppers. Red peppers tend to be sweeter, while green peppers retain more firmness.

A word of caution: These peppers emerge scalding hot from the oven. Prior to serving, let cool for 5 to 10 minutes before serving.

---

2 tablespoons extra-virgin olive oil
½ onion, diced
2 cloves garlic, minced
1 carrot, peeled and coarsely chopped
½ pound ground lamb
½ pound ground pork
3 green bell peppers
3 red bell peppers
3 plum tomatoes, diced
1½ teaspoons ground cumin
1 teaspoon salt, plus salt to taste
1½ cups cooked white or brown rice (page 206)
3 tablespoons tomato paste
½ cup water
Freshly ground pepper to taste

Preheat the oven to 400°F.

In a large skillet or sauté pan, heat the olive oil over medium heat. Add the onion and garlic and sauté until the onion is translucent, 3 to 4 minutes. Add the carrot and sauté 2 to 3 minutes. Stir in the lamb and pork, and sauté, breaking up the meat as needed, until cooked through, 5 to 8 minutes. The meats should be crumbly and well mixed.

While the meat is cooking, cut off ½-inch-thick slice from the stem end of each bell pepper. Discard the ends and remove the seeds. Rinse the bell peppers and pat dry.

Gently stir the tomatoes, cumin, and the 1 teaspoon salt into the meat mixture. Stir in the rice and reduce the heat to low. In a small bowl, dilute the tomato paste in the water. Stir the liquid into the meat and rice, mixing well. Season with the additional salt and with pepper. Remove from the heat.

Carefully fill each bell pepper with the meat mixture, dividing it evenly. Place the stuffed peppers in a baking dish or pan, standing them upright. Pour water to a depth of ½ inch in the bottom of the dish, and then cover the dish with aluminum foil.

Bake the peppers until tender when pierced with a fork, 30 to 40 minutes. Remove from the oven and let cool for 5 to 10 minutes before serving.

Serves 4 to 6

Zucchinius MAXIMUS

PREPARATION TIME: 15 minutes   **COOKING TIME:** 80 minutes

Each summer, without fail, certain zucchini in our garden grow out of control. Some of them attain a size that approaches two feet in length! The meat of these monsters is generally less sweet and firm than that of their smaller siblings, so we hollow them out and stuff the melonlike shells with a blend of seasoned meats. If you do not have leftover rice on hand, cook some rice while the whole zucchini is in the oven.

---

1 very large zucchini (15 to 18 inches long)
2 tablespoons, plus 1 teaspoon extra-virgin olive oil
1 onion, diced
2 cloves garlic, minced
1½ teaspoons dried thyme
1 teaspoon dried oregano
1 cup sliced mushrooms (optional)
½ pound ground lamb
½ pound ground beef
3 plum tomatoes, diced
½ cup chopped fresh parsley
3 cups cooked white or brown rice (page 206)
⅓ cup freshly grated Parmesan cheese
½ teaspoon salt
Freshly grated pepper to taste

Preheat the oven to 400°F.

Place the whole zucchini directly on the oven rack and bake until tender when pierced with a fork, about 30 minutes. Remove from the oven and let cool for 5 to 10 minutes.

Cut the zucchini in half lengthwise and, using a spoon, carefully scoop out the flesh, leaving a shell ¼ to ½ inch thick. Discard the scooped out flesh and reserve the shell. Reduce the oven temperature to 350°F.

In a large sauté pan or skillet, heat the 2 tablespoons olive oil over medium heat. Add the onion and garlic and sauté until the onion is translucent, 3 to 4 minutes. Stir in the thyme and oregano and then add the mushrooms, if using, and sauté for 2 more minutes.

Push the onion and mushrooms to the side of the pan and add the lamb and beef to the exposed pan surface. Using a spatula or wooden spoon, break up the meat and sauté until cooked through, 5 to 8 minutes. Stir in the tomatoes, parsley, and the onion and mushrooms, cover, reduce the heat to low, and cook for 15 minutes to blend the flavors.

Remove from the heat and stir in the rice, Parmesan, salt, and pepper. Coat a roasting pan with the remaining 1 teaspoon olive oil. Place the zucchini shells in the pan, trimming to fit if necessary, and gently fill them with the meat mixture. Cover the pan with aluminum foil.

Bake the stuffed zucchini for 10 minutes. Remove the foil and bake until the tops are crispy, about 10 more minutes. Cut each zucchini boat crosswise into halves or thirds and serve immediately.

Serves 4 to 6

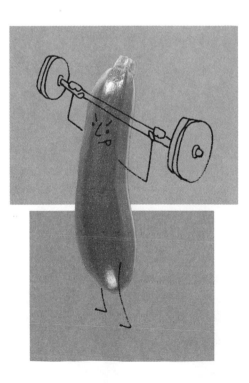

Chapter 7

PASTA
and
GRAINS

HEALTHY, SIMPLE TO MAKE, AND A FAVORITE AMONG YOUNG AND OLD, PASTA MAY BE THE ULTIMATE STAPLE FOR EVERY KITCHEN. Grains run a close second. We eat pasta at least twice a week. Because it reheats so easily, pasta retains added value at our house for leftovers.

How do we keep pasta from becoming boring? A varied repertoire of sauces helps, as well as a dedication to clear, clean flavors. We offer nineteen different pasta recipes in this chapter as evidence of this variety.

For us, pasta shape is not a prime consideration. Broader noodles, such as linguine and fettuccine, hold sauce more easily than wispy-thin angel hair pasta. But thinner noodles can be silkier on the palate. For children, short, round noodles are easiest to spear with a fork. Ultimately, personal preference should be the deciding factor in choosing pasta.

Rice and other grains also add substance to many meals. They soak up sauces while filling out the body of a dish. Whole grains contain the most fiber and nutrients, but they don t necessarily form the core of our home diet. We like white rice, and we also like whole-grain brown rice. So we eat them both, depending on our preference of the moment.

Risotto, made from short-grain, starchy Arborio rice, is also high on our list of favorites. Although it requires more attention than cooking regular rice, risotto is not difficult to make. The same goes for polenta, made from cornmeal. Other grains we enjoy include bulgur (cracked wheat) and couscous, which, from a diner s perspective, are excellent stand-ins for rice.

COOKING PASTA

Pasta may be the easiest of all foods to cook, and yet there is much discussion about how best to do it. Even we can t agree. Jodie likes to salt her water prior to boiling it because she says it boils faster and gives the pasta more flavor. Jeff takes a more minimalist approach and just boils the water as is without salt. Either way, no one complains about the end result. The skill is in making sure your pasta doesn't overcook and become mushy. It should be only slightly al dente, or kind of chewy, when removed from the water. Most dried pasta cooks in about 10 minutes. Fresh pasta cooks in only 2 to 3 minutes. Dried Japanese soba noodles are done in 3 to 4 minutes. Remember to use plenty of water, or your pasta will suffer from starch buildup and not separate or cook evenly. About 4 quarts of water is adequate for 1 pound of dried noodles, which we generally cook in a 6-quart soup pot.

About 4 quarts water
1 teaspoon salt (optional)
1 pound dried pasta

In a large pot, bring the water and the salt, if using, to a boil over high heat. Add the pasta all at once and stir it a bit as it softens. Reduce the heat slightly, but keep it high enough to maintain a boil without splattering the stove. When the pasta is no longer crunchy, but still firm and chewy, drain it in a colander and shake dry. Unless you want to bring it to room temperature quickly, don t rinse pasta with water to remove the starch like some of our parents did. Sauces will not adhere well to rinsed pasta.

REALLY Simple PASTA
WITH Olive Oil, THYME, AND Parmesan

PREPARATION TIME: 5 minutes

We often have leftover pasta, which we store for up to 4 days in the refrigerator. Invariably, it resurfaces sooner—cold and sticky. However, a little olive oil, cheese, and thyme can quickly transform these dull-edged noodles into a welcome snack or lunch. A touch of smoky-hot chipotle chile flakes adds high notes. Not just for leftovers, this simple dish works well with freshly cooked pasta, too. Add about 10 minutes to your kitchen time for cooking the pasta (see page 175). One pound dried pasta will serve 4 or 5.

Leftover cooked noodles for single portion
1 to 1½ tablespoons extra-virgin olive oil
½ teaspoon dried thyme
Freshly grated Parmesan cheese to taste
½ teaspoon chipotle chile flakes or red pepper flakes (optional)
Salt and freshly ground pepper to taste

Reheat leftover pasta in a microwave, or steam over boiling water.

Toss the noodles with the olive oil. Add the thyme and toss again, then toss with the Parmesan and the chile flakes, if using. Season with salt and pepper and serve at once.

Serves 1

Lemon AND Herb PASTA

PREPARATION TIME: 10 minutes   **COOKING TIME:** 10 minutes

Citrus and herbs are natural friends. When we make this pasta on very short notice, we use dried thyme. However, with a little foresight, we might remember to pick up a bunch of fresh basil on our way home from work. Fresh rosemary also adds an interesting twist. But less is more here; we recommend using only one herb at a time. Kids who like citrus flavors like lemon drops and lemon bars—will like this pasta, too.

¾ cup extra-virgin olive oil

1 cup freshly grated Parmesan cheese

Juice of 2 lemons

1 tablespoon dried thyme, or ½ cup coarsely chopped fresh basil,
  or ¼ cup minced fresh rosemary

1 pound dried linguine or other pasta

Coarse sea salt or kosher salt and freshly ground pepper to taste

---

In a large bowl, stir together the olive oil, Parmesan, lemon juice, and one of the herbs. Meanwhile, in a saucepan, cook the pasta in boiling water (lightly salted if desired) until the noodles are tender but still firm, about 10 minutes. Drain the pasta in a colander and shake dry.

Add the pasta to the bowl with the lemon and herb sauce and toss to coat evenly. Season with salt and pepper and serve at once.

Serves 4

Pasta WITH
SUMMER FRESH Tomato Sauce

PREPARATION TIME: 10 minutes　　　　　　　**COOKING TIME:** 25 minutes

Made with summertime's best tomatoes and basil, this simple sauce is light textured and pure pleasure on the palate. The secret to this sauce is the freshness of the ingredients and being careful not to overcook them.

2 tablespoons extra-virgin olive oil
4 cloves garlic, minced
2 pounds tomatoes, peeled (see page 32), blanching water reserved
½ teaspoon salt
1 cup coarsely chopped fresh basil
¼ cup freshly grated Parmesan cheese
1 pound dried pasta of choice
Freshly ground pepper to taste

In a large sauté pan or skillet, heat the olive oil over medium heat. Add the garlic and stir until golden brown, about 1 minute. Stir in the tomatoes and salt. Reduce the heat to low and simmer, uncovered, until the sauce has thickened, about 10 minutes. Add the basil and Parmesan and simmer for 5 more minutes.

While the sauce is simmering, bring the reserved water back to a boil, add the pasta, stir, and cook until it is tender but still firm, about 10 minutes. Drain the pasta in a colander and shake dry.

Transfer the pasta to individual serving bowls or plates. Spoon the tomato sauce over the top. Garnish with pepper and serve at once.

Serves 4 or 5

PARMESAN: PERFECT PASTA CHEESE

We eat more Parmesan than any other type of cheese. But because it is so sharp and forward in its flavors, we rarely eat it on its own. Most often, we toss it with pasta, although it also tastes terrific grated into hot soups, risotto, or other hot foods that might benefit from a hint of melted cheese.

In Italy, Parmesan cheese is called Parmigiano or Parmigiano-Reggiano, after the cities of Parma and Reggia from which it takes its name. True Italian Parmesan cheese bears little resemblance to the salty, powdery stuff often sold in green cylindrical packages in the United States. A small amount of freshly grated true Parmesan will add far more flavor and interest to your pasta than any domestic imposter. (There are, of course, many fine American cheeses, but we haven't found one yet that competes successfully in the Parmesan category.)

Italian Parmesan has a rich, nutty flavor that comes from the particular quality of the milk from which it is made and the one- to two-year-long aging process that brings out its flavors. It is produced in limited quantities—about 2.5 million large wheels annually—and only in the Emilia-Romagna region.

That's why Parmigiano-Reggiano costs more than many other hard cheeses suitable for grating. The good news is that you don't need to use a lot of it. Roughly a tablespoon per serving adds sufficient verve and character to any dish. Too much will overpower your pasta.

Some New World alternatives to Parmesan are reasonably good, but they still seem to rely more on salt than milk for their flavor. When the price of a chunk of Parmesan is too high for our budget, we turn to a more reasonably priced, hard Italian cheese called pecorino romano. Unlike Parmesan, which is made from cow's milk, pecorino is a sheep's milk cheese. It's saltier than Parmesan, and also serves up an almost flinty, or mineral, edge.

Pre-grated cheese does not retain as much flavor or moisture as freshly grated cheese. We use a small, handheld grater made by Zyliss to do the job tableside. It holds enough cheese for two or three servings, and employs an easy-turning crank mechanism. This tool is safer and more practical than the traditional flat grater that requires holding the cheese while scraping it across a sharpened surface. That often produces grated fingers as well as grated cheese! Our grater is safe for children of all ages. Parmesan can also be grated in a blender, but remember that any grated cheese that is not used immediately will lose its intensity.

Cold Sauce PASTA

PREPARATION TIME: 5 minutes   **COOKING TIME:** 10 minutes

This pasta sauce is a parent's dream come true. It serves up all the satisfaction that comes with tomato sauce, yet requires no cooking—aside from the pasta, of course. We created this sauce for our children when they were very young and couldn't wait for a hot sauce to cook. It remains one of their favorite pasta sauces today.

---

1 pound dried pasta of choice

¼ cup extra-virgin olive oil

1 teaspoon dried basil or 3 tablespoons coarsely chopped fresh basil

3 tomatoes, coarsely chopped (about 2 cups)

2 cloves garlic, minced

3 tablespoons freshly grated Parmesan cheese, plus extra cheese
    for serving (optional)

1 tablespoon fresh lemon juice

½ teaspoon salt

In a saucepan, cook the pasta in boiling water (lightly salted if desired) until tender but still firm, about 10 minutes. While the pasta is cooking, combine all the other ingredients in a large bowl. When the pasta is done, drain it in a colander and shake dry.

Add the pasta to the bowl with the cold sauce and toss to coat evenly. Serve immediately, with the additional Parmesan, if using.

Serves 4

Sage Butter PASTA

PREPARATION TIME: 5 minutes   **COOKING TIME:** 10 minutes

The sage butter that coats this pasta is simple, rich, and buttery, yet balanced by the mineral essence of fresh sage.

---

1 pound dried linguine, fettuccine, or other pasta
6 tablespoons unsalted butter
½ cup coarsely chopped fresh sage
½ teaspoon coarse sea salt or kosher salt, plus salt to taste
Freshly ground pepper to taste
Freshly grated Parmesan cheese for serving (optional)

In a saucepan, cook the pasta in boiling water (lightly salted if desired) until tender but still firm, about 10 minutes. While the pasta is cooking, melt the butter in a saucepan over low heat. Stir the sage and the ½ teaspoon salt into the butter, then remove from the heat and reserve. When the pasta is done, drain it in a colander and shake dry.

Transfer the pasta to a large bowl, add the sage butter, and toss to coat evenly. Season with the additional salt and with pepper. We grown-ups appreciate this dish without any cheese, but the kids require their ubiquitous Parmesan.

Serves 4

Linguine WITH Kale AND MARINATED Sun-Dried Tomatoes

PREPARATION TIME: 10 minutes   **COOKING TIME:** 10 minutes

When sautéed in olive oil with garlic, kale is one of our daughters' favorite greens. And when paired with squiggly linguine, plus bits of sun-dried tomato, their response is even keener. Sweet, tangy sun-dried tomatoes in olive oil can be found, jarred, in many grocery stores and specialty food shops.

---

1 pound dried linguine or other pasta
4 tablespoons extra-virgin olive oil
4 cloves garlic, minced
3 tablespoons water
1 large bunch kale, coarsely chopped
¼ cup sun-dried tomatoes packed in olive oil, coarsely chopped
Salt and freshly ground pepper to taste
½ cup freshly grated Parmesan cheese
Red pepper flakes to taste (optional)

In a saucepan, cook the pasta in boiling water (lightly salted if desired) until tender but still firm, about 10 minutes. Drain and reserve.

While the pasta is still cooking, in a large, deep skillet or Dutch oven, heat 3 tablespoons of the olive oil over medium heat. Add the garlic and sauté until light brown, about 1 minute. Add the water and stir to break up any clumps of garlic. Add the kale and stir until coated with the oil and garlic. Cover and cook over medium heat, stirring occasionally, until tender, about 5 to 7 minutes. Add a little water, 1 or 2 tablespoons at a time, to the pan if the kale begins to stick. Stir in the tomatoes.

Remove from the heat and add the freshly cooked pasta directly to the kale pan. Add the remaining 1 tablespoon olive oil and toss until all the ingredients are well blended. Season with salt and pepper.

Serve immediately. Garnish individual servings with the Parmesan and with the red pepper flakes, if using.

Serves 4

ONE-POT Broccoli PASTA

PREPARATION TIME: 5 minutes **COOKING TIME:** 10 minutes

Sometimes one pot is all we can handle at the end of the day. Here, we simply stretch our boiling pasta water by using it to cook our vegetable as well. Broccoli is a good choice because it is firm textured and doesn't fall apart when transferred to the colander with the noodles. But other vegetables, such as string beans or carrots, would work equally well. Or, for a more colorful approach, include both broccoli and sliced carrots.

1 pound dried pasta of choice
1 bunch broccoli (about 1 pound)
Extra-virgin olive oil for serving
Freshly grated Parmesan cheese for serving
Salt and freshly ground pepper to taste

In a saucepan, cook the pasta in boiling water (lightly salted if desired) for 5 minutes. During that time, trim the broccoli so that you keep the top florets. You may also cut the stems into slices ¼ inch thick.

Add the florets and the stems, if using, to the pasta and cook for 5 more minutes. Drain the pasta and broccoli in a colander and shake dry. Divide the pasta and broccoli among individual plates. Drizzle each serving with 1 to 2 teaspoons olive oil. Toss gently to coat the noodles, then sprinkle with the Parmesan, salt, and pepper and serve at once.

Serves 4 to 6

Pink Sauce PASTA

PREPARATION TIME: 15 minutes   **COOKING TIME:** 45 minutes

This creamy, pink tomato sauce gets it color from blending two sauces, one red and one white. For the white sauce, use an imported Italian Fontina for the best result. A bit of heat comes from red pepper flakes, but the amount is modest, with no cries of protest from our kids. Some picky palates might not like cream sauces, however. We suggest putting a little of the red sauce aside for them.

To save time, you can make the red sauce in advance, and then refrigerate it for up to 3 days.

RED SAUCE:

1 tablespoon extra-virgin olive oil
¼ pound pancetta or bacon, diced or cut into small pieces
1 onion, diced
3 cloves garlic, minced
¼ teaspoon red pepper flakes
3 tablespoons minced fresh rosemary
½ cup red wine or water
1 can (15 ounces) tomato purée
2 to 3 pounds fresh tomatoes (peeled if desired, see page 32),
*   coarsely chopped, or 1 can (28 ounces) plum tomatoes,*
*   drained and coarsely chopped*
½ teaspoon salt

WHITE SAUCE:

¾ cup heavy cream
¾ cup freshly grated Parmesan cheese
¾ cup freshly grated Italian Fontina cheese

1 pound dried pasta of choice

To make the red sauce, in a large saucepan or Dutch oven, heat the olive oil over medium heat. Add the pancetta and sauté until lightly browned, about 5 minutes. Add the onion, garlic, red pepper flakes, and rosemary and sauté until the onion is translucent, about 3 minutes. Add the wine, raise the heat to medium-high, bring to a boil, and boil for 2 to 3 minutes.

Stir in the tomato purée. (You can also make a purée by pulsing peeled tomatoes in a blender, but the canned version will be smoother.) Add the chopped tomatoes and salt and stir well. Reduce the heat to low and simmer, uncovered, until thickened, about 30 minutes.

To make the white sauce, in a small saucepan, combine the cream and cheeses over low heat. Cook, stirring continuously, until the cheeses are melted, 3 to 5 minutes.

Just before both sauces are ready, in a saucepan cook the pasta in boiling water (lightly salted if desired) until tender but still firm, about 10 minutes. Drain the pasta in a colander and shake dry. Transfer to a large bowl.

Stir the white sauce into the red sauce and mix well. Pour the now pink sauce over the pasta, toss to coat evenly, and serve at once.

Serves 4 to 6

Stoplight Pasta
WITH PEPPERS

PREPARATION TIME: 10 minutes   **COOKING TIME:** 30 minutes

The unusual name here refers to the fact that we use red, yellow, and green bell peppers. (If you can't find all three colors, substitute whatever colors are available.) A special bonus here is ease of eating. Ear-shaped orecchiette may not be easy to pronounce, but the bite-sized pasta requires no fancy fork work. The "ears" are eminently child friendly.

---

4 tablespoons extra-virgin olive oil

1 onion, diced

2 cloves garlic, minced

3 tablespoons finely chopped fresh rosemary

1 red bell pepper, seeded and cut lengthwise into narrow strips

1 yellow bell pepper, seeded and cut lengthwise into narrow strips

1 green bell pepper, seeded and cut lengthwise into narrow strips

½ teaspoon salt, plus salt to taste

¼ cup white wine or water

1 pound dried orecchiette pasta

6 slices feta cheese, each 2 inches thick

Freshly ground pepper to taste

In a Dutch oven or large, deep skillet, heat 3 tablespoons of the olive oil over medium heat. Add the onion and sauté until translucent, about 3 minutes. Stir in the garlic, rosemary, bell peppers, and the ½ teaspoon salt and mix well. Cover, reduce the heat to low, and simmer until the peppers have wilted, about 10 minutes. Add the wine and continue to simmer, uncovered, until most of the liquid has evaporated, about 10 more minutes.

While the sauce is cooking, cook the orechiette in boiling water (lightly salted if desired) until tender but still firm, about 12 minutes. Drain the pasta in a colander and shake dry.

Preheat the broiler. Place the feta slices in a baking dish or on a lightly oiled or nonstick baking sheet. Drizzle the feta slices evenly with the remaining 1 tablespoon olive oil. Place the cheese under the broiler and broil until it turns light gold, 3 to 4 minutes.

In a large bowl, combine the cooked pasta with the pepper mixture and the broiled cheese. Toss gently but thoroughly, which will make the cheese crumble. Season with the additional salt and with pepper and serve at once.

Serves 6

ROASTED Red Pepper
PASTA SAUCE

PREPARATION TIME: 10 minutes   **COOKING TIME:** 20 minutes

Here, the sweetness of red bell peppers gives a fresh face to red pasta sauce. We use a little optional white wine here, which loses all alcohol to evaporation while simmering on the stove. However, water makes an acceptable substitute should your wine cellar be bare. The kids like this sauce because it's red, like tomato sauce, but somehow refreshingly different.

---

3 tablespoons extra-virgin olive oil

1 onion, diced

2 cloves garlic, minced

¼ teaspoon chipotle chile flakes or red pepper flakes

½ cup white wine or water

5 roasted red bell peppers, peeled and seeded (see page 35),
*   then quartered lengthwise*

¼ teaspoon salt, plus salt to taste

Freshly ground pepper to taste

1 pound dried linguine, fettuccine, or other pasta

Freshly grated Parmesan cheese for serving

In a Dutch oven or large saucepan, heat the olive oil over medium heat. Add the onion and sauté until translucent, 3 to 4 minutes. Stir in the garlic and then the chile flakes. Add the wine and simmer for 3 minutes. Add the bell peppers and the ¼ teaspoon salt, cover, reduce the heat to low, and simmer for about 15 minutes to blend the flavors. Remove from the heat.

Transfer one-half to three-fourths of the pepper mixture to a blender or food processor and coarsely purée, leaving small bits of pepper. Return the puréed pepper to the Dutch oven and mix well. If the sauce seems too thick, stir in 2 to 3 tablespoons water. (If you have roasted your own peppers and retained the juice, use it here instead of water.) Place over medium heat and simmer to reheat thoroughly, 3 to 5 more minutes. Season with the additional salt and with pepper.

While the sauce is cooking, in a saucepan, cook the pasta in boiling water (lightly salted if desired) until tender but still firm, about 10 minutes. Drain the pasta in a colander and shake dry. You can spoon the sauce over the cooked pasta in a serving bowl, or toss the pasta in the pan with the sauce for even coating of the noodles. Garnish individual servings with Parmesan and serve at once.

Serves 4

SPICED Ginger Sesame NOODLES

PREPARATION TIME: 15 minutes   **COOKING TIME:** 10 minutes

These silky smooth sesame noodles are only mildly spicy, so they don't register any alarms on our kids' heat-sensitive palates. But they are loaded with seductive, exotic flavors and deliver a delightful crunch from toasted sesame seeds. Diced red bell pepper adds visual contrast and a mild sweetness.

Our older daughter, Skye, devours the noodles but leaves the tofu. Her sister, Zoë, can't get enough of the tofu but leaves the noodles. We grown-ups love the whole package.

Because these noodles are eaten chilled or at room temperature, they're great as leftovers. You can also easily take them to potlucks, where they will be quickly and efficiently consumed.

---

1 pound dried linguine, fettuccine, or other pasta

3 tablespoons Asian sesame oil

1 tablespoon sesame chile oil

6 tablespoons soy sauce or tamari

1 clove garlic, crushed or minced

½ teaspoon ground ginger

½ teaspoon ground allspice

12 to 14 ounces firm tofu, cut into ½-inch cubes

1 red bell pepper, seeded and cut into ¼-inch dice

4 green onions, white and green parts, thinly sliced

3 tablespoons sesame seeds, toasted (see page 32)

Pesticide-free edible flowers such as nasturtiums
*   for garnish (optional)*

In a saucepan, cook the pasta in boiling water (lightly salted if desired) until tender but firm, about 10 minutes. Meanwhile, in a large serving bowl, combine the sesame oils, soy sauce, garlic, ginger, and allspice and stir to blend evenly. Add the tofu and toss to coat thoroughly.

NOTES ON SESAME OIL AND SOY SAUCE:

Asian, or toasted, sesame oil is copper colored and richer than clear cold-pressed sesame oil. Sesame chile oil is simply chile-infused toasted sesame oil. Both are found among the oils or Asian condiments at your supermarket. In our kitchen, soy sauce and tamari are interchangeable. Tamari was originally a by-product of miso production, while soy sauce was made by extended maceration of soy beans, wheat, and salt in water. Today, however, the distinction is blurred because most tamari is also labeled soy sauce. Some are made with wheat and some are wheat-free. We use them both with similar results.

Drain the pasta in a colander and rinse with cold water to bring it to room temperature. Shake the noodles dry and add them to the tofu-sesame mixture, tossing until evenly coated.

Add the red bell pepper and green onions and toss to mix. Add the sesame seeds and toss again. Serve at room temperature in shallow bowls or on large plates. Garnish with edible flowers, if using.

Serves 4 to 6

Ginger **Shiitake** RICE NOODLES

PREPARATION TIME: 10 minutes, plus 20 minutes for soaking mushrooms   **COOKING TIME:** 10 minutes

Here these light-textured rice noodles are graced with the heady aromas of mushrooms and spice, yet they remain delicate on the palate. Chewy, meaty shiitake mushrooms add flavorful contrast. This dish is distinct from both our Italian-inspired pastas and our Spiced Ginger Sesame Noodles (page 190) primarily because of the use of rice noodles. Look for the noodles in the Asian or pasta section at your grocery store. For this recipe, we prefer thicker linguine-style rice noodles to very thin ones.

1 ounce dried shiitake mushrooms

1 package (7 ounces) dried flat rice noodles, about ¼ inch wide (linguini style)

3 tablespoons Asian sesame oil

4 tablespoons oyster sauce

2 teaspoons rice vinegar

2 tablespoons soy sauce or tamari

1 tablespoon sesame chile oil

3 cloves garlic, minced

1 tablespoon grated fresh ginger

6 green onions, white part only, thinly sliced

In a bowl, combine the mushrooms with hot water to cover. Let soak until the mushrooms are rehydrated, 15 to 20 minutes, then drain. Remove and discard the stems and slice the caps into narrow strips.

In a saucepan, cook the noodles in boiling water until they are just tender, 3 to 5 minutes. Drain the noodles in a colander and shake dry. Set aside.

In a small bowl, stir together the Asian sesame oil, oyster sauce, rice vinegar, and soy sauce. Set aside.

In a large sauté pan or skillet, heat the sesame chile oil, garlic, and ginger over medium-high heat. Stir rapidly for 30 seconds until fragrant.

Add the mushrooms, stir to mix well, and cook for 1 minute. Add the green onions and stir again to mix. Remove from the heat, add the sesame oil–oyster sauce mixture, and stir again. Add the noodles to the pan and toss until they are evenly coated with the sauce. Serve immediately.

Serves 4 as a light main course or side dish

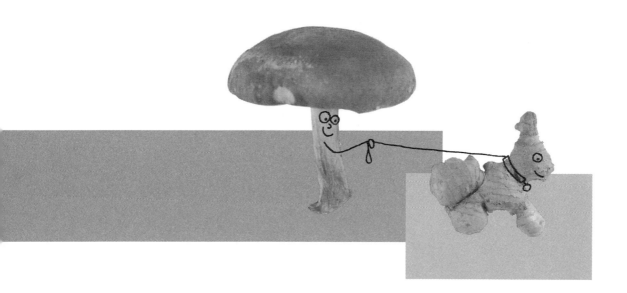

Bacon AND Spinach PASTA

PREPARATION TIME: 10 minutes   **COOKING TIME:** 10 minutes

Smoky, salty bacon elevates "lowly" spinach to a highly desirable status
in this family favorite. Vegetarians should note that we offer a similar
concept with our recipe for Linguine with Kale and Sun-Dried Tomatoes
(page 182).

---

1 pound dried pasta of choice
5 slices bacon, cut into matchsticks
1 tablespoon extra-virgin olive oil, plus extra if needed
4 cloves garlic, minced
1 pound spinach, rinsed and dried
Salt and freshly ground pepper to taste
Freshly grated Parmesan cheese for serving

In a saucepan, cook the pasta in boiling water (lightly salted if desired)
until tender but still firm, about 10 minutes. Drain the pasta in a
colander and shake dry.

While the pasta is cooking, in a large, deep skillet or Dutch oven, sauté
the bacon in the 1 tablespoon olive oil over medium heat until it begins
to brown, about 5 minutes. Stir in the garlic and cook for another
minute. (Sometimes a significant amount of bacon fat will collect in the
pan. You can drain it directly from the pan by holding the bacon and
garlic bits back with a knife or spoon. But don't pour it all out because it
adds flavor to the dish. More often than not, we don't drain off any fat.)

Add the spinach and stir gently until the leaves are coated with the oil.
Cover and cook until the leaves are wilted, 1 to 2 minutes. Remove from
the heat and add the pasta to the spinach pan. Toss to coat the pasta
evenly, then season with salt and pepper. If the pasta appears too dry,
drizzle with the additional olive oil.

Serve immediately. Garnish individual servings with Parmesan.

Serves 4

Basil PESTO

PREPARATION TIME: 10 minutes

Ideal for pasta, this sauce can also be served over tomato salads, in sandwiches, and with numerous other dishes, too. Some of us pour lots of it onto our pasta, while others prefer a small dollop gently tossed with the noodles. That's why we usually allow each diner to add it directly to his or her individual serving.

Pine nuts are a classic ingredient that weave a hint of tangy sweetness into the sauce. But if you don't happen to have any on hand, don't worry about it. Pesto without pine nuts is still absolutely delicious. The sauce can be stored in the refrigerator for several days.

¾ to 1 cup extra-virgin olive oil
4 cups firmly packed fresh basil leaves
2 tablespoons pine nuts (optional)
½ cup freshly grated Parmesan cheese, plus extra cheese
*   for serving (optional)*
2 cloves garlic, minced
Salt and freshly ground pepper to taste

In a blender or food processor, combine ¼ cup of the olive oil and the basil leaves and process until puréed, adding additional oil in ¼-cup increments as needed to achieve a smooth consistency. Add the pine nuts, if using, and the ½ cup Parmesan and continue to process until smooth. Add the garlic and pulse until it is incorporated. If the pesto is too thick, add a few tablespoons olive oil at the end. Season with salt and pepper.

When serving with pasta, garnish with additional Parmesan, if using.

Makes about 2 cups

Asparagus PESTO

PREPARATION TIME: 15 minutes   **COOKING TIME:** 15 minutes

This alternative to traditional basil pesto is refreshing. However, not all kids like asparagus. Happily, ours do. Accompany the pasta with Tomato, Mozzarella, and Basil Salad (page 135) for color contrast.

---

2 pounds asparagus
⅓ cup chicken stock (page 105) or canned low-sodium chicken broth
3 tablespoons freshly grated Parmesan cheese, plus extra cheese
    for serving
2 tablespoons extra-virgin olive oil
2 cloves garlic, halved
Salt and freshly ground pepper to taste
1 pound dried pasta of choice

Trim off and discard the tough ends from each asparagus spear—usually 1 to 2 inches. Fill a large sauté pan with water to a depth of 1 inch and bring to a boil over high heat. Lay the asparagus in the boiling water, cover, and cook until tender, 3 to 5 minutes. Drain in a colander and rinse immediately with very cold water to retain the color and stop the cooking, then pat dry. Alternatively, cook the asparagus in a steamer over boiling water until tender—the timing will be about the same—then rinse and dry.

Trim off the top 2 inches of each spear—the tips—and set them aside. In a blender or food processor, in batches if necessary, progressively purée the remaining spear portions with the stock until a thick "pea soup" consistency forms. (You will not be able to fit all the asparagus into a blender at once. Start with a small amount and pulse, adding more shoots as the first ones break down.) Add the 3 tablespoons Parmesan cheese and pulse again to mix.

In a large sauté pan, heat the olive oil over medium heat. Add the garlic and sauté, stirring occasionally, until it begins to brown, about 3 minutes. Using a slotted spoon, remove the garlic and discard. Pour the asparagus purée into the pan and stir gently for a few minutes to heat. Season to taste with salt and pepper.

Meanwhile, in a saucepan, cook the pasta in boiling water (lightly salted if desired) until tender but still firm, about 10 minutes. Drain the pasta in a colander and shake dry. Transfer to a serving bowl. Add the pesto and toss to coat evenly. Add the reserved asparagus tops, toss again, and serve at once. Garnish individual servings with the additional Parmesan.

Serves 4 to 6

Tomato, Eggplant,
AND Garlic RIGATONI

PREPARATION TIME: 20 minutes   **COOKING TIME:** 45 minutes

Pungent garlic is a powerful theme here, to which eggplant adds a soft-textured counterpoint. Flavors are smoky and tangy, while round, hollow rigatoni or penne are ideal shapes for cradling the sauce.

Salt
2½ pounds eggplant, unpeeled, cut crosswise into ¼-inch-thick slices
5 tablespoons extra-virgin olive oil, plus extra oil if needed
5 cloves garlic, minced
½ cup chopped fresh basil
⅛ teaspoon red pepper flakes
2 to 3 pounds fresh tomatoes (peeled if desired, see page 32),
    coarsely chopped, or 1 can (28 ounces) plum tomatoes,
    drained and coarsely chopped
1 pound dried rigatoni or penne pasta
¼ cup freshly grated Parmesan cheese
Freshly ground pepper to taste

Lightly salt the eggplant slices on both sides and set aside in a colander for 30 minutes. Meanwhile, in a Dutch oven or large, deep skillet, heat 2 tablespoons of the olive oil over medium heat. Add the garlic, basil, and red pepper flakes and sauté, stirring occasionally, until the garlic begins to turn golden, 2 to 3 minutes. Add the tomatoes, stir well, and simmer until thickened, about 15 minutes. Remove from the heat and cover to keep warm.

Rinse the eggplant slices and pat dry with a paper towel. In a second large skillet, heat the remaining 3 tablespoons olive oil over high heat. Working in batches, lay the eggplant slices in a single layer in the pan and sauté, turning once, until light brown and tender, 2 to 3 minutes on each side. Transfer the slices to a cutting board and cover them with paper towels to absorb the excess oil. Repeat until all the eggplant slices are cooked, adding more olive oil to the pan if necessary to prevent sticking.

While the eggplant slices are cooking, in a saucepan, cook the pasta in boiling water (lightly salted if desired) until tender but still firm, about 10 minutes. Drain the pasta in a colander and shake dry.

Return the tomato sauce to medium heat. Cut the eggplant slices into quarters and stir them into the sauce. Then mix in the cooked pasta and toss until evenly coated. Add the Parmesan and toss again. Season with salt and pepper, transfer to a serving bowl, and serve at once.

Serves 4

Sausage AND Peppers
WITH RIGATONI

PREPARATION TIME: 10 minutes   **COOKING TIME:** 30 minutes

Our neighborhood grocer always has a varied selection of Italian-style sausages. They are generally made with pork, chicken, turkey, or lamb, and we often use a combination for this dish. But any single variety will work here, too. Before we add the sausages to the sauce, we cook them in water to keep them moist.

Rigatoni pasta noodles are fat, round, hollow, and easy to spear with a fork. We also like them because they look like sausages. You can, however, substitute another pasta shape for the rigatoni.

---

4 to 6 sweet Italian sausages, about 1½ pounds total weight
3 tablespoons extra-virgin olive oil
1 large onion, halved and thinly sliced
3 cloves garlic, minced or chopped
2 green bell peppers, seeded and cut lengthwise into narrow strips
1 red bell pepper, seeded and cut lengthwise into narrow strips
2 teaspoons dried thyme
1 bay leaf
½ teaspoon salt, plus salt to taste
Freshly ground pepper to taste
1 pound dried rigatoni pasta
Freshly grated Parmesan cheese for serving

Using a fork, poke a series of holes in the opposite sides of each sausage. Pour water to a depth of about 1 inch in a skillet or sauté pan and bring to a boil over high heat. Place the sausages in the pan, cover, reduce the heat to medium, and simmer until cooked through, 5 to 7 minutes. Drain off the water and set the sausages aside.

In a large sauté pan or deep skillet, heat the olive oil over medium heat. Add the onion and garlic and sauté until translucent, about 3 minutes. Gently stir in the bell peppers, thyme, bay leaf, and the ½ teaspoon salt. Cover, reduce the heat to low, and cook until the peppers have wilted, 3 to 5 minutes.

Cut the sausages crosswise into 1-inch-thick slices. Push the onion and peppers to the side of the pan and place the sausages on the exposed pan surface. Cover the sausages with the onion and peppers. Cover the pan and continue to cook over low heat for 15 more minutes. Season with the additional salt and with pepper, and remove and discard the bay leaf.

While the sauce is cooking, in a saucepan, cook the pasta in boiling water (lightly salted if desired) until tender but still firm, about 10 minutes. Drain the pasta in a colander and shake dry. Transfer the pasta to a large serving bowl or individual plates.

Spoon the sausage and peppers over the pasta and garnish with Parmesan. Serve at once.

Serves 4 to 6

PASTA with Porcini, SAUSAGE, AND TOMATO SAUCE

PREPARATION TIME: 10 minutes   **COOKING TIME:** 40 minutes

Porcini and cèpes are two names for the same mushrooms; the former is the Italian term and the latter is the French. As this recipe calls for Italian sausages, we prefer to call these meaty-textured mushrooms by their Italian name. The mushrooms and sausages team up admirably in this robust sauce. Our daughters are not dedicated mushroom fans, but they like this dish anyway, probably because the mushrooms are subtly integrated into the sauce.

---

1 ounce dried porcini mushrooms

2 tablespoons extra-virgin olive oil

1 large onion, diced

3 cloves garlic, minced

2 sweet Italian sausages

1 teaspoon dried thyme

1 teaspoon dried oregano

½ cup red wine

1 can (28 ounces) plum tomatoes, drained and coarsely chopped

½ teaspoon salt

½ teaspoon freshly ground pepper

¼ cup freshly grated Parmesan cheese, plus extra cheese for serving

1 pound dried linguine or other pasta

In a small bowl, combine the mushrooms with hot water to cover and let stand for at least 15 minutes to rehydrate. Meanwhile, in a large skillet or sauté pan, heat the olive oil over medium-high heat. Add the onion and garlic and sauté until the onion is translucent, about 3 minutes.

While the onion and garlic are cooking, remove the sausage meat from its casings, and cut the meat into small chunks. Add them to the pan and sauté until cooked through, 4 to 5 minutes. Stir in the thyme and oregano, then stir in the wine. (All the alcohol will evaporate over the heat.)

Remove the mushrooms from the water, reserving the water, and cut into ¾-inch pieces. Stir the mushrooms into the sausage mixture. Strain the mushroom water through a fine-mesh sieve lined with cheesecloth or a coffee filter to remove any grit, and reserve ⅓ cup of the liquid. (If you don't have any cheesecloth or a coffee filter, just use a fine-mesh sieve alone.) Add the liquid to the pan, along with the tomatoes, salt, pepper, and the ¼ cup Parmesan cheese. Stir all the ingredients together. Reduce the heat to low and simmer, uncovered, until thickened, about 30 minutes.

While the sauce is simmering, in a saucepan, cook the pasta in boiling water (lightly salted if desired) until tender but still firm, about 10 minutes. Drain the pasta in a colander and shake dry.

Transfer the pasta to a large serving bowl or individual plates. Spoon the sauce over the pasta and top with the additional Parmesan. Serve immediately.

Serves 4

HEARTY (LEFTOVER) Lamb
AND Tomato PASTA

PREPARATION TIME: 10 minutes   **COOKING TIME:** 30 minutes

This rich, thick pasta sauce was born from leftover leg of lamb. We had a lot of meat sitting in the refrigerator, and there was a limit to how many lamb sandwiches we could eat, so we finished off the lamb in this pasta sauce. That decision did more than stretch our budget. It put a whole new face on three-day-old meat! However, if you don't have leftover leg of lamb, diced raw lamb will suffice.

This robust dish will warm up any dining room on a cold winter night. It's so tasty, we parents don't add Parmesan cheese. The kids, of course, insist on it.

---

2 teaspoons extra-virgin olive oil

1 onion, diced

1 clove garlic, minced

*3 to 4 cups cubed cooked lamb (¼-inch cubes) or 1 pound raw
    boneless lamb, cut into ¼-inch cubes*

*¼ pound fresh white button mushrooms (about 10 mushrooms),
    trimmed and quartered*

1 large carrot, peeled and diced

1 teaspoon ground cumin

1 teaspoon salt, plus salt to taste

1 teaspoon dried thyme

1 bay leaf (optional)

*2 to 3 pounds fresh tomatoes, or 1 can (28 ounces) plum tomatoes,
    with juice*

½ to 1 cup red wine or water

Freshly ground pepper to taste

1 pound dried pasta of choice

Freshly grated Parmesan cheese for serving (optional)

In a large sauté pan or Dutch oven, heat the olive oil over medium heat. Add the onion and sauté until translucent, about 3 minutes. Add the garlic and cook for 1 minute. Stir in the meat and cook until lightly browned,

3 to 5 minutes. Stir in the mushrooms, carrot, cumin, the 1 teaspoon salt, thyme, and bay leaf (if using) and cook for 1 to 2 minutes.

Coarsely chop the tomatoes and add them, along with their juices, to the pan. For added richness and color, add enough of the wine to submerge the ingredients halfway in the liquid. (If you are not using wine, add the water.) Raise the heat to high and bring the sauce to a boil, then reduce the heat to low. Cook uncovered, stirring occasionally, until the sauce thickens, about 20 minutes. Season with the additional salt and with pepper and remove and discard the bay leaf.

While the sauce is simmering, in a saucepan, cook the pasta in boiling water (lightly salted if desired) until tender but still firm, about 10 minutes. Drain the pasta in a colander and shake dry. Transfer the pasta to a large serving bowl.

Pour the sauce over the pasta and toss to coat evenly. Garnish with Parmesan, if using, and serve immediately.

Serves 4 to 6

BASIC Rice

COOKING TIME: 20 to 40 minutes (depending on type of rice)

Rice requires little more than boiling water to yield tender grains, yet there are many ways to cook it. Here is one of the simplest methods. (Brown rice typically takes up to twice as long as white rice to cook.)

---

*2 cups water, chicken stock (page 105), or canned low-sodium
    chicken broth*
½ teaspoon salt
1 cup long- or short-grain white or brown rice

In a saucepan, bring the water to a boil over high heat and add the salt. Stir in the rice, return to a boil, then cover, reduce the heat to low, and cook until all the water has been absorbed, 15 to 20 minutes for white rice and 30 to 40 minutes for brown rice.

Makes 2 cups; serves 4 as a side dish

Basic Rice, BUT **Better**

PREPARATION TIME: 5 minutes   **COOKING TIME:** 25 minutes

This method of preparing rice is almost as bare-bones as boiling it alone in water (see facing page). But the addition of a little olive oil and onion makes a big difference in flavor. Using chicken stock or broth is a big plus as well. (Vegetarians can substitute vegetable stock.) And if you have saffron on your shelf, drop in a pinch for added color and a slightly exotic profile.

---

1 tablespoon extra-virgin olive oil
½ onion, finely chopped
1 cup long- or short-grain white rice
2 cups chicken stock (page 105), or canned low-sodium chicken broth
½ teaspoon salt
Pinch of saffron threads (optional)

In a saucepan, heat the olive oil over medium heat. Add the onion and sauté until it begins to turn translucent, about 3 minutes. Add the rice and stir until the grains are thoroughly coated with the oil, about 1 minute.

Add the stock, salt, and the saffron, if using. Bring to a boil, then cover, reduce the heat to low, and cook until all the liquid has been absorbed, about 20 minutes.

Typically, the onion floats to the top of the cooked rice. Using a fork, stir it in gently, being careful not to break up the rice grains, before serving.

Serves 4 to 6 as a side dish

ASIAN **Fried** RICE

PREPARATION TIME: 5 minutes   **COOKING TIME:** 10 minutes

A pleasing blend of bright Asian-inspired flavors punctuates this sticky rice. Enjoy it on its own or alongside a vegetable, fish, or meat dish.

¼ cup canola oil

4 cups cooked white rice (page 206), cold or hot

3 green onions, white and green parts, chopped

1 red bell pepper, seeded and diced

2 tablespoons soy sauce or tamari

2 eggs, lightly beaten

In a large sauté pan or wok, heat the canola oil over high heat until it begins to bubble. Add the rice, breaking up any clumps, and stir frequently until it has absorbed most of the oil, 3 to 4 minutes. (The rice will become somewhat sticky.) Push the rice to the side of the pan, reduce the heat to medium, and add the green onions and bell pepper to the exposed pan surface. Sauté for 2 minutes, stirring often. Mix the pepper and onions with the rice, stir in the soy sauce, and mix thoroughly.

Push the rice mixture to the side of the pan again. Pour the eggs onto the bare, hot pan surface and stir until scrambled. Pull the rice back into the center of the pan and mix with the eggs until tiny pieces of egg are well distributed throughout. Serve at once.

Serves 4 to 6

BASIC Polenta

PREPARATION TIME: 2 minutes   **COOKING TIME**: 10 minutes

This quick-cooking cornmeal porridge can accompany many foods, from vegetables to fish to poultry to meats. You can also eat it unaccompanied, but it really shines as a side dish. Polenta is the name for both the grain and the finished dish.

You can buy instant polenta that cooks in about 5 minutes. But we prefer to use regular polenta, which hardly takes much longer, about 10 minutes. (It is mystifying to us that package instructions for cooking many brands of polenta give cooking times that range from 25 minutes to 45 minutes. This is simply unnecessary.)

Polenta becomes progressively thicker as it sits on a serving plate. We enjoy polenta best as a thick porridge within minutes after it has finished cooking.

---

4 cups water
1 teaspoon salt
1 cup polenta
½ cup half-and-half or heavy cream
2 tablespoons unsalted butter
½ cup freshly grated Parmesan cheese

Combine the water and salt in a 3- or 4-quart saucepan and bring to a boil over high heat. Slowly whisk in the polenta, then reduce the heat until the polenta gently bubbles. Stir in the half-and-half and continue to simmer, stirring occasionally with a wooden spoon as the polenta thickens.

After about 10 minutes, all the liquid should be absorbed and the polenta should have a smooth consistency. Remove from the heat. Add the butter and Parmesan cheese and stir until both have melted into the polenta.

Pour the polenta into a high-sided platter and allow it to settle for a few minutes, then serve immediately.

Makes about 4 cups; serves 4 to 6 as a side dish

CREAMY **Risotto**

PREPARATION TIME: 10 minutes   **COOKING TIME:** 30 minutes

It's no wonder the Italians love risotto. The creamy, smooth sauce makes a fine preparation for deliciously chewy Arborio rice. It's so tasty that Italians typically eat it as a first course, unaccompanied. But risotto also makes a fine side dish.

Contrary to what many people believe, risotto is not difficult to make. Some recipes require constant stirring. However, we have found that frequent stirring creates equally fine results while allowing greater flexibility in the kitchen.

Basic risotto can be enhanced by other ingredients such as mushrooms (page 212) or seafood (page 246). For this recipe, wine is not optional. It adds firmness and an essential acidity. However, there is no alcohol in the finished dish. The alcohol evaporates soon after the cooking process begins.

---

3 tablespoons extra-virgin olive oil
1 onion, finely chopped
2 cloves garlic, minced
1 cup Arborio rice
4 cups chicken stock (page 105) or canned low-sodium chicken broth
1 cup white or red wine
⅓ cup freshly grated Parmesan cheese
Salt and freshly ground pepper to taste

In a Dutch oven or heavy pot, heat the olive oil over medium heat. Add the onion and garlic and sauté until the onion is translucent, about 3 minutes. Add the rice and sauté for another 2 to 3 minutes. Add ½ cup of the stock and cook, stirring frequently—but not constantly—until most of the liquid is absorbed, about 3 minutes. Continue adding the stock ½ cup at a time, always stirring frequently until most of it is absorbed before adding more. After 2 cups of the stock have been incorporated, add the wine, stirring frequently until it is absorbed. Then add the remaining stock, ½ cup at a time, stirring as described above.

The rice is ready when it is tender but still slightly firm at the center of each grain and creamy. Remove from the heat and stir in the Parmesan, salt, and pepper. Serve at once.

Serves 4 to 6 as a first course or side dish

RISOTTO with Porcini

PREPARATION TIME: 15 minutes   **COOKING TIME:** 40 minutes

This risotto differs from our basic risotto recipe in that it uses only red
wine and serves up meaty, earthy flavors thanks to the porcini mushrooms.
The red wine is hardly hazardous to children, as all the alcohol evaporates.
Our children are not particularly fond of mushrooms, but they love this
dish. One of them eats the mushrooms, while the other picks them out
and enjoys the rice.

---

1 ounce dried porcini mushrooms
3 tablespoons extra-virgin olive oil
1 onion, finely chopped
2 cloves garlic, minced
1 cup Arborio rice
4 cups chicken stock (page 105) or canned low-sodium chicken broth
½ cup red wine
⅓ cup freshly grated Parmesan cheese
Salt and freshly ground pepper to taste

In a small bowl, combine the mushrooms with 1 cup hot water and let
stand for at least 15 minutes to rehydrate.

Meanwhile, in a Dutch oven or heavy pot, heat the olive oil over medium
heat. Add the onion and garlic and sauté until the onion is translucent,
about 3 minutes. Add the rice and sauté for another 2 to 3 minutes. Add
½ cup of the stock and cook, stirring frequently—but not constantly—
until most of the liquid is absorbed, about 3 minutes. Continue adding
the stock ½ cup at a time, always stirring frequently until most of it is
absorbed before adding more. After 2 cups of the stock have been incorporated, add the wine, stirring frequently until it is absorbed. Then add
the remaining stock, ½ cup at a time, stirring as described above.

When the mushrooms are rehydrated, remove them from the water,
reserving the water. Cut the mushrooms into smaller pieces, if desired,
and stir into the risotto. Strain the mushroom water through a fine-mesh

sieve lined with cheesecloth or a coffee filter to remove any grit, and reserve the water. (If you don't have any cheesecloth or a coffee filter, just use a fine-mesh sieve alone.) Add the reserved mushroom water to the risotto after most of the wine and stock have been absorbed. Continue to stir frequently.

The rice is ready when it is tender but still slightly firm at the center of each grain and creamy. Remove from the heat and stir in the Parmesan cheese, salt, and pepper. Serve at once.

Serves 4 to 6 as a first course or side dish

Chapter

8

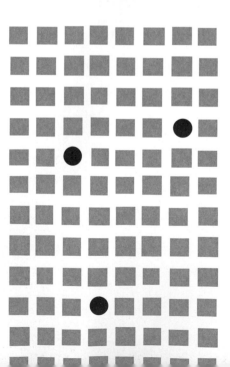

Pizza

and **Cheese**

Pizza is **MORE THAN A MEAL**. It is an invitation to group participation, depending on your child s level of interest. Our children enjoy kneading dough and covering their pizzas with whatever ingredients suit their fancy. If your child prefers nothing but cheese and tomato sauce on his or her pizza, there s a simple solution. Just make a Pizza Margherita (page 222) and leave off the basil. Indeed, when cooking pizza at home, **you can top your pizzas with anything you want**. In this chapter, we offer a selection of the pizzas most loved at our house.

Commercial packaged pizza dough is often less than inspiring. It usually contains unnecessary preservatives and unhealthy hydrogenated oils (see page 17). Some local pizzerias will sell you excellent, high-quality, freshly made dough a terrific option for busy parents. But if thats not the case in your neighborhood, pizza dough (page 218) is **easy to make** at home.

We've designed our recipes for round pizzas 12 to 14 inches in diameter. But you can also shape the dough into 9-inch-by-13-inch rectangles and bake them on baking sheets or pans.

Regardless of shape, pizzas cater to all tastes. Garnish them simply or adventurously and, if necessary, make one pizza for the grown-ups and a separate one for youthful palates. Our pizza dough recipe yields two crusts, so you can top each one differently. Keep in mind that the preparation times included with the pizza recipes do not include the time it takes to make and shape the dough or make the basic tomato sauce, if used.

And where there is pizza, there is usually **CHEESE**. In this chapter, we also offer suggestions for exploring the ever-expanding world of artisanal cheeses, some of which are perfect on pizza. Most, however, are best with country bread.

PIZZA Dough

PREPARATION TIME: 25 minutes, plus 2 hours for rising

Pizza dough is basically bread, so you'll have to allow time for it to rise. Be careful not to roll the dough out too thin, or you may find that your pizza slices will fall apart. That's not a problem for those who enjoy pizza with a knife and fork, of course, but for kids who eat pizza with their fingers, it's a sloppy proposition. If instead you purchase the dough, follow the instructions for shaping the crusts that appear here.

---

1 envelope (2½ teaspoons) active dry yeast
1¼ cups warm water
½ cup high-gluten flour (see sidebar, facing page)
2 cups unbleached all-purpose flour, plus extra flour
*   for kneading and rolling*
2 tablespoons extra-virgin olive oil, plus extra oil for the bowl
*   and pans*
½ teaspoon salt
Cornmeal for the work surface (optional)

In a large bowl, combine the yeast with 1 cup of the warm water. Using a wooden spoon, stir in the high-gluten flour. Add the all-purpose flour, the 2 tablespoons olive oil, and the salt. Stir with the wooden spoon until a sticky dough begins to form on the bottom of the bowl. Add the remaining ¼ cup warm water and, using your hands, shape the dough into a large ball.

When your hands become too sticky with dough, dust them with a little all-purpose flour. Continue kneading the dough in the bowl, pushing it down with the heel of your hand, then pulling it together in a mound and repeating until the dough becomes firm yet elastic, 4 to 5 minutes.

Lightly oil the surface of a large bowl. Place the dough in the bowl, cover the bowl with plastic wrap, and set it in a reasonably warm room to rise for 2 hours. It should double in size. (Standard room temperature of 70°F is adequate. Cooler temperatures will delay the rising process.)

Have ready 2 nonstick 12- to 14-inch round pans or two 9-by-13-inch baking sheets or pans. If you do not have nonstick pans, oil each pan with 1 teaspoon olive oil. Lightly flour a work surface or, for a crust with a crunchy exterior, dust it with cornmeal. Remove the risen dough from the bowl, set it on the prepared surface, and cut it in half. (If not using the dough immediately, place each half in a separate lightly oiled bowl. Cover the bowls with plastic wrap and place in the refrigerator for up to 8 hours. The dough will continue to rise somewhat, so use large bowls. Or wrap the dough in plastic or place it in a zippered plastic bag and freeze for up to 2 months.)

Set half of the dough aside. Using a rolling pin, roll out the dough to fit your pizza pans and raise the entire edge of the crust with your thumbs to make a rim. Transfer to one of the pans. Repeat with the remaining dough portion.

Makes 2 unbaked pizza crusts, each 12 to 14 inches in diameter or 9 by 13 inches

PIZZA CRUST AND HIGH-GLUTEN FLOUR

We do not like to use only all-purpose flour, which is a blend of hard- and soft-wheat flours, for making pizza dough. It doesn't contain enough gluten, a substance that gives structure to rising dough. High-gluten flour, which is milled from hard wheat, gives fresh country bread and pizza crust a chewy texture that is different from the more tender crumb of cakes and muffins. Too much gluten, however, will yield an overly weighty crust, so we recommend blending high-gluten flour, often simply labeled "gluten flour," with all-purpose flour.

And what about whole-wheat flour? It certainly contains more nutrients than white flour, but it doesn't rise as easily and makes a heavy crust. As a result, it's not our choice for pizza.

BASIC Tomato Sauce FOR PIZZA

PREPARATION TIME: 5 minutes   **COOKING TIME:** 15 minutes

Canned crushed tomatoes are the easiest thing to use here. But if you've got a summer garden full of beautiful ripe tomatoes, harvest them! Just make sure that when you chop the tomatoes, you capture all of the juice so that it can be added to the saucepan.

---

2 tablespoons extra-virgin olive oil
½ onion, diced
3 cloves garlic, minced
1 can (28 ounces) crushed tomatoes, or 2 to 3 pounds fresh tomatoes,
  peeled (see page 32) and finely chopped
1½ teaspoons dried oregano
1 teaspoon dried thyme
¾ teaspoon salt
½ teaspoon freshly ground pepper

In a large skillet or sauté pan, heat the olive oil over medium heat. Add the onion and garlic and sauté for 2 minutes. Stir in the tomatoes, oregano, thyme, salt, and pepper. Simmer uncovered, stirring occasionally, until the flavors are blended and the sauce is smooth and thick, 10 to 12 minutes. If the sauce becomes too thick, add water ¼ cup at a time to achieve the desired consistency, then simmer for a few more minutes. Remove from the heat, let cool, and use immediately or store for up to 3 days in the refrigerator or 3 months in the freezer.

Makes about 3 cups, or enough sauce for 3 round (12 to 14 inches in diameter) or rectangular (9 by 13 inches) pizzas.

Pissaladière (FRENCH ONION Pizza)

PREPARATION TIME: 15 minutes   **COOKING TIME:** 40 minutes

A staple of Nice, where it is consumed by many grown-ups and children daily, this marvelous French cheeseless pizza can be eaten hot or cold. The odd-sounding name is derived from *pissalat*, an anchovy purée from Nice that traditionally topped the pizza. Today, anchovy fillets have replaced it. Those with an aversion to anchovies can dispense with the fillets altogether.

---

1 prepared pizza crust (page 218)
3 tablespoons extra-virgin olive oil
4 cloves garlic, minced
4 teaspoons dried thyme
4 large onions, halved and thinly sliced
1 teaspoon salt
½ teaspoon freshly ground pepper
1 tin (6 ounces) anchovy fillets, packed in olive oil (optional)
20 to 25 Niçoise olives or pitted Kalamata olives

Prepare the pizza crust as directed. In a large skillet or sauté pan, heat the olive oil over medium heat. Add the garlic and thyme and stir for 30 seconds. Add the onions, separating the slices with a wooden spoon and stirring so that they are evenly coated with the oil, garlic, and thyme. Add the salt and pepper and stir well. Reduce the heat to low and cook, stirring every 5 minutes, until the onions are very soft, about 20 minutes.

While the onions are cooking, preheat the oven to 500°F.

Spread the cooked onions evenly over the prepared pizza crust. If using the anchovy fillets, arrange them on top in a diamond pattern. Dot the surface with the olives. Bake the pizza until the rim of the crust is golden brown, 12 to 15 minutes. Serve hot, warm, or at room temperature.

Makes one 12- to 14-inch pizza

PIZZA Margherita

PREPARATION TIME: 10 minutes   **COOKING TIME:** 15 minutes

This traditional Italian specialty was named after the late-nineteenth-century Queen Margherita, who is said to have been delighted by the pizza's color scheme—red (tomato), white (mozzarella cheese), and green (basil)—an echo of the Italian flag. We like it because it is simple and delicious.

1 prepared pizza crust (page 218)
1 cup Basic Tomato Sauce for Pizza (page 220)
½ pound fresh mozzarella cheese, shredded
1 large tomato, sliced
1 tablespoon extra-virgin olive oil
½ cup chopped fresh basil leaves

Prepare the pizza crust as directed. Preheat the oven to 500°F.

Spread the tomato sauce evenly over the prepared pizza crust. Distribute the cheese evenly over the sauce.

Bake the pizza for 8 to 10 minutes. Remove the pizza from the oven and evenly distribute the tomato slices over the cheese. Drizzle the 1 tablespoon olive oil over the tomatoes. Return the pizza to the oven and bake until the rim of the crust is golden brown, about 5 minutes. Remove the pizza from the oven again and garnish with the basil. Return the pizza to the oven and bake until the basil wilts, 30 to 45 seconds. Serve immediately.

Makes one 12- to 14-inch pizza

Pesto PIZZA WITH Ricotta
AND FRESH Goat CHEESE

PREPARATION TIME: 10 minutes   **COOKING TIME:** 12 minutes

It's refreshing to enjoy a pizza made with something other than a red sauce. This green and white pizza is simple to make, especially if you buy well-made basil pesto at your local grocery. If not, pesto is easy to make at home. Fresh ricotta and a soft, mild goat cheese add interesting flavors to the pie.

---

1 prepared pizza crust (page 218)
⅓ cup, plus 2 tablespoons basil pesto, homemade (page 195)
   or purchased
½ cup ricotta cheese
8 to 10 slices mild fresh goat cheese
Freshly ground pepper to taste

Prepare the pizza crust as directed. Preheat the oven to 500°F.

Spread the ⅓ cup pesto evenly over the pizza crust. Spread the ricotta cheese evenly over the pesto. In a circular pattern, drizzle the remaining 2 tablespoons pesto over the ricotta cheese. Distribute the goat cheese slices evenly over the pizza.

Bake the pizza until the rim of the crust is golden brown, 10 to 12 minutes. Remove from the oven, grind the pepper over the top, then serve immediately.

Makes one 12- to 14-inch pizza

WILD Mushroom AND Sausage PIZZA

PREPARATION TIME: 10 minutes

COOKING TIME: 15 minutes

For an earthy, forest-infused pizza, try this. Look for fresh wild mushrooms at a reputable food emporium. We love to use chanterelles, porcini, and black trumpets. Not all so-called wild mushrooms are really wild, however. For example, shiitakes are cultivated. If you can't find a suitable wild mushroom, try large, meaty portobellos, which are simply overgrown cremini, the small brown mushrooms that reside in most supermarket produce sections. In a pinch, just use whatever commercial mushrooms are available. When washing mushrooms, remember to rinse them quickly and pat them dry. Soaking them in water will make them soggy.

---

1 prepared pizza crust (page 218)
1 cup Basic Tomato Sauce for Pizza (page 220)
½ pound fresh mozzarella cheese, shredded
½ pound mixed wild mushrooms (see headnote), trimmed and sliced
1 hot Italian sausage, casing removed and chopped into small chunks
1 sweet Italian sausage, casing removed, chopped into small chunks
1 tablespoon extra-virgin olive oil
2 teaspoons dried oregano
Freshly ground pepper to taste

Prepare the pizza crust as directed. Preheat the oven to 500°F.

Spread the tomato sauce evenly over the pizza crust. Distribute the cheese evenly over the sauce. Spread the mushrooms evenly over the cheese. Dot the surface with the sausage chunks. Drizzle the olive oil evenly over the pizza, and sprinkle with the oregano.

Bake the pizza until the rim of the crust is golden brown, 12 to 15 minutes. Remove from the oven, grind the pepper over the top, then serve immediately.

Makes one 12- to 14-inch pizza

Prosciutto, FIG, AND Goat Cheese PIZZA

PREPARATION TIME: 5 minutes   **COOKING TIME:** 12 minutes

Here's another pizza that eschews traditional tomato sauce. We find there are few taste combinations as seductive as ripe fresh figs, fresh goat cheese, and salty-sweet prosciutto, Italy's famed dry-cured ham.

---

1 prepared pizza crust (page 218)
½ pound mild fresh goat cheese, sliced
⅓ pound sliced prosciutto, cut into julienne
8 fresh figs, sliced into rounds
1 tablespoon extra-virgin olive oil
2 tablespoons minced fresh rosemary

Prepare the pizza crust as directed. Preheat the oven to 500°F.

Distribute the goat cheese evenly over the pizza crust. Lay the prosciutto strips over the cheese. Dot the surface with the fig slices. Drizzle the olive oil evenly over the pizza, and sprinkle with the rosemary.

Bake the pizza until the rim of the crust is golden brown, 10 to 12 minutes. Serve immediately.

Makes one 12- to 14-inch pizza

TOMATO, Gruyère, SAUSAGE, Mushroom, AND Green Pepper PIZZA

PREPARATION TIME: 10 minutes   **COOKING TIME:** 15 minutes

Your selection of pizza cheese establishes your pizza's flavor profile. Instead of the standard mozzarella, we choose French or Swiss Gruyère cheese here. It has a toasty, nutty flavor that adds special character to this pizza with "the works." Remember to remove the sausage from its casing for thorough cooking.

---

1 prepared pizza crust (page 218)
1 cup Basic Tomato Sauce for Pizza (page 220)
2½ cups freshly grated Gruyère cheese
1 green bell pepper, seeded and cut lengthwise into narrow strips
½ white onion, sliced into thin crescents
6 white button mushrooms, trimmed and thinly sliced
1 hot Italian sausage, casing removed, chopped into small chunks
1 sweet Italian sausage, casing removed and chopped into
*   small chunks*
1 tablespoon extra-virgin olive oil
2 teaspoons dried thyme
1 teaspoon dried oregano

Prepare the pizza crust as directed. Preheat the oven to 500°F.

Spread the tomato sauce evenly over the pizza crust. Distribute the cheese evenly over the sauce. Spread the bell pepper, onion, and mushrooms evenly over the cheese. Dot the surface with the sausage chunks. Drizzle the olive oil evenly over the pizza, and garnish with the thyme and oregano.

Bake the pizza until the rim of the crust is golden brown, 12 to 15 minutes. Serve immediately.

Makes one 12- to 14-inch pizza

PASS THE CHEESE

Americans eat more cheese on pizzas than they do from the local cheese shop. Yet cheese in America has come a long way in the last twenty-five years. In the mid-1970s, Americans ate just under fourteen pounds of cheese annually per person. Today we eat twice that much, and it's not because we eat twice as much pizza. The current rising interest in fine cheese continues to deliver more exciting products to the market than ever before.

If you live in an area where eating well is a local priority, you probably know of at least one store that offers a broad array of French, Spanish, Italian, English, and fine American artisanal cheeses made from the milk of cows, goats, and sheep. They vary from creamy soft to hard and crumbly, and come in a range of colors, from soft white and ivory to blue veined and bright orange (the latter the result of naturally occurring carotene in certain grasses). These cheeses are not the plastic-wrapped, factory-formed, artificially colored, gooey gobs of yore. They are inspired by old-world traditions.

Americans, nonetheless, still consume a large quantity of factory-made cheeses that are not even true cheese. They are instead cheese by-products made from a combination of cheese, vegetable gums, dyes, emulsifiers, and stabilizing agents. Some are reasonably good, but they do not inspire us to eat more cheese at home. Instead, try tapping into the satisfying—and real—world of boutique cheeses made only with real milk by real people—not corporations.

The only problem with these boutique cheeses is that they are often expensive. But remember this: you're not supposed to eat a lot. Most cheese is made to be nibbled. It's rich and fattening, but also loaded with calcium and minerals. Simply put, a little goes a long way.

Perhaps the worst time to eat cheese is before dinner, when you're really hungry. It's a blueprint for overindulgence. But a little bit of blue cheese or goat cheese in a salad can heighten the pleasure of eating the greens. Grated cheeses, particularly Parmesan, enhance many hot dishes—again, in small doses.

At the end of a meal, we often choose from a modest selection—maybe just two or three cheeses—like diners do in France. It's a nice way to finish dinner when you're not that hungry but you want a little something savory before dessert. (Or maybe you don't want dessert at all. A small wedge of cheese often staves off a sweet craving nicely.)

Soft, runny cheeses may require crusty country bread for easy eating. Assertive, crumbly blue cheeses—like the famous Roquefort—taste best with unsalted butter. (No kidding. Butter softens their intensity.) Hard cheeses, like Gruyère and Gouda, also taste good with buttered country bread. But more often, we happily enjoy them on their own, as a small wedge.

Do kids like boutique cheeses? Ours do. Indeed, our greatest challenge is to prevent them from eating too much.

With literally thousands of cheeses to choose from, a working parent can quickly become overwhelmed. We suggest an unhurried approach that fits your budget and tastes. As your experience grows, so will your ability to find cheeses that please the whole family—at prices that work for you.

TIPS FOR BUYING CHEESES

The closer you get, the better you feel. Pick up a wrapped cheese. Press on it lightly with your thumb to see how soft or hard it is. Soft, creamy cheeses shouldn't feel hard, and aged, hard cheeses shouldn't feel soft. Smell your prospective cheese, too. Your nose knows what you'll like.

Shops that specialize in fine cheeses often let customers taste before they buy. Tasting is a reasonable request—particularly if the cheeses are openly displayed and cut to order. Don't be afraid to ask.

From a price point, be wary of heavily discounted cheeses. Like overripe fruit, bargain cheeses may be past their prime. As a rule, fresh, young cheeses are milder than older ones, which become more intensely flavored with age.

Are cow's milk cheeses different from goat's milk and sheep's milk cheeses? Yes, but the differences are not clear-cut. Goat's milk from one dairy may taste different than goat's milk from another, depending on what the goats are eating. The same holds true for cow's milk and sheep's milk. Goat's milk tends to be stronger flavored than cow's milk, and sheep's milk falls somewhere in between. But some fresh goat cheeses are very mild, while certain cow cheeses are intensely flavored. It all relates to the quality of the milk and the way the cheese is made.

Many people believe that variety is the spice of life. And we agree. Try not to get stuck on a few favorite cheeses when there are so many exciting shapes, sizes, textures, and flavors to discover.

sea

food

Seafood is a
first-rate source of
nutrition, packed with protein,
minerals, and vitamins. Even the fat in
fish seems to be good for us. The American
Heart Association has indicated that omega-3
fatty acids in fish reduce the risk of heart
disease and recommends at least two
servings of fish per week for a
heart-healthy diet.

**Not all seafood is
good for you, however. Some ocean
fish at the top of the food chain contain
relatively high amounts of mercury and should be
eaten in moderation. They include swordfish, shark,
and tuna. At the same time, other fish, mollusks, and
crustaceans, such as salmon, catfish, scallops,
oysters, and shrimp, contain little or virtually
no mercury at all. As a result, we tend
to eat more of the latter than
the former.**

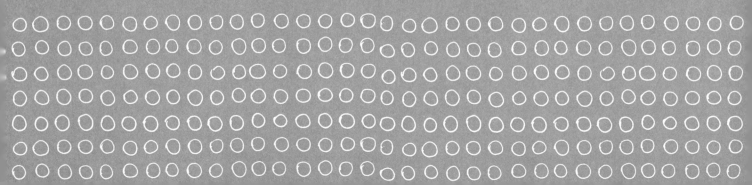

Nonetheless,
when beautifully fresh
swordfish appears at the market for
the right price, we buy it. It's hardly a
daily occurrence, and the nutritional benefits of
an occasional swordfish steak far outweigh the
hazards of mercury. Likewise, we wouldn't prepare
tuna fish sandwiches for our children every
day. But in moderation, tuna fits
safely and conveniently
into our diet.

Some parents
find fresh fish to be
especially challenging at the family
dinner table. In truth, our children are not
inspired by squiggly squid, mussels, and raw
oysters. But they happily devour mild, meaty fish like
salmon. And when we grill whole fish, such as trout (page
251), we fillet it for them and then, of course, double-
check for errant bones. This extra effort is worth
the opportunity to have the whole family
consume this flavorful, healthy
food group.

Seviche

Let's be honest about seviche. The kids probably won't want it when they hear it's raw fish—well, not really raw, but "cooked" by lime juice. The citric acid prompts a chemical reaction that produces a result similar to that of heat. Most children will keep their distance anyway, so we'll offer them an easy alternative such as Bruschetta (page 58).

For us grown-ups, seviche is easy to make and works beautifully as a deliciously refreshing appetizer or salad, especially for dinner parties. You can eat it unaccompanied, on crackers, or on a little plate garnished with a bit of diced red bell pepper and framed in baby lettuce greens.

---

1 pound firm white fish fillets such as snapper or cod, peeled shrimp,
*   or sea scallops, or a mixture, cut into ¼-inch cubes*
Juice of 3 limes (about ¾ cup)
2 serrano chiles, seeded and minced
½ cup finely chopped fresh cilantro
1 teaspoon coarse sea salt or kosher salt, plus salt to taste
½ red bell pepper, seeded and diced (optional)
¼ pound mixed baby salad greens (optional)

Place the fish, shrimp, and/or scallops in a glass or porcelain bowl. In a small bowl, stir together the lime juice, chiles, cilantro, and the 1 teaspoon salt. Pour the mixture over the fish and stir well.

Cover and refrigerate, stirring lightly every 30 minutes until the flesh is opaque, about 2 hours.

Season with the additional salt to taste. If using, garnish individual servings with the diced bell pepper and baby greens.

Serves 4 to 6 as an appetizer or first course

TANGY FRIED Oysters

PREPARATION TIME: 5 minutes   **COOKING TIME**: 5 minutes per batch

Not far from a cottage we rent by the sea, there is an oyster farm that shucks a portion of its plump, juicy oysters each day and sells them by the quart jar. We've noticed many food markets around the country now sell similarly jarred fresh-shucked Pacific and Atlantic oysters, and we can imagine no better way to enjoy them than fried in chile-laced cornmeal.

Canola oil for deep-frying
3 cups cornmeal
2 teaspoons chipotle chile flakes or red pepper flakes
2 teaspoons salt
1 quart fresh-shucked oysters (about 30 medium-sized oysters)
Juice of 2 or 3 lemons for drizzling

Pour the canola oil to a depth of 1 inch into a deep, heavy, large sauté pan or skillet and heat over medium-high heat until it begins to bubble slightly. Meanwhile, in a bowl, stir together the cornmeal, chile flakes, and salt.

Reduce the heat to medium. Quickly dredge the oysters—2 to 4 at a time—in the cornmeal mixture and immediately place them in the hot oil. (If necessary, reduce the heat to prevent the oil from splattering and smoking.) Repeat until the pan is filled with oysters. Depending on the size of your oysters and pan, you should be able to fry 8 to 12 at once. Using tongs, a slotted spoon, or wooden chopsticks, flip the oysters when they turn golden brown at their edges, after 2 to 3 minutes. The second side will cook more quickly than the first side, within 1 to 2 minutes. Do not overcook the oysters or they will dry out. They should remain moist and plump inside their golden, crisp cornmeal crust.

Using the tongs, spoon, or chopsticks, transfer the oysters to a serving plate lined with paper towels. Drizzle with some of the lemon juice and serve immediately. Fry the remaining oysters in 2 or 3 batches.

Serves 4

Clam AND Corn FRITTERS

PREPARATION TIME: 10 minutes   **COOKING TIME:** 5 minutes per batch

These plump little fritters are a marvelous appetizer or side dish. With a green salad (page 122) on the side, they make a meal. Our kids love these, perhaps because we don't harp on the fact that the fun, chewy stuff inside is made of clams. Enjoy piping hot with aioli (page 34), sour cream, or plain.

Canola oil for deep-frying
2 cups unbleached all-purpose flour
1 teaspoon salt
¼ teaspoon cayenne pepper
1½ cups buttermilk
3 green onions, white part only, chopped
1 egg
2 ears corn, kernels removed
1 can (6½ ounces) minced clams, drained

Pour the canola oil to a depth of 2 inches into a deep, heavy, large sauté pan or skillet and heat over high heat until it begins to bubble slightly.

Meanwhile, in a bowl, stir together the flour, salt, and cayenne. In a small bowl, stir together the buttermilk, green onions, and egg until blended. Add the buttermilk mixture to the flour mixture to create a batter. Add the corn and clams and mix thoroughly.

Reduce the heat to medium-high. Using a tablespoon, spoon out a fritter from the batter and drop it into the hot oil. Repeat until the pan is filled with fritters, being careful not to crowd them. Using tongs, a slotted spoon, or wooden chopsticks, flip the fritters when they turn golden brown at their edges, after 2 to 3 minutes. The second side will cook more quickly than the first side, within 1 to 2 minutes.

Using the tongs or spoon, transfer the fritters to paper towels to drain briefly, then serve immediately. Fry the remaining fritters in 1 or 2 batches.

Makes about 24 fritters; serves 6

SEARED DAY-BOAT Scallops
WITH Lemon AND Capers

PREPARATION TIME: 10 minutes   **COOKING TIME:** 10 minutes

Day-boat (or diver) scallops are hand-harvested by divers and shucked right on the boat. Unlike some commercial varieties, which are induced to hold up to 25 percent more water, these plump, wild mollusks harbor more flavor than liquid.

But don't worry if you can't find true diver scallops. Just look for fresh, moist big scallops at your fish counter. Be careful not to cook them too long or they will become rubbery. After searing, the interior should remain translucent. In this recipe, these firm, silky shellfish serve up a briny sweetness balanced by tangy lemon and capers. Serve with Basic Rice, but Better (page 207).

---

1 cup unbleached all-purpose flour
1 pound day-boat or large sea scallops
4 tablespoons unsalted butter
Salt and freshly ground pepper to taste
Juice of 1 lemon
2½ teaspoons capers

Place the flour in a large bowl. Dredge the scallops in the flour until they are lightly and evenly coated. Shake off excess flour and set aside.

In a large sauté pan or skillet, melt the butter over medium-high heat. Place the scallops in the pan and sauté, turning once, until golden brown, 2 minutes per side. Remove from the heat and, using a slotted spoon or spatula, transfer to a serving platter. Season with salt and pepper.

With the pan still off the heat, add the lemon juice and stir to scrape up any browned bits from the pan bottom. Stir in the capers.

Divide the scallops among individual plates and drizzle with the lemon-caper sauce. Serve immediately.

Serves 4

Gravlax (CURED SALMON)

PREPARATION TIME: 5 minutes, plus 3 days for curing

We admit that gravlax takes a while to cure, but it only takes five minutes to prepare. So if you plan in advance and have the patience to wait, you'll impress dinner guests by telling them you cured the salmon yourself! You'll also save money on this otherwise pricey prepared food, which is cheap to make at home.

Gravlax is the perfect party food. It can be served in bite-sized portions as an appetizer, or in larger slices artfully displayed on a plate as a first course. You can enjoy it topped with a dollop of crème fraîche or sour cream and capers, or more simply with lemon juice. Or forget about the party: Gravlax is delicious for any mundane occasion. Thinly sliced, it makes a fine sandwich on lightly buttered bread. Our kids like it best on bagels with cream cheese.

---

2 salmon fillets from the tail of the fish with skin intact,
  1 to 1¼ pounds total weight
¼ cup sugar
¼ cup salt
1 tablespoon coarsely ground pepper
1 cup chopped fresh dill
1 tablespoon gin or vodka

Lay the fillets, skin-side down, on a large plate. Cover the flesh evenly with the sugar, salt, pepper, and dill. Drizzle evenly with the gin. Lay 1 fillet on top of the other fillet, flesh sides together and skin on the outside.

Wrap the sandwiched fillets tightly in plastic wrap, place them in a shallow bowl, and top with a heavy weight. (We use a 28-ounce can of tomatoes.)

Refrigerate the salmon for 3 days. Once each morning and once each night, flip the sandwiched fillets over, empty the bowl of any collected liquid, and replace the weight. After 3 days, unwrap the fillets, peel or slice away the skin, scrape away the seasonings if desired, then thinly slice the gravlax and serve as suggested above.

Serves 6 to 8

EASY BRAISED Salmon AND
White Butter SAUCE

PREPARATION TIME: 5 minutes   **COOKING TIME:** 12 minutes

This elementary dish is our "ace in the hole" when we are just too pooped or frazzled to deal with much of anything at dinnertime. We make some rice (page 206) as a side dish while the salmon is cooking, and start off the meal with a quick green salad (page 122). Any thick, meaty fish such as halibut or cod will also work here. The white wine is essential. It not only cooks the fish, but it's also the base for the butter sauce, which our kids enjoy enormously. Parents should remember that the wine's alcohol disappears within minutes through evaporation. Not surprisingly, what's left in the bottle makes a fine adult beverage for the evening.

---

2 tablespoons extra-virgin olive oil
2 salmon steaks or fillets, about 2 pounds total weight, skin removed
½ teaspoon salt, plus salt to taste
2 cups white wine
3 tablespoons unsalted butter
Freshly ground pepper to taste

In a large skillet or sauté pan, heat the olive oil over medium-high heat. Sprinkle the salmon on both sides with the ½ teaspoon salt and place it in the pan. Add the wine, reduce the heat to medium, cover, and cook until the fish is opaque throughout but still moist, about 10 minutes. Transfer the steaks or fillets to individual plates, dividing them into serving pieces.

Stir the butter into the liquids remaining in the pan and return to medium-high heat. When the butter has melted, stir well and pour the butter sauce over the fish (and the rice, if serving rice on the side). Season with the additional salt and with pepper and serve immediately.

Serves 4 to 6

BUYING AND COOKING FRESH FISH

When buying fish, look for freshness first. There should be no dullness in the flesh or skin. The color should be shiny or translucent. In whole fish, the eyes should be clear and the flesh firm and buoyant to the touch. Scales should not be flaking.

Shop only at reputable fish markets where the product turnover is brisk. Also, don't be afraid to ask when a fish arrived, or what is freshest among the counter selections.

Fish cooks quickly and dries out easily when overcooked. Certain meaty fish, such as tuna or salmon, are sometimes cooked rare. But, as with meat, that's a matter of taste. Most fish should be cooked until the flesh is opaque and firm but still flaky and moist.

BAKED Salmon FILLETS

PREPARATION TIME: 5 minutes   **COOKING TIME:** 15 minutes

Fish doesn't get much easier than this recipe. Thick salmon fillets quickly bake in the oven, remaining moist and flavorful with minimal attention and mess. As always, we recommend double-checking for bones before serving to children, who devour this dish with gusto.

1½ tablespoons extra-virgin olive oil
Salt and freshly ground pepper to taste
4 salmon fillets with skin intact, about 2 pounds total weight
1 tablespoon dried thyme or dried rosemary
4 to 6 lemon wedges

Preheat the oven to 400°F.

Lightly oil a baking dish or pan with ½ tablespoon of the olive oil. Lightly salt and pepper the salmon on both sides. Drizzle the remaining 1 tablespoon olive oil over the fillets. Sprinkle them, flesh side only, with the thyme.

Place the fillets, skin-side down, in the pan and bake until opaque throughout but still moist, about 15 minutes. Using a spatula, transfer the fillets to individual plates, dividing them into serving pieces. (Most of the skin, which can be discarded, will remain in the pan.) Garnish each serving with juice from a lemon wedge, then serve immediately.

Serves 4 to 6

POCKET Salmon Steaks
WITH Lemon, FENNEL, AND Capers

PREPARATION TIME: 10 minutes   **COOKING TIME:** 25 minutes

We call these "pocket" salmon steaks because we cook them in little disposable aluminum-foil pockets. The technique simplifies cleaning up and keeps the baked fish moist and firm. The fennel offers a subtle hint of anise. Try this recipe with other fish as well, such as halibut and tuna.

4 salmon steaks or fillets, 6 to 8 ounces each, skin removed
Salt and freshly ground pepper to taste
4 teaspoons extra-virgin olive oil
4 slices fennel, each ¼ inch thick
4 slices lemon, each ⅛ inch thick
4 teaspoons capers

Preheat the oven to 400°F.

Place 1 salmon steak on a piece of aluminum foil about 8 by 12 inches. Sprinkle the salmon with salt and pepper and drizzle it with 1 teaspoon of the olive oil. Lay 1 fennel slice on top of the salmon, then lay 1 lemon slice on top of the fennel. Top with 1 teaspoon of the capers. Pull the edges of the aluminum foil together and crimp them to make a sealed pocket that fits loosely around the salmon. Repeat with the remaining fish steaks and other ingredients, to make 4 pockets in all.

Arrange the pockets on a baking sheet and bake for 25 minutes. Remove from the oven and, when the foil can be handled, carefully unwrap the first pocket so that the juices are not lost. Using a spatula, lift the salmon and its garnishes out of its wrapping and place on an individual plate, then pour the juices over the top. Repeat with the remaining pockets. Serve immediately.

Serves 4

SESAME-COATED Tuna STEAKS

PREPARATION TIME: 10 minutes, plus
    15 to 30 minutes for marinating

COOKING TIME: 4 minutes

These meaty tuna steaks are coated with crunchy sesame seeds. The tuna is almost sweet, with a briny, nutty edge that comes from the soy marinade. Don't sell your kids short. They will, indeed, eat tuna that doesn't come from a can. (But they might balk at the sesame seeds, so consider deleting this ingredient from their servings.)

Any fresh, high-quality tuna steaks will work here. Black sesame seeds, also known as *kuro goma,* are found in the Asian food sections of many supermarkets. If you can't find them, use all white sesame seeds. Serve the tuna steaks with Asian Slaw (page 132).

¼ cup soy sauce or tamari
2 tablespoons Asian sesame oil
1 tablespoon grated fresh ginger
Pinch of cayenne pepper
1½ pounds tuna steaks
½ cup white sesame seeds
½ cup black sesame seeds
Canola oil for frying
Coarse sea salt or kosher salt to taste

In a bowl large enough to hold the tuna, stir together the soy sauce, sesame oil, ginger, and cayenne. Place the tuna in the soy mixture, turn to coat both sides, and marinate at room temperature for 15 to 30 minutes—no longer or the fish will become mushy.

In a large, shallow bowl, stir together the white and black sesame seeds. Remove the tuna from the marinade and generously and evenly coat on all sides with the sesame seeds. Set aside.

Pour the canola oil to a depth of ½ inch into a large skillet or sauté pan and heat over high heat until almost smoking. (You can tell if the oil is hot enough by dropping in a few sesame seeds; they will make a sizzling noise on contact.) Add the tuna and sear for 1 to 2 minutes on each side for rare, or longer if you prefer your tuna cooked more thoroughly.

Transfer to individual plates, dividing into serving pieces, and season with salt. Serve immediately.

Serves 4 to 6

SEAFOOD Aioli

In Mediterranean countries, the garlic mayonnaise aioli is eaten with a variety of fish. This version is simple to prepare, whether for a weeknight family supper or a weekend dinner party, yet makes a striking, colorful presentation. Here the fish is grilled, but you may bake it (page 240) or braise it (page 239) instead.

---

6 red potatoes, about 3 pounds total weight, unpeeled, quartered
4 carrots, about 1½ pounds total weight, peeled and cut into
  2-inch lengths
1 pound string beans, trimmed
Salt and freshly ground pepper to taste
2 pounds meaty fish steaks such as salmon, halibut, or swordfish
2 teaspoons extra-virgin olive oil
1½ cups aioli (page 34)

Prepare a fire in a grill.

Bring a saucepan three-fourths full of water to a boil, add the potatoes and carrots, and cook until tender, about 15 minutes. Drain in a colander and cover to keep warm.

While the potatoes and carrots are cooking, steam the string beans or boil them in water until tender, 6 to 8 minutes. Drain and cover to keep warm.

When the grill is ready, lightly salt and pepper the fish on both sides, then brush on both sides with the olive oil. Place the fish on the grill rack and grill, turning once, until opaque throughout, 4 to 5 minutes per side. Remove from the grill and cut into serving pieces.

To serve, arrange the vegetables, grouped separately, on a large serving platter. Place the fish on a separate platter and the aioli in a serving bowl. Diners help themselves to fish, vegetables, and aioli. Each bite of fish or vegetable should be eaten with a small amount of the rich aioli.

Serves 4 to 6

GRILLED Swordfish
WITH Fruit Salsa

Meaty swordfish is perfect for the grill. (You may also panfry the swordfish over medium-high heat in an extra tablespoon of olive oil.) When paired with a snappy fruit salsa, this swordfish yields a satisfying family meal or grown-up dinner party. Any meaty fish, such as salmon or shark, can be served in the same way. Serve with Yellow Rice and Black Bean Salad (page 142) on the side.

FRUIT SALSA:

4 cups peeled (if necessary) and cubed (½-inch cubes) mixed ripe
*   fruits such as peach, nectarine, mango, and papaya*
3 tablespoons diced red onion
3 tablespoons fresh lime juice
¼ teaspoon salt
⅛ teaspoon cayenne pepper
⅓ cup chopped fresh cilantro

Salt and freshly ground pepper to taste
2 large swordfish steaks, about 1 pound each
2 teaspoons extra-virgin olive oil

Prepare a fire in a grill.

To make the salsa, in a large bowl, toss together the fruits, onion, lime juice, salt, and cayenne. Add the cilantro and toss again. Taste and adjust the seasoning. Cover and refrigerate until ready to use.

When the grill is ready, lightly salt and pepper the fish steaks on both sides, then brush on both sides with the olive oil. Place the steaks on the grill rack and grill, turning once, until opaque throughout, 4 to 5 minutes per side.

Remove the steaks from the grill and remove the skin from each steak. Cut each steak in half lengthwise to create 4 portions. Place the portions on individual plates and garnish with the salsa. Serve immediately.

Serves 4

SEAFOOD Risotto

PREPARATION TIME: 15 minutes   **COOKING TIME:** 40 minutes

This variation on our basic risotto recipe turns a simple side dish into a full-blown main course that's well suited to home entertaining.

---

3 tablespoons extra-virgin olive oil
1 onion, finely chopped
2 cloves garlic, minced
1 cup Arborio rice
4 cups chicken stock (page 105) or canned low-sodium chicken broth
1 cup white wine
20 to 25 medium-sized shrimp, peeled and deveined
8 large sea scallops, quartered
16 clams, scrubbed
⅓ cup freshly grated Parmesan cheese
Salt and freshly ground pepper to taste

In a Dutch oven or other large, heavy pot, heat the olive oil over medium heat. Add the onion and garlic and sauté until the onion is translucent, about 3 minutes. Add the rice and sauté for another 2 to 3 minutes. Add ½ cup of the stock and cook, stirring frequently—but not constantly—until most of the liquid is absorbed, about 3 minutes. Continue adding the stock ½ cup at a time, always stirring frequently until most of it is absorbed before adding more. After 2 cups of the stock have been used, add the wine, stirring frequently until it is absorbed. Then add the remaining stock, ½ cup at a time, stirring as described above. When the last of the stock is added, stir and wait 2 minutes, then gently stir in the shrimp and scallops and continue to cook, stirring occasionally, until the shrimp are pink and the scallops are opaque, about 4 minutes.

Meanwhile, pour water to a depth of 1 inch into a saucepan and bring to a boil over high heat. Add the clams, cover, reduce the heat to medium, and cook until they open, 4 to 5 minutes. Discard any clams that remain closed.

Check the risotto, which should be finished cooking or nearly so. It is ready when the rice is tender but still slightly firm at the center of each grain and creamy. Remove from the heat and stir in the Parmesan, salt, and pepper. Spoon into broad, shallow bowls and top each serving with 4 clams. Serve immediately.

Serves 4

SEAFOOD Pasta

PREPARATION TIME: 20 minutes   **COOKING TIME:** 40 minutes

A favorite among our friends, this dish may look complicated, but it's really quite easy, making it the perfect solution for a dinner party. If you have the opportunity, make the tomato sauce in advance (without the seafood), and then reheat to a simmer and add the seafood. And if you don't think your kids will appreciate squiggly squid tentacles, don't place those curlicues on their plates. (If you buy your squid already cleaned, they probably won't have their heads and tentacles. Thus, the potential problem is solved.)

TOMATO SAUCE:

3 tablespoons extra-virgin olive oil
½ onion, diced
2 cloves garlic, minced
1 small jalapeño chile, seeded and finely chopped (about 1 tablespoon)
1 teaspoon dried thyme
1 teaspoon dried oregano
½ teaspoon salt, plus salt to taste
Freshly ground pepper to taste
¼ cup red wine or water
6 tomatoes, peeled (see page 32), or 1 can (28 ounces) whole tomatoes,
    drained
½ cup freshly grated Parmesan cheese

20 medium-sized shrimp, peeled and deveined
3 squid, cleaned with bodies cut into rings and tentacles (optional)
    left whole
4 large sea scallops, quartered
1 pound linguine or other dried pasta
10 littleneck or other small clams, scrubbed
10 mussels, scrubbed and debearded

To make the tomato sauce, in a Dutch oven or other large, heavy pot, heat the olive oil over medium heat. Add the onion, garlic, and chile and sauté until the onion is translucent, about 3 minutes. Stir in the herbs, the ½ teaspoon salt, pepper, and wine.

Add the tomatoes and gently mash them to a coarse purée using a potato masher or large serving fork. Stir in the Parmesan, reduce the heat to low, and simmer, uncovered, until the sauce thickens, about 30 minutes. Taste and adjust the seasoning.

About 10 minutes before serving, stir the shrimp, squid, and scallops into the simmering sauce, cover, and cook until tender.

At the same time, in a saucepan, cook the pasta in boiling water (lightly salted if desired) until it is tender but still firm, about 10 minutes. Drain the pasta in a colander and shake dry.

While the pasta is cooking, pour water to a depth of 1 inch into a saucepan and bring to a boil over high heat. Add the clams and mussels, cover, reduce the heat to medium, and cook until they open, 4 to 5 minutes. Discard any mollusks that remain closed.

Add the drained pasta to the pot with the tomato-seafood sauce and toss to coat well. To serve, divide the pasta and sauce among individual large, shallow bowls. Top each serving with the mussels and clams. Serve immediately.

Serves 4 to 6

GRILLED Shrimp Teriyaki KABOBS

PREPARATION TIME: 20 minutes, plus 1 hour for marinating

COOKING TIME: 8 minutes

These savory kabobs combine a hint of sweetness with the gentle heat of cayenne. We use metal skewers, but you can also use wooden ones, which need to be soaked in water prior to grilling. Kids love to help us put the skewers together. Just remember to monitor this activity to avoid any accidents.

⅓ cup soy sauce or tamari
1 tablespoon rice vinegar
1 clove garlic, minced
1 tablespoon grated fresh ginger
3 green onions, white and green parts, diced
⅛ teaspoon cayenne pepper
18 large shrimp, peeled and deveined
12 medium or large mushrooms, stems trimmed but caps left whole
2 tablespoons extra-virgin olive oil
⅛ teaspoon salt
12 large cherry tomatoes
4 slices bacon, cut into 2-inch-wide pieces (12 pieces total)

In a large bowl, stir together the soy sauce, vinegar, garlic, ginger, green onions, and cayenne. Place the shrimp in the bowl and toss until evenly coated with the soy mixture. Cover and refrigerate for 1 hour.

Prepare a fire in a grill. Just before it is ready, in a bowl, toss together the mushrooms, olive oil, and salt.

Using 6 metal skewers, thread a shrimp, a tomato, a mushroom, and a bacon slice onto each skewer. Repeat and then finish with a shrimp. Each skewer will have 3 shrimp on it: 1 at each end and 1 at the midpoint. Place the skewers on the grill rack and grill, turning as needed, until the shrimp turn orange-pink, about 8 minutes total. Remove from the grill and serve immediately.

Serves 4 to 6

GRILLED Whole Trout
WITH Lemon AND Garlic

PREPARATION TIME: 10 minutes   **COOKING TIME:** 15 minutes

Invariably, whole trout are among the cheapest fish at our fish counter. They're gutted, but with their heads and tails attached, and ready to cook. We find meaty, yet delicate, fresh trout particularly delicious when they take on the smoky nuance of the grill.

Some trout aficionados love the skin of the fish, while others don't, including our daughters. So, we remove the skin, bones, and heads in the kitchen and serve them nice little white fillets in the dining room.

---

1 tablespoon extra-virgin olive oil
½ teaspoon coarse sea salt or kosher salt, plus salt to taste
½ teaspoon dried thyme
2 whole trout, ¾ to 1 pound each, cleaned
3 slices lemon, each cut in half
3 cloves garlic, coarsely chopped
Freshly ground pepper to taste

Prepare a fire in a grill.

In a small bowl, stir together the olive oil, the ½ teaspoon salt, and the thyme. Rinse the fish under cold water and pat dry with a paper towel. Rub the fish, inside and out, with the olive oil mixture and place equal amounts of lemon and garlic inside the cavity of each fish.

Place the trout in a lightly oiled grill basket or directly on the grill rack and grill, turning once, until the skin is crispy and begins to detach itself from the flesh, about 7 minutes per side. If using a grill basket, briefly flip a few more times to heat both sides evenly. Without a basket, skip that step, as the trout will start to fall apart. Serve the trout whole or filleted (see sidebar). Garnish each serving with the cooked lemon and garlic and season with the additional salt and with pepper. Serve immediately.

Serves 4

FILLETING WHOLE COOKED FISH

It's no big deal to remove the backbone and head from a fish once it is cooked. You can fillet the fish all at once, or eat one side, lift out the backbone, and then enjoy the second half.

To remove the flesh, simply cut down the center of the side facing upward on your plate. (A sharp knife is helpful but not required.) Peel away the soft flesh on each side of the incision for an initial serving. Detach the little flap of skin that connects the tail on the downward facing side, and pull up the entire backbone and rib cage, tail first. The head usually comes right off with the bones, leaving a nice fillet remaining on your plate.

As with all fish, we strongly recommend double and triple checking for bones, not only along where the backbone once lay, but also for small bones where the fins are attached.

Chapter

10

POULTRY
and
EGGS

When in doubt, try chicken.

Like the egg it hatched from, chicken provides home cooks with myriad opportunities for fast-cooking, flavor-filled meals. From the stove top to the oven to the grill, chicken and other poultry are tops in their category as satisfying centerpieces.

Roasted with herbs, chicken is a culinary anchor for our household. It's also accommodating to other flavors, from curry to ginger to soy sauce. As a bonus, versatile chicken is one of the rare leftovers that can actually be reborn as a totally new dish, such as **Second-Day Chicken Soup (page 112)**.

Perhaps best of all, chicken is cheap. Even relatively expensive organically raised birds don't come close in price to their equivalents in the meat department.

Chicken may be the star of the poultry section in your supermarket, but other birds, such as turkey and duck, should also find favor in your kitchen. Try them out as burgers, too (Chapter 12). And for more about the eggs from which all these birds spring, see pages 273 to 279.

BASIC **Roast** Chicken

PREPARATION TIME: 10 minutes   **COOKING TIME:** 20 minutes per pound

The kids never complain when roast chicken is on the menu. Best of all, it may be one of the easiest recipes this side of scrambled eggs. At its simplest, a chicken can be salted and cooked in the oven for about an hour. However, we like to coat our bird with a little olive oil and herbs, which deliver added flavor.

Plan on roasting your chicken for 20 minutes per pound at 400°F. Most young birds run between 3 and 4 pounds, large enough to feed a family with two or three children. The only tools required are a roasting pan and rack. You don't need to tie up the legs or pin back the wings. (Who cares if the wing tips come out crunchy? No one eats them anyway.) Basting is not required either. Most chickens contain enough fat to be "self-basting."

1 chicken, 3 to 4 pounds, rinsed and patted dry
Salt and freshly ground pepper to taste
1 tablespoon extra-virgin olive oil
1 tablespoon dried rosemary or dried thyme

Preheat the oven to 400°F.

Lightly season the outside of the chicken with salt and pepper. Gently rub the skin with the olive oil and rosemary. Set the chicken, breast-side up, on a rack in a roasting pan.

Roast the chicken until the skin is crisp and the juices run clear when a thigh is pierced, 1 hour to 1 hour and 20 minutes.

Transfer the chicken to a cutting board and let rest for 10 minutes before carving (see sidebar, page 258). If desired, reserve some of the drippings at the bottom of the pan to drizzle over the carved chicken, or make a quick gravy (page 36.)

Serves 4 to 6

Garlic AND Lemon ROAST Chicken

PREPARATION TIME: 10 minutes   **COOKING TIME:** 20 minutes per pound

This chicken is almost as simple as our Basic Roast Chicken (facing page). To make this into a one-pot dinner, toss some coarsely cut potatoes (quartered or smaller) in olive oil with a little salt, then place them in the bottom of the roasting pan. They'll cook along with the bird. If you like, squeeze some extra lemon juice over the carved chicken.

---

1 chicken, 3 to 4 pounds, rinsed and patted dry
3 cloves garlic, cut into thick slivers
1 large lemon
Salt and freshly ground pepper to taste
2 tablespoons extra-virgin olive oil

Preheat the oven to 400°F.

Using the tip of a paring knife, make small incisions at regular intervals in the breast of the chicken and insert a garlic sliver into each cut as it is made. Place the lemon in the chicken cavity. Lightly season the outside of the bird with salt and pepper, then, using your hands, coat it with the olive oil. Set the chicken, breast-side up, on a rack in a roasting pan.

Roast the chicken until the skin is crisp and the juices run clear when a thigh is pierced, 1 hour to 1 hour and 20 minutes.

Transfer the chicken to a cutting board. Using a fork, spear the hot lemon and remove it from the cavity. Slice it in half and squeeze the juice over the chicken, then let the chicken rest for 10 minutes before carving (see sidebar, page 258).

Serves 4 to 6

Garlic AND HERB ROAST Chicken
WITH Potatoes AND Carrots

PREPARATION TIME: 20 minutes   **COOKING TIME:** 20 minutes per pound

The scent of roasting olive oil and rosemary fills the house and whets the appetite for this dish, a favorite among children and grown-ups alike.

---

1 chicken, 3 to 4 pounds, rinsed and patted dry
3 or 4 cloves garlic, cut into slivers ⅛ inch thick, plus 5 to
  10 unpeeled whole garlic cloves (optional)
Salt and freshly ground pepper to taste
3 tablespoons extra-virgin olive oil
3 tablespoons dried rosemary
5 potatoes, unpeeled, quartered or cut into 1- to 2-inch cubes
4 carrots, peeled and cut crosswise into 1-inch lengths

Preheat the oven to 400°F.

Using the tip of a paring knife, make incisions at regular intervals in the breast of the chicken and insert a garlic sliver into each cut as it is made.

Lightly season the outside of the bird with salt and pepper, then, using your hands, coat it with 1 tablespoon of the olive oil. Finally, gently rub 2 tablespoons of the rosemary evenly over the entire bird. Set the chicken, breast-side up, on a rack in a roasting pan.

In a large bowl, toss the potatoes, carrots, and the whole garlic cloves (if using), with the remaining 2 tablespoons olive oil and 1 tablespoon rosemary. Sprinkle with some salt and pepper and toss again.

Place the vegetables in the roasting pan around the rack and under the chicken. Roast the chicken until the skin is crisp and the juices run clear when a thigh is pierced, 1 hour to 1 hour and 20 minutes. The potatoes and carrots should be firm but tender, and the garlic should be soft.

Transfer the chicken to a cutting board and let rest for 10 minutes before carving (see sidebar). Use the pan drippings to make gravy (page 36), if desired. Serve the chicken with the vegetables and roasted garlic on the side.

Serves 4 to 6

CARVING CHICKEN

Chickens are the easiest birds to carve, as long as they are fully cooked. After roasting, let the chicken rest for 10 minutes to firm up. It will make carving easier. But if you don't have time to wait, just carve immediately.

Start with the drumsticks, which should be loose at their joints. Using a sharp knife, cut down, away from yourself, and toward the joint. Then slice through the soft cartilage. Do the same with the wings.

There are a couple of options for the breast. One way is to remove the entire breast by slicing down and around it from the top of the breastbone. Using your hands—or a carving knife and a fork—you can then lift the meat off the bird and carve it into slices ½ inch thick. (Note that the meat may still be very hot; be careful not to burn your fingers.) Alternatively, thinly slice the meat directly off the bird. This works just fine, but it's slower, and the slices cool off faster.

Like the drumsticks, the thighs should also come off easily at the joint, but we often cut off thick slices directly, without removing the bone.

Curried CHICKEN in Coconut Milk

PREPARATION TIME: 15 minutes   **COOKING TIME:** 35 minutes

The flavors of curry and coconut milk are sensual and seductive, and the spices used here are readily available at your supermarket. We prefer regular coconut milk, which is thicker and more flavorful than "lite" coconut milk.

---

3 tablespoons canola oil

1 large onion, finely chopped

4 cloves garlic, minced

2½ teaspoons ground coriander

1½ teaspoons ground cumin

2½ teaspoons curry powder

1 teaspoon ground turmeric

⅛ teaspoon cayenne pepper

*4 boneless, skinless whole chicken breasts, about 3 pounds total
    weight, quartered*

1 can (14 ounces) coconut milk

1 teaspoon salt

1½ pounds baby spinach

¾ cup chopped fresh cilantro

4 cups hot cooked white rice (page 206)

In a large skillet or sauté pan, heat the canola oil over high heat. Add the onion and garlic and sauté for 2 minutes. Add the coriander, cumin, curry powder, turmeric, and cayenne and stir well. Add the chicken pieces and sear on each side for 3 to 4 minutes. Add the coconut milk and salt, stir well, cover, and reduce the heat to low. After 10 minutes, flip the chicken pieces, re-cover, and cook until the chicken is opaque throughout, about 10 more minutes.

Stir in the spinach, re-cover, and cook until wilted, about 5 minutes. Stir in the cilantro, cover, and cook for 2 minutes to blend the flavors. Serve the chicken over the rice.

Serves 6

E A S Y **Chicken Stew**

PREPARATION TIME: 20 minutes   **COOKING TIME:** 1 hour 10 minutes

Here is a chicken stew with all the good-tasting benefits of chicken soup but a lot more substance. It's even better on the second day and makes a terrific warm lunch for kids.

We remove the chicken skin for this dish, which lowers the fat content substantially. Vegetables are added in stages to prevent them from getting soggy or mushy. White wine is our cooking liquid of choice, as its natural acidity gives the stew a bit of brightness and zip. Water is an acceptable substitute, however. With its rich broth, chicken, and vegetables, this recipe can serve as an entire meal, or you can accompany it with rice (page 206).

---

2 tablespoons extra-virgin olive oil

1 onion, diced

3 cloves garlic, minced

1 chicken, 3 to 4 pounds, cut into 8 pieces (legs, thighs, wings, and breasts) and skin removed

Salt to taste, plus 1 teaspoon

Freshly ground pepper to taste

1 tablespoon dried rosemary

4 cups white wine or water

3 carrots, peeled and sliced

3 small red or white potatoes, unpeeled, cut into ½-inch cubes

3 small zucchini, cut into ½-inch-thick rounds

In a Dutch oven or other large, heavy pot, heat the olive oil over medium heat. Add the onion and garlic and sauté until the onion is translucent, about 3 minutes. Season the chicken pieces with salt and pepper and place them in the pot. Cook, turning occasionally, until lightly browned on all sides, 2 to 4 minutes. Stir in the rosemary and pour in the wine. Raise the heat to high and bring to a boil. Reduce the heat to low, add the 1 teaspoon salt, cover, and cook, stirring occasionally, for 40 minutes.

Add the carrots and potatoes, re-cover, and simmer for another 20 minutes. At this point, the chicken will be opaque throughout and all the vegetables will be tender. Add the zucchini, re-cover, and simmer for 10 more minutes. Season with salt and pepper. Serve piping hot.

Serves 4 to 6

Coq AU VIN

PREPARATION TIME: 30 minutes   **COOKING TIME:** 1½ hours

It may have a fancy French name, but *coq au vin* simply means chicken with wine. The boiled wine tenderizes the chicken, but the alcohol evaporates almost immediately. As a result, this rich, moist, and delicious dish can be enjoyed by everyone in the family, young and old. It is our daughter Zoë's most often requested dish.

Coq au vin is not hard to make, but it does require a bit more time than you might allocate to an average weeknight. Try this on Saturday night with friends. Accompany the chicken with mashed potatoes (page 164) or pasta (page 175).

1 bay leaf

1 teaspoon dried thyme

1 teaspoon dried rosemary

3 tablespoons extra-virgin olive oil

3 slices bacon, cut into matchsticks

1 pound white button mushrooms, trimmed and halved or quartered

2 onions, diced

4 cloves garlic, minced

1 chicken, about 5 pounds, cut into 8 pieces (legs, thighs, wings, and breasts) and skin removed

Salt to taste, plus 1 teaspoon

Freshly ground pepper to taste

1 cup, plus 2 tablespoons unbleached all-purpose flour

3 cups red wine

1 carrot, peeled and cut into 3-inch-long matchsticks

4 tablespoons unsalted butter

Fresh parsley or rosemary sprigs for garnish

Wrap the bay leaf, thyme, and rosemary in a 5-inch-square piece of cheesecloth. Tie the cheesecloth closed with string and set aside. (This little pouch is called a bouquet garni.)

In a large, deep skillet or Dutch oven, heat the olive oil over medium heat. Add the bacon and sauté until it browns, about 5 minutes. Add the mushrooms, onions, and garlic, stir gently, cover, and cook until the mushrooms are soft, about 5 minutes. Transfer the mushroom mixture to a bowl, cover, and reserve.

Season the chicken pieces with salt and pepper and then dredge the pieces in the 1 cup flour, shaking off the excess. Discard any unused flour. Return the skillet to medium-high heat, add the chicken pieces, and brown for about 2 minutes on each side. Add the wine, the bouquet garni, and the 1 teaspoon salt and bring to a boil. Cover, reduce the heat to low, and cook, stirring occasionally, for 1 hour.

While the chicken is simmering, plunge the carrot slices into boiling water for 2 minutes. Rinse in cold water, cover, and set aside.

After the chicken has cooked for 1 hour, add the carrot along with the reserved mushroom mixture and cook for 15 more minutes. At this point the chicken will be cooked through and dark in color on the outside (from the red wine).

Remove the chicken pieces from the pan, set them on a serving platter, and cover with aluminum foil to retain the heat. Discard the bouquet garni, but let the vegetables continue to simmer.

Meanwhile, in a small sauté pan, melt the butter over low heat and gently whisk in the 2 tablespoons flour until the mixture thickens, about 1 minute. Whisk the flour-butter mix into the vegetable-wine sauce and simmer for another minute until slightly thickened.

Remove the aluminum foil from the chicken and cover it with the vegetable-wine sauce. Garnish with parsley sprigs and serve.

Serves 4 to 6

CHICKEN Kabobs MARINATED in Yogurt AND SPICES

PREPARATION TIME: 10 minutes, plus 2 to 4 hours for marinating

COOKING TIME: 15 minutes

Try these savory, moist kabobs with white rice (page 206) and Spiced Carrot and Raisin Salad (page 131) for an exotic taste treat. We use metal skewers to make kabobs. If you use wooden skewers, remember to soak them in water first. Let the kids help put the chicken on the skewers, but supervise them to avoid accidents.

2 tablespoons fresh lemon juice
½ cup plain yogurt
3 tablespoons chopped fresh cilantro
1 tablespoon grated fresh ginger
2 cloves garlic, minced
1 teaspoon ground cumin
1 teaspoon ground coriander
2 tablespoons canola or other vegetable oil
1 teaspoon salt
2 pounds boneless, skinless chicken breasts, cut into 2-inch cubes

In a large glass or ceramic bowl, combine the lemon juice, yogurt, cilantro, ginger, garlic, cumin, coriander, 1 tablespoon of the canola oil, and the salt. Stir in the chicken cubes, cover, and refrigerate for 2 to 4 hours.

Prepare a fire in a grill or preheat the broiler. Remove the chicken cubes from the marinade and thread onto metal skewers. Brush the chicken with the remaining 1 tablespoon canola oil. Place the skewers on the grill rack, or on a broiler pan and slip the pan under the broiler. Grill or broil, turning occasionally, until the chicken is opaque throughout, 12 to 15 minutes. If using a grill, close the top for the last 5 minutes to ensure thorough cooking. Serve the skewers immediately.

Serves 4

CHICKEN Adobo

PREPARATION TIME: 15 minutes   **COOKING TIME:** 50 minutes

This sweet and spicy chicken is our version of the national dish of the Philippines. For extra heat, double the amount of cayenne pepper. You may also substitute pork for the chicken.

---

2 cups water
½ cup soy sauce or tamari
2 tablespoons distilled white vinegar
1 teaspoon brown sugar
1 onion, diced
2 cloves garlic, minced
1 teaspoon ground ginger
2 bay leaves
1 teaspoon peppercorns
⅛ teaspoon cayenne pepper
1 chicken, about 4 pounds, cut into 8 to 10 pieces (legs, thighs,
    wings, breasts in halves or quarters), skin removed
Salt to taste
2 tablespoons canola or other vegetable oil
3 cups hot cooked white rice (page 206)

In a bowl, stir together the water, soy sauce, vinegar, brown sugar, onion, garlic, ginger, bay leaves, peppercorns, and cayenne. Set aside.

Lightly sprinkle the chicken pieces with salt. In a Dutch oven or a large, deep skillet, heat the canola oil over medium heat. Add the chicken pieces and brown lightly, turning occasionally, for about 3 minutes.

Stir the water-soy mixture and pour it into the pot with the chicken. Raise the heat to high and bring to a boil, then cover, reduce the heat to low, and simmer until the chicken is opaque throughout, about 45 minutes. (For a thicker sauce, simmer uncovered for the final 10 to 15 minutes.) Serve immediately spooned over the rice.

Serves 4 to 6

Chicken **Stir-Fry** WITH **LEMON BUTTER** AND **Broccoli**

PREPARATION TIME: 15 minutes   **COOKING TIME:** 15 minutes

Kids and grown-ups alike will tuck into this tangy chicken with enthusiasm. It is not a classic stir-fry, which requires more stirring. But for us, the key is *less* stirring. That gives us a few moments to deal with other pressing requirements, whatever they may be.

½ teaspoon salt, plus salt to taste
2 boneless whole chicken breasts, about 1½ to 2 pounds total
    weight, skin removed and cut into ¾-inch squares
3 tablespoons extra-virgin olive oil
4 cups small broccoli florets
10 cherry tomatoes, cut in half
3 tablespoons water
1 tablespoon dried rosemary
5 cloves garlic, thinly sliced
¼ cup fresh lemon juice
3 tablespoons unsalted butter
Freshly ground pepper to taste
2 cups hot cooked white rice (page 206)

Sprinkle the ½ teaspoon salt evenly over the chicken pieces and set them aside. In a large sauté pan, heat 1 tablespoon of the olive oil over medium-high heat. Add the broccoli and tomatoes and stir to coat evenly with the oil. Add 2 tablespoons of the water, cover, and cook until the tomatoes are soft and the broccoli is fairly tender, about 3 minutes. Transfer the broccoli and tomatoes to a large bowl and reserve.

Add another tablespoon of the olive oil to the pan and heat over medium-high heat. Stir in the chicken chunks and rosemary, cover, and cook for 2 minutes. Flip the chicken pieces over, re-cover, and cook until the chicken is opaque throughout, another 3 to 4 minutes. Transfer the chicken to the bowl holding the broccoli and tomatoes.

Reduce the heat to medium and add the remaining 1 tablespoon olive oil. Add the garlic and cook, stirring occasionally to prevent burning, until golden brown, about 1 minute. Add the lemon juice and the remaining 1 tablespoon water for added moisture, then stir in the butter until it melts. Return the chicken, broccoli, and tomatoes to the pan, stir well, and reheat to serving temperature, 30 to 45 seconds.

Remove from the heat and season with the additional salt and with pepper. Serve immediately with the rice.

Serves 4 or 5

CHICKEN STIR-FRY WITH Snow Peas

PREPARATION TIME: 15 minutes   **COOKING TIME:** 15 minutes

If your kids like Chinese food, they will love this recipe. It's redolent of ginger and garlic and loaded with chicken. Shrimp or pork can take the place of the chicken here. Snow peas, also known as Chinese pea pods, are broad, flat peas that are eaten pod and all.

½ teaspoon salt

2 boneless, skinless whole chicken breasts, 1½ to 2 pounds total weight, cut into ¾-inch squares

2 teaspoons cornstarch

¼ cup chicken stock (page 105) or canned low-sodium chicken broth

2 tablespoons Asian sesame oil

½ pound snow peas, trimmed (about 3 cups)

2 tablespoons grated fresh ginger

6 green onions, white part only, diced

2 cloves garlic, minced

3 tablespoons soy sauce or tamari

2 tablespoons rice vinegar

¼ pound bean sprouts

⅓ cup chopped fresh cilantro

Freshly ground pepper to taste

2 cups hot cooked white rice (page 206)

Sprinkle the salt evenly over the chicken pieces and set them aside. In a small bowl, stir the cornstarch into the stock to dissolve. Set aside.

In a large sauté pan, heat 1 tablespoon of the sesame oil over medium-high heat. Add the snow peas and stir gently. Cover, reduce the heat to low, and cook until slightly wilted, about 3 minutes. Transfer the snow peas to a bowl and set aside.

Add the chicken to the pan, raise the heat to medium, cover, and cook for 2 minutes. Flip the chicken pieces over, re-cover, and cook until the chicken is opaque throughout, another 3 to 4 minutes. Transfer the chicken to the bowl holding the snow peas.

Reduce the heat to medium-low and add the remaining 1 tablespoon sesame oil to the pan. Add the ginger, green onions, and garlic and cook for 1 minute, stirring occasionally. Quickly stir the cornstarch mixture, then stir it into the pan with the soy sauce and rice vinegar. Bring to a gentle boil and boil, stirring, for a minute or two to thicken the pan sauce. Return the chicken and snow peas to the pan, stir well, and reheat to serving temperature, 30 to 45 seconds.

Remove from the heat and mix in the bean sprouts. Transfer to a serving dish and garnish with the cilantro. Grind a little pepper over the top. Serve immediately with the rice.

Serves 4

ROAST Turkey Breast

PREPARATION TIME: 15 minutes   **COOKING TIME:** 45 minutes

Here is a fine way to feature turkey without waiting four hours for a whole bird to cook. It's moist on the inside, with a crisp, savory red-hued skin that the kids will probably fight over. Fashion the leftovers into lunchtime sandwiches, or use them to make a great "chicken" soup (page 112). Accompany this dish with Braised Red Cabbage with Apple and Bacon (page 166).

---

*1 turkey breast, about 5 pounds, cut in half lengthwise, with skin
    and bones intact*
2 teaspoons salt
1 teaspoon freshly ground pepper
1 teaspoon paprika
2 teaspoons garlic powder
1 tablespoon extra-virgin olive oil

Preheat the oven to 400°F.

Season each turkey breast half with half of the salt, pepper, paprika, and garlic powder. (Try this over the sink to facilitate cleanup.) Then rub each breast half with half of the olive oil until the oil and spices are evenly distributed over the skin. Place the breast halves, skin-side up, directly in a roasting pan (without a rack).

Roast the breast halves until the skin is crisp and the juices run clear when pierced at the thickest point with a fork, about 45 minutes. For extra-crispy skin, slip the pan under the broiler for 2 to 3 minutes at the end. Transfer to a cutting board and let rest for 10 minutes before carving.

Serves 6

CRISPY PANFRIED Duck Breasts

PREPARATION TIME: 5 minutes   **COOKING TIME:** 15 minutes

Duck breast may be poultry, but it sure tastes like steak. When cooked, the dark red meat is topped with a rich, crispy layer of skin that adds texture and flavor.

Duck is easy to cook, but it tends to smoke and splatter a bit, so wear your apron. The breasts will seem very flat prior to cooking, but they plump up in the pan. Like steak, we enjoy our duck medium to medium-rare, with Caramelized Onions (page 159) and mashed potatoes (page 164) on the side.

2 boneless duck breasts, about 1 pound each
Salt and freshly ground pepper to taste
1 tablespoon canola oil

Cut each duck breast in half lengthwise and trim away excess fat from around the edges of the skin. Do not, however, remove the skin. Using a fork, poke the skin of each half breast 5 or 6 times to create holes that will allow the fat to drain. Sprinkle both sides of the breasts generously with salt and pepper.

In a large skillet or sauté pan, heat the canola oil over medium-high heat. Place the duck, skin-side down, in the pan and cook until the skin is crisp, 7 to 8 minutes. Spoon off and discard excess fat in the pan. Reduce the heat to medium, flip the breasts over, and cook for 3 to 4 more minutes for medium-rare. Serve at once.

Serves 4

EGGS: NOT JUST FOR BREAKFAST

Scrambled eggs (page 42) are practical in the morning because they cook quickly. But they are equally advantageous at noon, on their own or as filling for tortillas or other sandwiches. Hard-boiled eggs (page 34) fit easily into sandwiches or salads, too, while raw eggs are quickly whisked into mayonnaise or garlicky aioli (page 34). Two more elaborate preparations, the omelet and the quiche (pages 273 to 279), provide fast-to-assemble main courses at dinnertime.

Most commercial eggs, the shells of which have been coated with a natural mineral oil to make them less porous, remain edible for periods of up to six months when stored in the refrigerator. However, we don't recommend storing eggs at home for more than three to four weeks. (If you buy your eggs in a supermarket, they are probably already three to seven days old.) With eggs, freshness equals flavor. Buy your eggs from a reputable purveyor and check the carton for a sell-by date. When an egg is cracked, it should reveal a plump, deep yellow or orange yolk and "thick" whites.

OMELETS

Because we eat omelets for lunch or dinner, our kids would be surprised to discover that many people enjoy them for breakfast. They do make great breakfasts, of course, but we don't usually have time to cook them on weekday mornings. Nonetheless, omelets are relatively easy to prepare for dinner, and quite versatile.

You can fill omelets with almost anything: onions, garlic, tomatoes, kale, spinach, apples, plantains, broccoli, leeks, cheese, mushrooms, leftover pasta, zucchini, red or green bell peppers, avocado, sausage, ham—you name it. Just remember that most raw vegetables need to be briefly sautéed prior to combining with the egg. The recipes featured here are among our favorites.

We're not talking about so-called Parisian-style omelets made as individual servings. It would take a long time to make a separate omelet for everyone in our house, so we create omelets to fill an entire frying pan. These large egg dishes never need to be flipped. One, alone, serves the entire family.

Skye and Zoë love omelets with Roasted Rosemary Potato Crisps (page 162) on the side. Mashed potatoes (page 164) or rice (page 206) are also in demand. You might consider a green vegetable, like String Beans with Tomato and Garlic (page 153), as an accompaniment as well.

Tomato, CHEESE, and Herb OMELET

PREPARATION TIME: 10 minutes   **COOKING TIME:** 20 minutes

This is our standard "house" omelet. It's really an egg pizza. No garlic in the house? Just use onion. No garlic or onion? Well, it won't be quite as tasty, but the kids won't complain.

---

2 tablespoons extra-virgin olive oil

1 clove garlic, minced

1 small onion, diced (optional)

8 eggs

1 tomato, sliced

¼ pound cheese such as Gruyère, Swiss, or Cheddar, sliced or grated

1 teaspoon dried thyme

Salt and freshly ground pepper to taste

Dijon mustard for serving (optional)

In a large sauté pan or skillet, heat the olive oil over medium heat. Add the garlic and sauté until it is golden, about 1 minute. If using the onion, sauté with the garlic until translucent, 2 to 3 minutes. While the garlic and onion are cooking, beat the eggs with a whisk or fork in a bowl until blended.

Push the garlic (and onion) to the side of the pan and pour in the eggs, which will fill the pan. Reduce the heat to low, and spread the garlic (and onion) over the surface of the eggs. Evenly distribute the tomato slices over the top, and then sprinkle evenly with the cheese, and finally the thyme. Cover the pan and cook until the eggs are firm, 12 to 15 minutes. (The bottom will not burn over low heat. It will simply brown and become slightly crisp.)

Remove the pan from the heat. While the omelet is still in the pan, cut it into pie-shaped wedges (like pizza). Then, using a spatula, transfer the wedges to individual serving plates. Sprinkle with salt and pepper and serve immediately with a dollop of Dijon mustard on the side, if using.

Serves 4 or 5

Kale OMELET

A popular variation on our basic omelet, this kale-rich omelet fills a broad spectrum of nutritional requirements while serving up plenty of satisfaction on the palate.

---

2 tablespoons extra-virgin olive oil
2 cloves garlic, minced
1 small bunch kale, about ½ pound, coarsely chopped
3 tablespoons water
8 eggs
¼ pound Gruyère cheese, sliced or grated
1 teaspoon dried thyme
Salt and freshly ground pepper to taste
Dijon mustard for serving (optional)

In a large sauté pan or skillet, heat the olive oil over medium heat. Add the garlic and sauté until golden, about 1 minute. Add the kale and stir to coat with the oil and garlic. Add the water to the pan, cover, and cook until the kale is wilted, about 3 minutes. While the kale is cooking, beat the eggs with a whisk or fork in a bowl until blended.

Push the kale to the side of the pan and pour in the eggs, which will fill the pan. Reduce the heat to low and spread the kale over the surface of the eggs. Evenly distribute the cheese over the kale and top with the thyme. Cover the pan and cook until the eggs are firm, 10 to 15 minutes.

Remove the pan from the heat. While the omelet is still in the pan, cut it into pie-shaped wedges (like pizza). Then, using a spatula, transfer the wedges to individual serving plates. Sprinkle with salt and pepper and serve immediately with a dollop of Dijon mustard on the side, if using.

Serves 4 or 5

Apple OMELET

PREPARATION TIME: 5 minutes   **COOKING TIME:** 20 minutes

Here, we like the sweetness of apple mixed with savory eggs and cheese. It's a little like having a cheese course with fruit and makes a great omelet for a Sunday morning brunch.

---

2 tablespoons extra-virgin olive oil
1 apple, unpeeled, halved, cored, and sliced
8 eggs
¼ pound Gruyère or Swiss cheese, sliced or grated
1 teaspoon dried thyme
Salt and freshly ground pepper to taste

In a large sauté pan or skillet, heat the olive oil over medium heat. Add the apple slices and sauté, turning as needed, until they begin to soften, about 2 minutes per side.

While the apple is cooking, beat the eggs with a whisk or fork in a bowl until blended.

Push the apple slices to the side of the pan and pour in the eggs, which will fill the pan. Reduce the heat to low and spread the apple over the surface of the eggs. Evenly distribute the cheese on top and sprinkle with the thyme. Cover and cook until the eggs are firm, 10 to 15 minutes.

Remove the pan from the heat. While the omelet is still in the pan, cut it into pie-shaped wedges (like pizza). Then, using a spatula, transfer the wedges to individual serving plates. Sprinkle with salt and pepper and serve immediately.

Serves 4 or 5

Plantain OMELET

PREPARATION TIME: 5 minutes   **COOKING TIME:** 25 minutes

Ripe plantains are firmer and easier to cook than bananas. Look for a plantain with a dark yellow or browning skin. Its flesh will be yellow or slightly pink.

---

2 tablespoons canola oil
1 ripe plantain, peeled and cut into ¼-inch-thick slices
8 eggs
Salt and freshly ground pepper to taste

In a large sauté pan or skillet, heat the canola oil over medium heat. Add the plantain slices and sauté, turning once, until golden brown on both sides, about 4 minutes per side. While the plantain slices are cooking, beat the eggs with a whisk or fork in a bowl until blended.

Push the plantain slices to the side of the pan and pour in the eggs, which will fill the pan. Reduce the heat to low and spread the plantain slices over the surface of the eggs. Cover and cook until the eggs are firm, about 10 to 15 minutes.

Remove the pan from the heat. While the omelet is still in the pan, cut it into pie-shaped wedges (like pizza). Then, using a spatula, transfer the wedges to individual serving plates. Sprinkle with salt and pepper and serve immediately.

Serves 4 or 5

Quiche THREE WAYS

PREPARATION TIME: 15 minutes   **COOKING TIME:** 45 minutes

A quiche is a savory egg custard pie. It's versatile—perfect for brunch, lunch, or dinner—and easy to make if you use a commercial pie crust, which can be found in the freezer section at your supermarket. Look for one made in a "deep-dish" style with real butter (check the ingredient list).

Quiche teams up wonderfully with stray leftovers, like a few slices of ham, a piece of grilled salmon, or some vegetables. We offer three possibilities following the basic recipe, but you should experiment with what you have on hand.

---

4 eggs
2 cups heavy cream
¼ teaspoon ground nutmeg
½ teaspoon salt
½ teaspoon freshly ground pepper
1 purchased pie crust, 9 inches in diameter

Preheat the oven to 425°F.

In a bowl, whisk together the eggs and cream until blended. Stir in the nutmeg, salt, and pepper.

Bake the pie crust for 6 minutes. Remove from the oven and pour the egg mixture into the crust. Return the filled crust to the oven and bake for 15 minutes. Reduce the heat to 375°F and continue to bake until a fork or toothpick inserted into the center comes out dry, 20 to 25 minutes.

Remove the quiche from the oven and let cool on a rack for 10 to 12 minutes. The quiche firms up as it cools down. Cut into wedges and serve.

To make any one of the following quiches, stir the additional ingredients into the basic custard before pouring it into the pie crust, then bake as directed.

HAM AND CHEESE QUICHE: Add ½ cup grated Gruyère or any Swiss-style cheese and ½ cup diced ham to the custard.

SALMON AND DILL QUICHE: Add ½ cup finely diced raw or smoked salmon and 2 tablespoons finely chopped fresh dill to the custard.

MUSHROOM QUICHE: In a small skillet or sauté pan, heat 1 tablespoon unsalted butter or canola oil over medium heat. Add 1 cup sliced mushrooms and 2 tablespoons finely chopped onion and sauté until the mushrooms are tender, about 5 minutes. Remove from the heat, let cool slightly, and then add to the custard.

Chapter **11**

MEATS

There is something primal about eating a good piece of meat: The soft firmness as we bite down, the rich juices that flow across our tongues. As we chew, we savor a tradition as old as humanity.

Our kids love meat. And we're talking more than burgers (for those, see chapter 12). They love to tuck into a rich stew of lamb and vegetables (page 296), or a more esoteric cassoulet (page 288). They're crazy about pork chops (page 284) and oxtail stew (page 304).

Meat can take center stage or fill a supporting role. In many recipes in this book, we use a bit of bacon or sausage to add flavor to an otherwise meatless dish. But in this chapter, meat is the star, and each type displays its own character. Lamb is more assertive and earthy than beef. Pork is sweeter than either beef or lamb.

ts

Occasionally, we'll follow our prehistoric muse and throw some ribs on the grill for a quick, fire-driven treat. At other times, there is nothing so satisfying as a slow oven-cooked casserole. Either way, meat adds a special touch to everyday dining.

A NOTE ABOUT CARVING:

In a perfect world, we let meat sit for about **10** minutes before carving it. This allows the meats natural juices to redistribute themselves evenly. The meat also becomes firmer, making it easier to carve. However, we have found that hungry children do not necessarily appreciate these fine points. As a result, we often carve immediately, with results that are still eminently edible.

PANFRIED Pork Chops WITH
CRUNCHY Garlic

PREPARATION TIME: 10 minutes   **COOKING TIME:** 20 minutes

We like these quick and easy chops best with mashed potatoes (page 164). If desired, serve with an optional wine sauce (see below), or forgo the wine and simply use the butter to dress your meat and potatoes.

---

2 tablespoons extra-virgin olive oil
8 large cloves garlic, thickly sliced
4 pork chops, each about 1 inch thick
Salt and freshly ground pepper to taste
2 tablespoons unsalted butter
1½ cups red or white wine (optional)

In a large sauté pan or skillet, heat the olive oil over medium heat. Add the garlic and sauté until golden brown, about 3 minutes. Remove the garlic slices with a slotted spoon and set aside in a small bowl.

Season the pork chops on both sides with salt and pepper. Put them in the oil remaining in the hot pan, raise the heat to medium-high, and cook until lightly browned on the underside, about 10 minutes. (If the pan starts to smoke, add a few tablespoons of water.) Reduce the heat to medium, flip the chops over, cover, and cook until the meat is opaque throughout but still moist, another 5 to 10 minutes.

Transfer the chops to individual plates. Cut the butter into 4 equal pats, and top each chop with a pat of butter and the reserved garlic slices.

Or, to serve the chops with a wine sauce, transfer the chops to a plate and cover to retain the heat. Add the wine to the pan over high heat and stir to scrape up any browned bits from the bottom. Cook over high heat until the liquid is reduced by half, about 3 minutes. Add the butter, reduce the heat to low, and stir until the butter melts. Place the pork chops on individual plates, top with the garlic slices, and drizzle with the sauce.

Serves 4

Pork Loin AND TANGY Apples

PREPARATION TIME: 10 minutes   **COOKING TIME:** 20 minutes

Creamy, sweet apples and onions provide a fine foil for these tender, lean pork loin rounds. Simply cooked white or brown rice (page 206) pairs well with this saucy dish.

---

2 tablespoons extra-virgin olive oil
2 pounds pork tenderloin, sliced into ¾-inch-thick rounds
1 onion, thinly sliced
1 red apple, unpeeled, halved, cored, and thinly sliced
¼ cup white wine, chicken stock (page 105), canned low-sodium
    chicken broth, or water
3 tablespoons heavy cream
Salt and freshly ground pepper to taste

In a large, heavy skillet or sauté pan, heat the olive oil over high heat. Add the pork slices and sear on both sides to brown, about 1 minute per side. Transfer the meat to a plate and set aside.

Reduce the heat to medium, add the onion to the oil remaining in the pan, and sauté until translucent, about 3 minutes. Stir in the apple, cover, and cook until the apple has softened somewhat, about 3 minutes. Pour in the wine and stir to scrape up any browned bits from the bottom. Reduce the heat to low and return the pork rounds to the pan, laying them over the apple-onion mixture. Cover and simmer until the meat is opaque throughout, about 8 minutes.

Remove the meat from the pan and place on a serving platter. Stir the cream into the apple-onion mix and continue to simmer for 30 seconds to thicken slightly.

Pour the apple-onion sauce over the pork rounds and season with salt and pepper. Serve immediately.

Serves 4 to 6

Braised PORK ROAST
with Garlic and Rosemary

PREPARATION TIME: 15 minutes   **COOKING TIME:** 50 minutes

Pork roast is deliciously cheap and easy, especially when cooked in this traditional Italian manner. Enjoy with Basic Rice, but Better (page 207) on the side.

---

7 cloves garlic, minced

3 tablespoons finely chopped fresh rosemary

2½ teaspoons coarse sea salt or kosher salt

½ teaspoon freshly ground pepper

5 tablespoons extra-virgin olive oil

1 boneless pork roast, about 3 pounds

1½ cups whole milk, plus more if needed

Preheat the oven to 400°F.

In a small bowl, combine the garlic, rosemary, salt, pepper, and 3 tablespoons of the olive oil. Using a wooden spoon, mix well to form a paste. Set aside.

In a Dutch oven or other large, ovenproof pot, heat the remaining 2 tablespoons olive oil over medium-high heat. Place the pork roast in the oil and brown on all sides, about 2 minutes per side. Remove the pot from the heat, pour in the 1½ cups milk and stir it into the pan juices. Spread the garlic and rosemary paste on top of the pork roast. If you have a probe-type meat thermometer, insert it into the thickest part of the roast, then cover the pot.

Place the pot in the oven and cook the roast, basting occasionally with the pan juices, for 45 minutes. (If the pan juices look like they are going to evaporate, add more milk ½ cup at a time.) Check the temperature on the thermometer, or insert an instant-read thermometer. The roast is ready when the thermometer registers 155°F.

Transfer the roast to a cutting board and let rest for 5 to 10 minutes before carving. Meanwhile, whisk the pan juices to break up any solids that might remain on the bottom. These savory juices are your sauce. If it seems too thin, simmer on the stove top over high heat for a few minutes to thicken.

Slice the roast and serve with the sauce spooned over the top.

Serves 6

Cassoulet QUICKLY

PREPARATION TIME: 20 minutes   **COOKING TIME:** 45 minutes

With cassoulet, the French have taken pork and beans to precipitous culinary heights. This streamlined version better suits our schedule and budget. It nonetheless serves up plenty of soulful, heartwarming flavors. If you want to use dried beans instead of canned beans, you will need to cook 2 cups dried white navy or cannellini beans (see page 34). Include the time necessary to soak and cook them in your schedule.

8 to 10 sweet or hot Italian sausages, about 3 pounds total weight
2 tablespoons extra-virgin olive oil
1 onion, diced
3 cloves garlic, coarsely chopped
2 teaspoons dried thyme
1 teaspoon dried rosemary
2 cups sliced white button mushrooms
2 pounds fresh tomatoes, unpeeled and coarsely chopped, or 1 can
    (28 ounces) whole tomatoes, coarsely chopped, with juice
2 cans (15 ounces each) white beans, rinsed and drained
2 teaspoons salt
Freshly ground pepper to taste
2 bay leaves

Preheat the oven to 400°F.

Using a fork, poke a series of holes in the opposite sides of each sausage. Pour water to a depth of about 1 inch in a large skillet or sauté pan and bring to a boil over high heat. Place the sausages in the pan, cover, reduce the heat to medium, and simmer until cooked through, 5 to 7 minutes. Drain off the water and set the sausages aside.

In a Dutch oven or other large, ovenproof pot, heat the olive oil over medium heat. Add the onion and garlic and sauté until the onion is translucent, about 3 minutes. Stir in the thyme, rosemary, and mushrooms, cover, and cook until the mushrooms are tender, about 5 minutes. Add the tomatoes and their juices to the pan along with the beans. Stir well, then add the salt and season with pepper. Remove from the heat.

Cut the sausages into 2-inch-long sections and incorporate them into the bean mixture. Insert the bay leaves into the top. Bake, uncovered, for 45 minutes. Serve immediately.

Serves 8

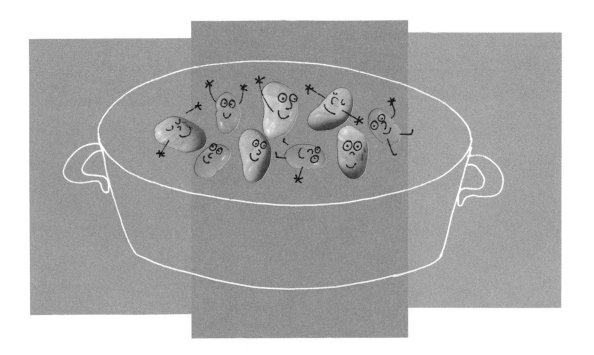

Standing Pork Roast
WITH Sage AND ROAST Potatoes

PREPARATION TIME: 10 minutes   **COOKING TIME:** 1 hour

A standing pork roast is simply a group of pork chops that remain attached to one another. Here, the potatoes roast with the pork, for added flavor and ease of preparation. Try this dish accompanied with Caramelized Onions (page 159).

---

1 standing pork roast with 4 bones, 2½ to 3 pounds
1 teaspoon salt
1 teaspoon freshly ground pepper
6 tablespoons extra-virgin olive oil
⅓ cup minced fresh sage
2½ pounds new potatoes, unpeeled, coarsely chopped

Preheat the oven to 350°F.

Season the pork with ½ teaspoon each of the salt and pepper. Drizzle 1 tablespoon of the olive oil on each side of the roast, and rub the oil evenly over the meat. Cover the roast with the sage, and place the roast, bone-side facing down, on a rack in a roasting pan.

In a large bowl, toss the potatoes with the remaining 4 tablespoons olive oil. Add the remaining salt and pepper and toss again. Place the potatoes in the roasting pan at the base of the rack. If you have a probe-type meat thermometer, insert it into the thickest part of the roast (do not let it touch the bones).

Place the roast in the oven and roast for 1 hour. Check the temperature on the thermometer, or insert an instant-read thermometer (again, not touching the bones). The roast is ready when the thermometer registers 155°F. For a crisper exterior, turn the oven to broil and place the roast under the broiler for 2 minutes.

Transfer the roast to a cutting board and let rest for 10 minutes before carving, then carve between the bones, serving 1 chop for each person. Accompany with the potatoes.

Serves 4

MEAT AND GOOD HEALTH

Vegetarians will disagree, but meat is good for us. Theories regarding diets rich or low in animal fats vary widely. But the fact remains that our bodies thrive on protein. Moderation is the key to a balanced diet, and that extends to meat.

What's moderate? Depending on your size and perspective, it's a concept open to discussion. But if you take a proactive role in the quality of the foods you eat, the chances are good that common sense will direct you to a reasonably healthy outcome.

Our greatest questions regarding consumption of meat revolve less around meat's natural nutritional qualities than its somewhat unnatural additives. America's beef (and poultry) industries are big business today, and the bottom line leans toward profit—not your health or animal rights. Many animals are raised under deplorable conditions. They are often pumped

GRILLED **Baby Back** Ribs

PREPARATION TIME: 10 minutes, plus 6 hours to overnight for marinating   **COOKING TIME:** 15 minutes

up with antibiotics and growth hormones. In addition, most cattle are fed a diet not intended for animals that naturally graze on grass. The repercussions inevitably ricochet right up the food chain—possibly into our waistlines and clogged arteries.

But we humans are natural omnivores, designed to eat just about everything. As such, we continue to enjoy meat. When possible, look for beef and poultry that are free-range and raised without antibiotics or hormones. It's a dietary tradition that dates back to the dawn of history.

You must grill these meaty pork ribs so that they are crisp on the outside, yet remain juicy and sweet inside, and are brimming with smoky flavors. For ease, begin marinating the ribs the night before you plan to serve them.

1½ cups soy sauce or tamari
¼ cup rice vinegar
¼ cup Asian sesame oil
¼ cup firmly packed brown sugar
3 tablespoons sliced green onion, white and green parts
2 cloves garlic, minced
⅛ teaspoon cayenne pepper
5 to 6 pounds baby back pork ribs

To make the marinade, in a large bowl, stir together the soy sauce, vinegar, sesame oil, brown sugar, green onion, garlic, and cayenne. Cut the ribs into serving sections, 3 to 4 ribs per section. Divide the sections into 2 batches and place each batch in a large zippered plastic bag. Pour half the marinade into each bag and close securely. Turn each bag over to coat the meat fully. Refrigerate the bags for at least 6 to 8 hours or for up to overnight. If possible, turn the bags every few hours.

Prepare a fire in a grill. Remove the ribs from the marinade and place on the grill rack. Grill the ribs until they are well done and crisp on the outside but still juicy inside, 12 to 15 minutes. Grill each side for about 5 minutes—the meaty side requires 2 to 3 more minutes than the bony side—and then flip the ribs on the grill a few more times to retain heat. For quicker results and smokier flavor, cover the grill, but watch for smoke and uncover the ribs after 3 to 4 minutes per side.

Remove the ribs from the grill and serve at once.

Serves 4 or 5

Shepherd's PIE

A pie in name only, this robust dish features a mashed-potato crust on the top. A surefire child-pleaser, this hearty and filling dish makes a great leftover lunch, too. We don't peel the potatoes before boiling and mashing them; just scrub the skins clean prior to cooking. If you are using fresh tomatoes, the same applies to them.

---

*3 pounds new potatoes or other thin-skinned potatoes such as
    Yukon Gold*

8 tablespoons extra-virgin olive oil

1 onion, diced

2 cloves garlic, minced

8 large white button mushrooms, trimmed and coarsely chopped

1 pound ground beef

¾ pound ground lamb

2 teaspoons dried rosemary

1 teaspoon dried thyme

2 teaspoons salt

*2 pounds fresh tomatoes, unpeeled, coarsely chopped, or 1 can
    (28 ounces) whole tomatoes, drained and coarsely chopped*

1½ cups fresh or frozen shelled peas

½ cup red wine (optional)

Wash the potatoes, but leave the skins intact. Cut the potatoes into quarters or eighths, depending on their size. In a saucepan three-fourths full of water, boil the potatoes until they are tender, about 20 minutes. You should be able to pierce them easily with a fork.

While the potatoes are cooking, preheat the oven to 300°F. In a Dutch oven or other large, ovenproof pot, heat 3 tablespoons of the olive oil over medium-high heat. Add the onion and garlic and sauté until the onion is translucent, 2 to 3 minutes. Add the mushrooms, stir, cover, and cook until tender, 3 to 4 minutes.

Raise the heat to high and add the beef, lamb, rosemary, thyme, and 1 teaspoon of the salt. Sauté, stirring frequently, until the meat has browned, 5 to 7 minutes. Reduce the heat to medium and add the tomatoes, peas, and the wine, if using. Stir thoroughly, cover, and simmer for 10 minutes.

When the potatoes are ready, drain them, return them to the pot, add the remaining 5 tablespoons olive oil and 1 teaspoon salt, and mash them with a hand masher. (Lumpy potatoes are acceptable—even desirable. They add texture.)

Spread the mashed potatoes evenly over the meat and vegetables in the Dutch oven or pot. Cover, place in the oven, and bake for 20 minutes. Serve immediately.

Serves 4 to 6

MARINATED Lamb Chops WITH Rosemary AND Sea Salt

PREPARATION TIME: 5 minutes, plus 1 hour to overnight for marinating

COOKING TIME: 15 minutes

Rosemary always reminds us of southern France, where the hillsides are studded with this aromatic plant. Fortunately, most supermarket produce shelves in the United States are also blessed with fresh rosemary, which gracefully lends its distinctive flavor to lamb. If you have some on hand, use *fleur de sel*, the excellent sea salt from the Brittany coast of France. White Bean Salad with Sun-Dried Tomatoes and Arugula (page 140) makes a fine accompaniment. These chops are the perfect size for little hands to pick up and eat.

---

4 cloves garlic, sliced

4 fresh rosemary sprigs, 6 to 8 inches long

¼ cup extra-virgin olive oil

¼ teaspoon freshly ground pepper

8 to 10 center-cut lamb chops

Coarse sea salt or kosher salt to taste

In a shallow bowl or large zippered plastic bag, combine the garlic, rosemary, olive oil, and pepper. Place the lamb chops in the marinade and turn to coat. Cover the bowl or close the bag and let stand for 1 hour at room temperature or overnight in the refrigerator. If refrigerated, remove 30 minutes prior to grilling.

Prepare a fire in a grill or preheat the broiler. Remove the chops from the marinade and place on the grill rack, or on a broiler pan and slip under the broiler. Grill or broil, turning once, until nicely browned on the outside but still pink inside, 5 to 7 minutes per side.

Transfer to individual plates and sprinkle the top of each lamb chop with salt. Serve immediately.

Serves 4

ROSEMARY Leg OF Lamb

Lamb and rosemary are natural partners. The heady scent of the herb highlights the powerful, earthy flavors of the meat. As it roasts, this leg of lamb fills the kitchen with mouthwatering aromas, setting the stage for a fine feast. Accompany it with White Beans with Tomatoes, Fresh Rosemary, and Parmesan Cheese (page 160).

---

1 bone-in leg of lamb, 6 to 7 pounds
4 cloves garlic, sliced into thin slivers
½ teaspoon salt
½ teaspoon pepper
1 tablespoon extra-virgin olive oil
5 teaspoons dried rosemary
⅓ cup water

Preheat the oven to 425°F.

Using a paring knife, make a ½-inch-deep incision in the lamb and stuff a garlic sliver into the cut. Repeat at regular intervals all over the leg until all the garlic slivers are used. Season the lamb with the salt and pepper, then rub the surface evenly with the olive oil and cover with the rosemary.

Place the meat on a rack in a roasting pan. Pour the water into the pan to prevent the juices from burning. If you have a probe-type meat thermometer, insert it into the thickest part of the leg of lamb (do not let it touch the bone).

Place the leg of lamb in the oven and roast for 20 minutes. Reduce the heat to 350°F and continue to roast for about 50 minutes. Check the temperature on the thermometer, or insert an instant-read thermometer (again, not touching the bone). The roast is ready when the meat thermometer registers 145°F for medium-rare. Transfer the lamb to a cutting board and let rest for 10 minutes before carving.

Meanwhile, if desired, use the pan juices to make a quick gravy (page 36), then pass the gravy at the table.

Serves 6 to 8

Lamb STEW

PREPARATION TIME: 20 minutes   **COOKING TIME:** 1¼ hours

This straightforward stew showcases the distinctive flavor of lamb. Red wine adds richness and balance to the sauce, and its alcohol evaporates long before the meat has finished cooking.

A tip regarding the carrots and potatoes: They are not added until the stew is half-cooked. But if you want to chop them early, while preparing the other ingredients, reserve them in a bowl of cold water to prevent discoloring.

---

3 tablespoons extra-virgin olive oil
2 onions, coarsely chopped
4 cloves garlic, minced or coarsely chopped
10 mushrooms, trimmed and quartered
3 tablespoons dried rosemary
1 cup unbleached all-purpose flour
2½ pounds boneless lamb, cut into 1-inch-square chunks
2½ cups red wine
1 teaspoon salt, plus salt to taste
4 carrots, peeled and cut into 1-inch pieces
5 red potatoes, about 2 pounds total weight, unpeeled, cut into
*   quarters or eighths*
Freshly ground pepper to taste

In a Dutch oven or other heavy pot, heat the olive oil over medium-high heat. Add the onions and garlic and sauté until the onions are translucent, about 3 minutes. Stir in the mushrooms and rosemary, reduce the heat to medium, and cook, stirring occasionally, until the mushrooms are soft and reduced in size, about 5 minutes.

Meanwhile, pour the flour onto a large plate. Dredge the lamb pieces in the flour, covering them with a thin layer. Discard any unused flour.

Push the onions and mushrooms to the side of the pot and place the meat on the exposed pan surface. Cook, stirring occasionally, until browned on all sides, 3 to 5 minutes. Add the wine and the 1 teaspoon salt. Raise the heat to high, stir, and bring the liquid quickly to a boil. Cover, reduce the heat to low, and cook for 40 minutes.

Add the carrots and potatoes, stir, and continue to simmer, uncovered, until the liquid thickens, about 30 minutes.

Season with the additional salt and with pepper. Serve immediately.

Serves 4 to 6

GRILLED Flatiron Steak

PREPARATION TIME: 10 minutes, plus 1 hour for marinating

COOKING TIME: 10 minutes

If you don't have a grill to cook this tender cut of meat, just broil it in the oven. Look for the sweet and spicy Jamaican Pickapeppa sauce in the condiment section of your supermarket. Serve this dish with String Bean and Potato Salad (page 133).

---

3 tablespoons extra-virgin olive oil
2 tablespoons Worcestershire sauce
2 tablespoons Pickapeppa sauce
1 clove garlic, minced
½ teaspoon salt
Freshly ground pepper to taste
2 flatiron steaks, about 1 pound each

In a bowl, stir together the olive oil, Worcestershire sauce, Pickapeppa sauce, garlic, salt, and a few grinds of pepper. Using a fork, poke several holes in both sides of each steak and place the steaks in a zippered plastic bag. Pour in the marinade, secure, and marinate at room temperature for 1 hour, turning the bag over once after 30 minutes.

Prepare a fire in a grill. Remove the meat from the marinade and place on the grill rack. Grill, turning once, for about 5 minutes per side for medium-rare. Transfer to a cutting board and let rest for 5 minutes before carving into thin slices.

Serves 4

Beef STIR-FRY WITH Broccoli

PREPARATION TIME: 15 minutes   **COOKING TIME:** 12 minutes

This recipe pairs nutritious broccoli with tender, bite-sized morsels of beef in a light sauce of soy and rice vinegar. Serve with Asian Fried Rice (page 208).

½ cup canned low-sodium beef broth
1 tablespoon soy sauce or tamari
1 tablespoon rice vinegar
1 tablespoon cornstarch
1 pound broccoli florets
2 tablespoons canola oil
1 pound flatiron steak, cut into strips 1 inch long and ¼ inch thick
Pinch of red pepper flakes (optional)

In a small bowl, stir together the broth, soy sauce, vinegar, and cornstarch. Set aside.

Bring a saucepan three-fourths full of water to a boil, add the broccoli and boil for 1 minute. Drain in a colander.

In a large sauté pan or wok, heat the canola oil over high heat until it begins to smoke. Add the broccoli and stir for 2 minutes. Cover, reduce the heat to low, and cook, stirring occasionally, until tender, about 2 more minutes.

Push the broccoli to the side of the pan, add the steak to the exposed area, and cook, stirring, until the pink meat is lightly browned, 3 to 5 minutes. Mix in the pepper flakes, if using, then quickly stir the soy mixture and add to the pan. Raise the heat to high and stir the broccoli and meat together until the sauce thickens, about 2 minutes.

Transfer to a serving dish and serve at once.

Serves 4

Slow-Braised **Beef** WITH EXOTIC Spices

PREPARATION TIME: 20 minutes   **COOKING TIME:** 1¼ hours

Don't be discouraged by the cooking time here. This Indian-inspired stew is really quite easy to prepare and is loaded with fresh and exotic flavors. They are not too exotic, however, for our children, who love this dish. Enjoy it with rice (page 206).

---

3 tablespoons canola or other vegetable oil

1¾ pounds boneless stewing beef, cut into 1-inch cubes

3 onions, diced

1 tablespoon grated fresh ginger

2 cloves garlic, minced

2 tablespoons ground coriander

1 tablespoon paprika

½ teaspoon cayenne pepper

¾ cup plain yogurt

2 tomatoes, diced

1 cup water

1½ teaspoons salt, plus salt to taste

1 pound spinach

½ cup chopped fresh cilantro

Freshly ground pepper to taste

In a Dutch oven or other large, heavy pot, heat 2 tablespoons of the canola oil over medium-high heat. Add the beef cubes and sear on all sides, about 5 minutes. (You can do this in batches if the cubes are too crowded to sear well.) Transfer the beef to a plate and set aside.

Add the remaining 1 tablespoon canola oil to the pot and reduce the heat to medium. Add the onions and sauté until translucent, about 3 minutes. Mix in the ginger, garlic, coriander, paprika, cayenne, and yogurt. Reduce the heat to low and simmer, uncovered, for 3 to 4 minutes. Return the meat to the pot and add the tomatoes, water, and the 1½ teaspoons salt. Raise the heat to medium-high and bring to a boil. Cover, reduce the heat to low, and cook until the meat is very tender, about 1 hour.

Once the meat is nearly done, rinse the spinach and steam until wilted, 3 to 4 minutes. (If you don't have a steamer, place the rinsed, wet spinach leaves into a pot, cover, and cook over medium-high heat until wilted, about 2 minutes.) Drain off the excess water and coarsely chop.

Stir the chopped spinach and cilantro into the stew and simmer, uncovered, for another 5 minutes. Taste and adjust the seasoning with the additional salt and with pepper, then serve.

Serves 4 to 6

ALMOST-OUTLAW Chili

PREPARATION TIME: 20 minutes

COOKING TIME: 1¾ hours

The real Outlaw Chili is made by our good friend Judge Snowden, who's more comfortable wearing his cowboy hat and boots than his judge's robes. He makes his chili Texas style, with lots of heat and lots of meat. We've toned down the heat and added rice and beans for a family-style dish that still conjures up an aura of the West.

---

4 tablespoons extra-virgin olive oil

3 hot Italian sausages, casings removed, cut into small chunks

2 yellow onions, diced

4 cloves garlic, minced

4 pounds boneless marbled beef, such as tri-tip or top sirloin,
    cut into ¾-inch squares

4 cups chicken stock (page 105) or canned low-sodium chicken broth

3 tablespoons chili powder

2 tablespoons ground cumin

2 teaspoons dried oregano

1 tablespoon salt

6 to 8 tablespoons sour cream

4 green onions, green and white parts, thinly sliced

3 to 4 cups hot cooked white or brown rice (page 206)

3 to 4 cups drained cooked black or red beans,
    home cooked (see page 34) or canned, heated

In a Dutch oven or other large, heavy pot, heat 1 tablespoon of the olive oil over medium heat. Add the sausages and sauté, stirring occasionally, until browned, about 5 minutes. Remove the sausage with a slotted spoon and reserve. Add another tablespoon olive oil to the pot, add the yellow onions and garlic, and sauté until the onions are translucent, about 3 minutes. Using the slotted spoon, remove the onions and garlic and reserve with the sausages.

Add the remaining 2 tablespoons olive oil to the pot over medium-high heat. Add the beef, and cook, stirring occasionally, until browned, 6 to 8 minutes. Return the sausage, onions, and garlic to the pot and stir well.

Stir in the stock, chili powder, cumin, oregano, and salt and bring to a boil. Reduce the heat to medium-low and cook, uncovered, until the meat is very tender, about 1½ hours.

Serve the chili in soup bowls or deep plates. Garnish each serving with 1 tablespoon of sour cream and top with the green onions. Serve the rice and beans on the side, or serve the chili over the rice with the beans on the side.

Serves 6 to 8

Oxtail STEW

PREPARATION TIME: 15 minutes   **COOKING TIME:** 1½ hours

Like many stews, this one features an inexpensive cut from the butcher counter. But don't underestimate the quality of the flavor. Slowly cooked, the tender, richly textured meat is steeped in a savory tomato and red wine sauce. Potatoes and carrots round out this robust main course. Ask your butcher to cut the oxtail into 2-inch-thick segments.

---

3 tablespoons extra-virgin olive oil

1 large onion, diced

3 cloves garlic, minced

1 cup unbleached all-purpose flour

5 pounds oxtail, cut into 2-inch segments

4 cups canned low-sodium beef broth

2 cups red wine

1 can (28 ounces) whole tomatoes, coarsely chopped, with juice

1 bay leaf

2 teaspoons dried thyme

1 teaspoon salt, plus salt to taste

3 tablespoons tomato paste

*5 red potatoes, about 2 pounds total weight, unpeeled, cut into
    quarters or eighths*

5 carrots, peeled and cut into 1-inch pieces

Freshly ground pepper to taste

In a Dutch oven or other large, heavy pot, heat the olive oil over medium-high heat. Add the onion and garlic and sauté until the onion is translucent, about 3 minutes.

Meanwhile, pour the flour onto a large plate. Dredge the oxtail pieces in the flour, covering them evenly with a thin layer. Push the onion and garlic to the side of the pot, and reduce the heat to medium. Add the oxtails to the exposed pot surface and cook, stirring occasionally, until browned, about 5 minutes. Add the broth, wine, tomatoes and juice, bay leaf, thyme, and the 1 teaspoon salt. Raise the heat to medium-high and bring to a boil. Cover, reduce the heat to low, and simmer, skimming off any foam or fat, for 1 hour.

Ladle 1 to 2 cups of the broth from the pot into a small bowl. Stir the tomato paste into the broth to dilute it, then return the broth to the pot. Add the potatoes and carrots, re-cover the pot, and cook until the potatoes are tender, another 20 to 25 minutes.

For a thicker sauce, remove the cover and continue to simmer for another 10 minutes. Taste and adjust the seasoning with the additional salt and with pepper. Serve immediately.

Serves 4 to 6

bur

CHAPTER
12

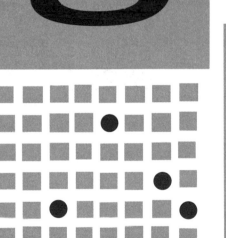

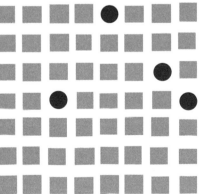

Who doesn't love burgers? Originally introduced to America by German immigrants, the hamburger has become our quintessential national dish. Because we can find this classic beef patty at virtually every snack shop and restaurant in America, we rarely make traditional hamburgers at home. But we do love to cook burgers. We just make them with ingredients other than beef.

Fresh tuna, salmon, chicken, turkey, duck, pork, and lamb are among our favorite alternatives. These burgers are just as easy to prepare as their beef counterparts, plus they provide us with refreshing new tastes. Try them without ketchup, which masks their distinctive qualities. For some recipes, we recommend alternative condiments.

We're not high on hamburger buns either. These soft, sweet, packaged breads dilute flavor in the name of convenience. As a result, we generally eat our burgers with a knife and fork, alongside pasta, rice, beans, potatoes, or possibly fried plantains.

If you need
a bun to appreciate
your burger, try fresh
country breads, rolls, or toasted
English muffins in place of the light-
weight commercial buns sold in many
grocery stores. With your burger sandwiched
inside a bun, potatoes or pasta might be a
heavy side order. Think instead about a green
salad (page 122) or a vegetable dish like String
Beans with Tomato and Garlic (page 153).

Pork and lamb burgers have higher fat content and hold their shape better than poultry and fish patties. For the leaner burgers, we thicken the mix with light-textured panko, Japanese "bread crumbs" made from rice flour. Panko is available in Japanese markets and in many supermarkets and specialty food shops. Traditional fine dried bread crumbs can be substituted for panko. To firm up our low-fat patties a bit more, we dip them lightly in flour and refrigerate them for 30 minutes before frying in olive or vegetable oil.

Cooking times for burgers vary dramatically depending
on the temperature of the grill or skillet and the thickness
of the patties. Cook some burgers—like pork—well
done, or 8 to 9 minutes per side. Other burgers—such
as tuna or duck—are best medium-rare, or about 4
minutes per side. With a little practice, you'll
know what timing works best
with your equipment.

medium well

FRESH Tuna BURGERS
WITH Wasabi Soy SAUCE

PREPARATION TIME: 20 minutes, plus 30 minutes for chilling

COOKING TIME: 8 minutes

Any fresh tuna, such as ahi or albacore, makes a fine burger. Be careful not to overcook it or it will dry out and lose its rich sweetness. Tuna can be enjoyed quite rare, just like meat, or can be cooked according to your preference.

Wasabi, sometimes called Japanese horseradish or mustard, is made from the root of the wasabi plant, which is related to mustard. It is sold in most supermarkets today, in both powder and paste forms. We buy it as a paste, ready to eat. Too much fiery wasabi can quickly overwhelm sensitive palates, but in modest amounts, it adds lift to other natural flavors. Another often-used Japanese condiment is pickled ginger, which can also be found in the Asian section of most supermarkets. It's not required for this recipe, but it adds a bright, spicy note.

Try these flavorful burgers with Asian Fried Rice (page 208).

WASABI SOY SAUCE:

4 teaspoons soy sauce, plus extra soy sauce for garnish (optional)
¼ teaspoon wasabi paste, plus extra wasabi for garnish (optional)

1 egg
3 tablespoons panko or fine dried bread crumbs
4 green onions, white part only, thinly sliced
1 pound tuna fillet, minced or ground
2 tablespoons all-purpose flour
3 tablespoons extra-virgin olive oil
Pickled ginger for garnish (optional)

To make the Wasabi Soy Sauce, put the 4 teaspoons soy sauce in a small bowl and stir in the ¼ teaspoon wasabi until dissolved.

In a large bowl, beat the egg with a fork until blended. Stir in the panko, green onions, and the wasabi–soy sauce mixture until well mixed, then stir in the tuna. Evenly divide the mixture into 4 balls. Flatten into patties ½ inch thick.

Place the flour on a plate and gently dredge each patty in the flour, coating both sides. Pat the patties with both hands to distribute the flour evenly. Place them on a plate, cover with plastic wrap, and refrigerate for 30 minutes

In a large skillet or sauté pan, heat the olive oil over medium-high heat. Add the patties and cook until golden brown on the first side, about 4 minutes. Flip the patties over, reduce the heat to medium, and cook until golden on the second side and medium-rare to medium, depending on your taste, 3 to 4 more minutes.

Meanwhile, if desired, mix together a small additional amount of soy sauce and wasabi for serving. When the burgers are ready, transfer to individual plates and spoon a little wasabi soy sauce over each burger, if using.

Garnish with the pickled ginger, if using, and serve immediately.

Serves 4

Salmon BURGER WITH Aioli

PREPARATION TIME: 20 minutes, plus 30 minutes for chilling

COOKING TIME: 10 minutes

Fresh, full-flavored salmon makes a marvelous burger. Use caution, however, even with fillets. Run your fingers over them to find any errant bones, then remove them with your fingers or tweezers. If you still miss some, mincing or grinding will break them up into harmless bits.

---

1 egg
½ onion, finely chopped
3 tablespoons panko or fine dried bread crumbs
1 clove garlic, minced
1 teaspoon dried thyme
1 teaspoon salt
1 pound salmon fillet, skin removed, then minced or ground
2 tablespoons all-purpose flour
2 tablespoons extra-virgin olive oil
Aioli (page 34) or mayonnaise (page 33) for serving

In a large bowl, beat the egg with a fork until blended. Stir in the onion, panko, garlic, thyme, and salt. Add the salmon and again mix well with the fork. Evenly divide the mixture into 4 balls. Flatten each ball into a patty ½ inch thick.

Place the flour on a plate and gently dredge each patty, coating both sides. Pat the patties with both hands to distribute the flour evenly. Place them on a plate, cover with plastic wrap, and refrigerate for 30 minutes.

In a large skillet or sauté pan, heat the olive oil over medium-high heat. Add the patties and cook until golden brown on the first side, about 6 minutes. Flip the patties over, reduce the heat to medium, and cook until they are golden brown on the second side and medium to medium-well, depending on your taste, 4 to 5 more minutes. Serve the burgers immediately, garnished with the aioli.

Serves 4

Pork BURGERS
WITH Apple AND Cilantro

PREPARATION TIME: 10 minutes   **COOKING TIME:** 15 minutes

It's no accident that roast suckling pig is traditionally served with an apple in its mouth. Indeed, pork and apples go so well together that we've paired them here, too. If you feel like firing up the backyard grill, these burgers will benefit from the smoky flavors it will impart. Enjoy the burgers with Asian Slaw (page 132) on the side.

---

1 egg
½ red onion, finely chopped
½ Granny Smith or other tart apple, peeled, cored, and
   finely chopped
1 teaspoon salt
½ teaspoon freshly ground black pepper
⅛ teaspoon cayenne pepper
½ cup chopped fresh cilantro
1 pound ground pork shoulder
2 tablespoons extra-virgin olive oil

In a large bowl, beat the egg with a fork until blended. Stir in the onion, apple, salt, black pepper, cayenne, and cilantro. Mix in the pork. (The meat is rich and thick. For best results, use your hands to mix.) Evenly divide the mixture into 4 balls. Flatten each ball into a patty about ½ inch thick.

In a large skillet or sauté pan, heat the olive oil over medium-high heat. Add the patties and cook until golden brown on the first side, about 8 minutes. Flip the patties over, reduce the heat to medium, and cook until golden brown on the second side and opaque throughout, about 7 minutes. Serve immediately.

Serves 4

Curried **Chicken** BURGER

Despite the use of a variety of spices, these fragrant Indian-inspired burgers are sufficiently mild for children's sensitive palates. If your kids like spicy foods, you can add heat here by doubling the amount of cayenne. A purchased sweet mango chutney makes the perfect garnish. Other types of chutney—many of which are also now available in most supermarkets—would work as well. Serve the burgers with Yellow Rice and Black Bean Salad (page 142).

---

3 tablespoons canola or other vegetable oil
½ onion, chopped
1 clove garlic, minced
1 egg
6 tablespoons panko or fine dried bread crumbs
1 teaspoon curry powder
½ teaspoon ground cumin
½ teaspoon salt
¼ teaspoon cayenne pepper
1 pound ground chicken or turkey breast
2 tablespoons all-purpose flour
Mango chutney for garnish

In a large skillet or sauté pan, heat 1 tablespoon of the canola oil over medium heat. Add the onion and garlic and sauté until the onion is translucent, about 3 minutes. Transfer to a large bowl. Reserve the pan for cooking the burgers.

Add the egg, panko, curry powder, cumin, salt, and cayenne to the onion mixture and mix thoroughly with a fork. Add the chicken and again mix well with the fork. Evenly divide the mixture into 4 balls. Flatten each ball into a patty about ½ inch thick.

BUYING GROUND MEATS AND FISH

If possible, ask your butcher to grind your meats for you. That way you actually see what cuts you're getting, and you know how fresh the meat is. Otherwise, to ensure freshness, rely on a good meat department where some types of meat are ground and wrapped for sale daily.

Because of a low demand for certain ground poultry—such as duck—and most fish, it's hard to find these items already ground. If your butcher grinds them for you, you can lose up to a quarter of the total purchased weight in the grinder because unusual meats and fish can't be pushed through at the end with other scraps of the same meat. For this reason, it's best to mince your salmon or tuna fillets or duck breasts at home with a large, sharp knife or (if you have one) your own meat grinder.

Place the flour on a plate and gently dredge each patty in the flour, coating both sides. Pat the patties with both hands to distribute the flour evenly. Place them on a plate, cover with plastic wrap, and refrigerate for 30 minutes.

In the reserved pan, heat the remaining 2 tablespoons canola oil over medium-high heat. Add the patties and cook until golden brown on the first side, about 6 minutes. Flip the patties over, reduce the heat to medium, and cook until golden brown on the second side and opaque throughout, about 6 minutes. Serve immediately, topped with a little mango chutney.

Serves 4

Duck BURGERS

PREPARATION TIME: 20 minutes, plus 30 minutes for chilling   **COOKING TIME:** 8 minutes

These burgers pair well with traditional commercial sauces or garnishes like Worcestershire, Pickapeppa, and chutney. They're also a fine match for the Wasabi Soy Sauce served with the tuna burgers (page 310). And if ketchup is the only condiment your kids will accept, that's fine too. We also like these burgers plain (and simple). Serve them with White Beans with Tomatoes, Rosemary, and Parmesan (page 160). They're also good alongside Really Simple Pasta with Olive Oil, Thyme, and Parmesan (page 176) or Fried Plantains (page 152).

---

1 boneless duck breast, about 1¼ pounds

1 egg

6 tablespoons panko or fine dried bread crumbs

4 green onions, white part only, thinly sliced

1 clove garlic, minced

1 teaspoon salt

½ teaspoon freshly ground pepper

2 tablespoons all-purpose flour

2 tablespoons extra-virgin olive oil

To remove the skin from the duck breast, place the breast skin-side down. With your free hand, press down firmly on the breast and, using a sharp knife, carefully slice the skin away from the meat. Mince the meat with a large, sharp knife or grind it in a meat grinder. Set aside.

In a large bowl, using a fork, beat the egg until blended. Stir in the panko, green onions, garlic, salt, and pepper. Add the duck meat and again mix well. Evenly divide the mixture into 4 balls. Flatten each patty into a ball ½ inch thick.

Place the flour on a plate and gently dredge each patty in the flour, coating both sides. Pat the patties with both hands to distribute the flour evenly. Place them on a plate, cover with plastic wrap, and refrigerate for 30 minutes.

In a large skillet or sauté pan, heat the olive oil over medium-high heat. Add the patties and cook until golden brown on the first side, about 4 minutes. Flip the burgers over, reduce the heat to medium, and cook until they are golden brown on the second side and medium-rare to medium, depending on your taste, 3 to 4 more minutes. Serve immediately.

Serves 4

■ ● ■ ■ ■ ● ■ ● ■ ■ ■ ● ■ ● ■ ■ ■ ● ■ ● ■ ■ ■ ● ■ ● ■ ■ ■ ● ■ ● ■ ■ ■ ● ■ ● ■ ■ ■ ● ■ ● ■ ■ ■ ● ● ○

BURGERS—COOKED TO KILL

Every so often we hear of illnesses related to salmonella, E. coli, or other microbial pests that wreak havoc in digestive tracts across the nation. The truth is, much of our meat supply is tainted by fecal matter or other contaminants during processing or storage. Children or individuals with compromised immune systems are most vulnerable to the ravages of these microscopic monsters.

That's why prudent parents cook meats well enough to kill off any potential microorganisms that could harm their children. Ground meats are particularly insidious because you cannot always know how clean the butcher's grinder was, where the meat came from, or under what conditions the meat was stored before and after grinding.

Unfortunately, meats that are cooked "to death" don't always taste best. If you know your butcher well and have confidence in his or her ability to provide you with untainted meats from reputable sources, then you can cook your red meats—and that includes duck—on the rare side. Yes, there's a small risk here, but there are similar risks with many fresh foods, including fresh vegetables.

We cook our chicken and pork burgers well done. We take liberties with lamb and beef, although the kids like theirs best well done anyway. The same applies for duck burgers. Fresh salmon and tuna burgers dry out quickly when overcooked. Since we mince these fish by hand at home and have confidence in our fishmonger, we generally eat these meaty fish burgers medium to medium-rare.

Remember to wash your hands and all utensils, plates, and cutting boards that come in contact with raw meats and fish thoroughly with soap and warm water.

Lamb BURGER WITH Cumin

PREPARATION TIME: 15 minutes   **COOKING TIME:** 15 minutes

This burger delivers the satisfaction of any good burger, but with the added twist of fragrant cumin and earthy lamb. Yes, even our kids love these, but maybe that's because they insist on drowning them in ketchup, which hides the flavor of the lamb. Instead of ketchup, we prefer a steak sauce such as Worcestershire or Jamaican Pickapeppa. You can, of course, use ground beef instead of lamb—with or without cumin—for a more traditional hamburger, and you can cook them on your grill rather than on the stove top.

Garnish these robust patties with Caramelized Onions (page 159) and serve with Roasted Rosemary Potato Crisps (page 162). Or accompany them with Lentil Salad (page 141) for a summertime barbecue.

½ onion, finely chopped
1 clove garlic, minced
1 egg
1 pound ground lamb
1 teaspoon ground cumin
1 teaspoon salt
½ teaspoon freshly ground pepper
2 teaspoons extra-virgin olive oil

In a large bowl, using a fork, mix together the onion, garlic, and egg. Add the lamb, cumin, salt, and pepper and again mix well with the fork. Evenly divide the mixture into 4 balls. Flatten each ball into a patty about ½ inch thick.

In a large skillet, heat the olive oil over medium-high heat. Add the patties and cook until browned on the first side, 5 to 7 minutes. Flip the patties over, reduce the heat to medium, and cook until browned on the second side and light pink on the inside, 5 to 7 more minutes, or longer for well done. Serve immediately.

Serves 4

Notes

CHAPTER

13

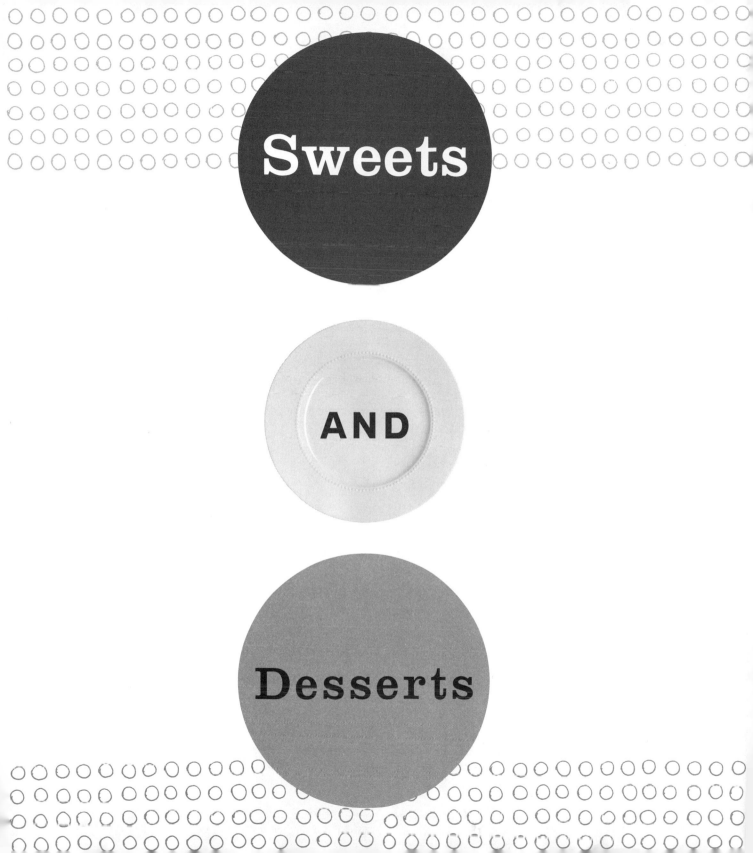

Sweets

AND

Desserts

Desserts may be an exception to the rule of better nutrition. Sugar and saturated fats, such as those found in many desserts, are easily converted to fat in our bodies. That can impact circulation, blood pressure, and many other facets of our health (see pages 16 to 17). But let s face it, **LIFE WITHOUT DESSERT JUST ISN'T FUN**. When eaten in moderation and on the heels of a balanced diet, dessert shouldn t compromise your health.

We all know that a good dessert in the wings can act as an incentive for children to finish their vegetables. But we don't recommend this kind of bribery. It can create an unhealthy relationship between parents and children and an unhealthy attitude toward food. Nonetheless, our kids have learned if they don't eat their dinner, dessert is hardly an option. That's just common sense. Our children enjoy baking with us. It's a family activity that feeds their creative juices—along with their sweet tooth. But not all desserts are cakes and cookies. Poached pears, baked apples, and peach crisp serve up refreshing flavors that are best when these fruits are in season. The desserts in this chapter run the gamut from sweet to sweeter, SO LET'S LIVE A LITTLE!

HONEY BAKED Apples WITH
Maple WHIPPED CREAM

PREPARATION TIME: 15 minutes   **BAKING TIME:** 1 hour

Select Granny Smith, Braeburn, or another good baking apple for this recipe. They hold their shape in the oven and taste delicious bathed in a caramel-like sauce and topped with the maple syrup–infused whipped cream. These baked apples remind us of an apple pie without the crust!

---

2 cups apple juice
1 cinnamon stick
5 whole cloves
¼ cup honey
¼ cup firmly packed brown sugar
¼ teaspoon ground nutmeg
5 tablespoons unsalted butter
4 large, firm apples
½ cup heavy cream
1 tablespoon maple syrup

Preheat the oven to 400°F.

In a saucepan, combine the apple juice, cinnamon stick, and cloves, bring to a boil over high heat, and boil for 10 minutes. Add the honey, brown sugar, nutmeg, and butter and stir until the butter melts. Remove from the heat and reserve.

With a paring knife, core the apples in a circular motion, digging out all the seeds but stopping short of the bottoms, then peel them. In a small baking pan or dish, arrange the apples standing upright. Fill the cavity of each apple with the juice-honey mixture, being careful not to include any cloves or the cinnamon stick, then pour the remaining liquid with the cinnamon and cloves into the baking pan.

Bake the apples, basting every 15 minutes with the pan juices, until tender when pierced with a knife, about 1 hour.

Prior to serving, pour the cream and the maple syrup into a bowl and, using an electric mixer or a whisk, beat until the cream holds stiff peaks. (You can do this immediately prior to serving, or whip the cream up to 2 hours in advance and cover and refrigerate until ready to use.)

Serve the apples warm, at room temperature, or chilled. Top each apple with a big dollop of the whipped cream.

Serves 4

POACHED Pears
IN A Chocolate BATH

PREPARATION TIME: 15 minutes   **COOKING TIME:** 40 minutes

Here is a good example of opposites that attract. Soft, delicate pears meet rich, dense chocolate in a classy embrace that not only tastes elegantly sweet, but also looks impressive. While we call it a chocolate "bath," it's really more of a shower, as dripping chocolate oozes downward to hug the round-shouldered pears.

You can poach these pears in advance and refrigerate overnight to simplify preparations for an upcoming dinner party. Then make the chocolate sauce the night of the event.

---

4 cups water
1 cup sugar
3 tablespoons fresh lemon juice
5 whole cloves
2 cinnamon sticks
¼ teaspoon almond extract
4 Bosc pears, peeled with stems intact
2 tablespoons unsalted butter
3 ounces semisweet chocolate, coarsely chopped

In a wide 6-quart saucepan, combine the water, sugar, lemon juice, cloves, cinnamon sticks, and almond extract over medium heat and heat, stirring until the sugar dissolves. Cover, reduce the heat to low, and simmer for 10 minutes.

Cut a ¼-inch-thick slice off the blossom end of each pear so it will stand upright. Lay the pears on their sides in the sugar-spice mixture, cover, and simmer until tender when pierced with a knife, about 30 minutes.

While the pears are cooking, in a small saucepan, combine the butter and chocolate and melt over low heat, stirring often until smooth. Remove from the heat and cover to keep warm.

When the pears are ready, remove them with a slotted spoon and stand them on their bottoms on individual plates. Discard the sugar-spice mixture.

Spoon 2 tablespoons of the warm chocolate sauce over each pear. Serve the pears warm or at room temperature. Or cook the pears in advance, refrigerate for up to 1 day, and then serve chilled, topped with freshly made, warm chocolate sauce.

Serves 4

DAD'S Apple Tart

PREPARATION TIME: 30 minutes, plus 1 hour for chilling

BAKING TIME: 50 minutes

Here is an elegant tart that is exceedingly simple to make. That's why Jeff and our daughters enjoy making it together. The kids love to roll out the dough and carefully arrange the apple slices in a circular pattern. Not too sweet, our apple tart can also stand in for breakfast—albeit only occasionally and with parental approval.

PASTRY CRUST:

½ cup (1 stick), plus 1 tablespoon unsalted butter, at room temperature
⅓ cup sugar
1 egg
1 cup unbleached all-purpose flour
½ teaspoon salt

3 red or yellow apples, unpeeled, halved, cored, and cut lengthwise
  into ¼-inch-thick slices
2 tablespoons unsalted butter, cut into small pieces
1 tablespoon sugar

To make the pastry crust, in a large bowl, using a wooden spoon, beat together the ½ cup butter and the sugar until fluffy. Stir in the egg. Add the flour and salt and mix thoroughly until a dough forms. Transfer the mound of dough to a floured work surface. Push down on the dough with the heel of your hand and spread it forward over the floured surface, extending it about 6 inches. Fold it back onto itself and repeat the spreading and folding action several times, lightly flouring your palms as needed to prevent the dough from sticking, until the dough is smooth and elastic.

Form the dough into a ball, then flatten it slightly into a fat disk. Wrap it with plastic wrap or place it in a zippered plastic bag. Refrigerate for at least 1 hour or for up to 2 days.

Remove the dough from the refrigerator and let stand at room temperature for about 10 minutes. On a floured work surface, roll out the dough into a thin round 14 inches in diameter. Using the 1 tablespoon butter, grease the bottom of a 12-inch tart pan with a removable bottom. Carefully transfer the dough round to the pan and fit it into the bottom and sides. Roll the rolling pin over the top edge to cut away excess dough. (Let the kids shape a few cookies from the excess dough. Place the cookies on a small baking sheet and bake later with the tart. They will cook in 10 minutes or less.)

Preheat the oven to 350°F.

Starting at the outer edge of the crust bottom, arrange the apple slices in concentric circles or in a spiral to cover the bottom completely. Dot the apples with the 2 tablespoons butter, then sprinkle with the 1 tablespoon sugar.

Bake the tart until the edges of the crust are golden brown, 45 to 50 minutes. Let cool completely on a rack, then remove the pan sides and transfer to a serving plate to serve.

Makes one 12-inch tart; serves 6 to 8

Peach AND Nectarine CRISP

PREPARATION TIME: 15 minutes   **BAKING TIME:** 20 minutes

Serve this fruit-rich, crunchy-topped summertime specialty on its own or with whipped cream or ice cream on the side. The key here is finding juicy, ultrafresh peaches and nectarines.

---

4 cups cubed (1-inch cubes) unpeeled peaches
4 cups cubed (1-inch cubes) unpeeled nectarines
1 teaspoon fresh lemon juice
1 tablespoon, plus ½ cup granulated sugar
½ cup (1 stick) unsalted butter, at room temperature
½ cup firmly packed brown sugar
1 teaspoon vanilla extract
½ teaspoon ground cinnamon
1¼ cups unbleached all-purpose flour
Whipped cream (page 37) or ice cream for serving

Preheat the oven to 425°F.

In a large bowl, combine the peaches, nectarines, lemon juice, and the 1 tablespoon granulated sugar. Toss to mix and set aside.

In a bowl, using an electric mixer, cream together the butter, the remaining ½ cup granulated sugar, the brown sugar, vanilla, and cinnamon. Add the flour and, using a wooden spoon, mix until crumbly.

Spread the fruits evenly in an 8-inch-square baking dish. Distribute the butter-sugar mixture loosely over the top. Bake the crisp until the topping is crunchy and toasty brown, about 20 minutes. Serve hot, warm, or at room temperature with whipped cream.

Serves 6 to 8

Banana NUT BREAD

PREPARATION TIME: 15 minutes   **BAKING TIME:** 1 hour

This moderately sweet bread is a good way to use up bananas that have been sitting around for a few too many days. The riper the banana, the better!

---

1 tablespoon, plus ½ cup (1 stick) unsalted butter, at room temperature
2 cups unbleached all-purpose flour
1 teaspoon baking powder
½ teaspoon baking soda
½ teaspoon salt
1 teaspoon ground cinnamon
1 cup sugar
2 eggs
1 teaspoon vanilla extract
3 ripe bananas, peeled
½ cup walnut bits

Preheat the oven to 325°F. Using the 1 tablespoon butter, grease a 9-by-5-inch loaf pan.

In a medium bowl, sift or stir together the flour, baking powder, baking soda, salt, and cinnamon. Set aside.

In a large bowl, using an electric mixer, cream together the ½ cup butter and the sugar until fluffy. Beat in the eggs and vanilla. Add the flour mixture and beat just until blended. In a separate shallow bowl or on a plate, mash the bananas with a fork. Add the mashed banana to the butter-flour mixture and mix until evenly distributed. Add the walnuts and mix again.

Spoon the batter into the prepared loaf pan, spreading it evenly. Bake the bread until a fork or toothpick inserted into the center comes out dry, about 1 hour. Let cool in the pan on a rack for about 10 minutes, then turn out onto the rack to cool, for at least another 10 minutes. Serve warm or at room temperature.

Serves 6 to 8

Almond–Poppy Seed CAKE

PREPARATION TIME: 15 minutes   **BAKING TIME:** 45 minutes

Poppy seeds give this dessert a refreshingly crunchy texture. The cake is not particularly sweet, which makes it fine for snacks or breakfast as well as dessert.

---

2 tablespoons, plus ½ cup (1 stick) unsalted butter, at room temperature
3 tablespoons, plus 2 cups unbleached all-purpose flour
½ cup poppy seeds
½ cup milk
2 teaspoons baking powder
¼ teaspoon salt
1 teaspoon ground cinnamon
½ teaspoon ground allspice
1 cup sugar
4 eggs
1 tablespoon minced orange zest
1 teaspoon almond extract

Preheat the oven to 325°F. Grease a 9-inch Bundt pan with the 2 tablespoons butter. Add the 3 tablespoons flour to the pan and tilt and rotate to cover evenly. Flip the pan upside down over your sink and tap out any excess flour.

In a small bowl, combine the poppy seeds and the milk and set aside.

In a medium bowl, sift or stir together the 2 cups flour, the baking powder, salt, cinnamon, and allspice. Set aside.

In a large bowl, using an electric mixer, cream together the ½ cup butter and the sugar until fluffy. Add the eggs one at a time, mixing well after each addition. Add the orange zest and almond extract and mix again. Add the flour mixture and beat just until blended. Add the milk and poppy seeds and mix once more.

Spoon the batter into the prepared pan, spreading it evenly. Bake the cake until a fork or toothpick inserted into the center comes out dry, about 45 minutes. Let cool in the pan on a rack for 10 minutes, then unmold and transfer to a serving platter. Serve warm or at room temperature.

Serves 6 to 8

BLUEBERRY Scone Cake

PREPARATION TIME: 15 minutes   BAKING TIME: 40 minutes

Although a bit lighter in texture than a true scone, this cake nonetheless reminds us of one. Only mildly sweet, it's loaded with moist blueberries that give it a bright purple hue. The cake is equally good for breakfast, a snack, or dessert.

---

1 tablespoon, plus ½ cup (1 stick) unsalted butter, at room temperature
3 tablespoons, plus 1½ cups unbleached all-purpose flour
1½ teaspoons baking powder
½ teaspoon salt
¾ cup sugar
1 egg
1 teaspoon vanilla extract
½ cup milk
2½ cups fresh or frozen blueberries

Preheat the oven to 375°F. Grease an 8-inch-square baking pan with the 1 tablespoon butter. Add the 3 tablespoons flour to the pan and tilt and rotate to cover evenly. Flip the pan upside down over your sink and tap out any excess flour.

In a medium bowl, sift or stir together the 1½ cups flour, the baking powder, and salt. Set aside.

In a large bowl, using an electric mixer, cream together the ½ cup butter and the sugar until fluffy. (If you forget to take the butter out of the refrigerator in advance to bring it to room temperature, zap it in the microwave for 10 seconds.) Beat in the egg and vanilla until well mixed. Stir half the flour mixture into the butter-sugar mixture. Then stir in half the milk. Repeat with the remaining flour mixture and milk. Using a wooden spoon, gently fold in the blueberries. (The batter will be quite thick.)

Spoon the batter into the prepared baking pan, spreading it evenly. Bake the cake until a fork or toothpick inserted into the center comes out dry, 35 to 40 minutes. Let cool in the pan on a rack for 5 minutes, then turn out onto the rack to cool for at least another 15 minutes. Serve warm or at room temperature.

Serves 8

Blueberry MUFFINS

PREPARATION TIME: 15 minutes   **BAKING TIME:** 20 minutes

These light-textured muffins aren't too sweet, which means they make great snacks and breakfasts, too. They can also be frozen for up to 3 months. For thawing, leave them at room temperature overnight. Or, for quicker results, defrost them in a microwave.

---

2 cups unbleached all-purpose flour
2 teaspoons baking powder
½ teaspoon baking soda
½ teaspoon salt
½ cup sugar
2 eggs
1 cup plain yogurt
½ cup canola oil
1 cup fresh or frozen blueberries

Preheat the oven to 375°F. Line 12 muffin-pan cups with paper liners.

In a medium bowl, sift or stir together the flour, baking powder, baking soda, and salt. Set aside.

In a large bowl, using an electric mixer, beat together the sugar and eggs until pale yellow. Add the yogurt and canola oil, mixing well. Add the flour mixture and beat only until blended. Using a wooden spoon, gently fold in the blueberries just until evenly distributed.

Spoon the batter into the lined muffin cups, filling them three-fourths full. Bake the muffins until a fork or toothpick inserted into the center comes out dry, about 20 minutes. Let cool in the pan on a rack for about 5 minutes, then turn out onto the rack. Serve warm or at room temperature.

Makes 12 muffins

FLOUR: TO SIFT OR NOT TO SIFT?

In our parents' and grandparents' day, flour was more caked, or solid, than it is today. Sifting helped to break it up into a fine powder. Nowadays, running flour through a sifter is no longer as necessary as it once was. But sifting flour with other dry ingredients, such as salt or baking soda, will help blend them evenly. In our family, Jodie does most of the baking. She swears by sifting, and so we generally include it in our recipes.

However, if you don't have a sifter, don't worry. It is not essential. You can use a fine-mesh sieve in place of a sifter or simply stir your dry ingredients thoroughly to mix them well.

Pecan Butter BALL COOKIES

PREPARATION TIME: 15 minutes, plus 30 minutes for chilling

BAKING TIME: 18 minutes

Airy and light, these cookies are refreshing, yet sweet enough to satisfy anyone's craving for sugar.

---

1 cup (2 sticks) unsalted butter, at room temperature
1½ cups confectioners' sugar
1 teaspoon vanilla extract
2 cups unbleached all-purpose flour
½ cup pecan bits

In a large bowl, using an electric mixer, cream together the butter and ½ cup of the confectioners' sugar until fluffy. Beat in the vanilla. Sift or simply pour the flour directly into the butter-sugar mixture and mix well. Add the pecans and mix again. (The dough will be quite thick. If desired, use a wooden spoon at any time during the mixing process.) Cover the bowl with plastic wrap and refrigerate for 30 minutes.

Preheat the oven to 350°F.

Using your palms, roll the chilled dough into balls about 1½ inches in diameter and place them on a nonstick baking sheet, spacing them about 1 inch apart. Bake the cookies until lightly browned, 15 to 18 minutes. Remove from the oven and let the cookies cool on the baking sheet on a wire rack for 3 to 5 minutes. Meanwhile, put the remaining 1 cup confectioners' sugar in a shallow bowl. One at a time, roll the warm cookies in the sugar to coat evenly. Place the cookies on another wire rack to cool completely. Store in an airtight container at room temperature for up to 4 days.

Makes about 36 cookies

LACY Chocolate Chip COOKIES

Elegant and buttery, these delectable cookies are packed with wholesome calories and mounds of flavor. But they taste lighter on the palate than your average chocolate chip cookie—they're not heavy or dense—simply because they use less flour. If you're on a diet, however, steer clear of these gems. They are addictive.

1½ cups (3 sticks) unsalted butter
2 cups unbleached all-purpose flour
1 teaspoon baking soda
¾ teaspoon salt
¾ cup granulated sugar
½ cup firmly packed brown sugar
½ teaspoon vanilla extract
2 eggs
2 cups semisweet chocolate chips
1 cup walnuts, coarsely chopped

Preheat the oven to 375°F.

In a saucepan, melt the butter over low heat. Remove from the heat and reserve.

In a small bowl, sift or stir together the flour, baking soda, and salt. In a large bowl, stir together the granulated and brown sugars. Stir in the melted butter and the vanilla.

In another small bowl, beat the eggs with a fork until blended. Stir the eggs into the butter-sugar mixture, then add into the flour mixture, stirring thoroughly. Add the chocolate chips and the walnuts and stir thoroughly until a dough forms.

Scoop up tablespoon-sized dollops of cookie dough and place on a nonstick baking sheet, spacing them about 2 inches apart. (The cookies will spread in the oven.) Bake the cookies until golden and somewhat flat, 8 to 10 minutes. Remove from the oven and let sit for a minute or two on the baking sheet to firm up, then, using a spatula, transfer to a wire rack and let cool completely. Repeat with the remaining cookie dough. Store the cookies in an airtight container at room temperature for up to 4 days.

Makes about 30 cookies

Oatmeal CHOCOLATE CHIP COOKIES

PREPARATION TIME: 20 minutes   **BAKING TIME:** 10 minutes per batch

Here are traditional oatmeal cookies, but with a chocolate hook. They're also made with another twist—maple syrup, nutmeg, cinnamon, and allspice—which creates a wonderfully fragrant biteful.

1 cup (2 sticks) unsalted butter
1 cup unbleached all-purpose flour
1 teaspoon baking soda
1 teaspoon ground cinnamon
1 teaspoon ground nutmeg
1 teaspoon ground allspice
¼ teaspoon salt
2 eggs
1 cup firmly packed brown sugar
¼ cup granulated sugar
3 tablespoons maple syrup
1 teaspoon vanilla extract
3 cups quick-cooking rolled oats
1 cup semisweet chocolate chips

Preheat the oven to 350°F.

In a saucepan, melt the butter over low heat. Remove from the heat and reserve. In a small bowl, sift or stir together the flour, baking soda, cinnamon, nutmeg, allspice, and salt. Set aside.

In a large bowl, beat the eggs with a whisk or fork until blended. Using a wooden spoon, mix in the sugars. Add the melted butter and stir until the mixture is smooth. Stir in the maple syrup and vanilla and then stir in the flour mixture. Finally, stir in the rolled oats and chocolate chips. The dough will be thick.

Scoop up tablespoon-sized dollops of the cookie dough and place on a
nonstick baking sheet, spacing them about 2 inches apart. (The cookies
will spread in the oven.) Bake the cookies until golden brown, about
10 minutes. Remove from the oven and let sit for a minute or two on the
baking sheet to firm up, then, using a spatula, transfer to a wire rack
and let cool completely. Repeat with the remaining cookie dough. Store
the cookies in an airtight container at room temperature for up to 4 days.

Makes about 36 cookies

Lemon BARS

PREPARATION TIME: 20 minutes   BAKING TIME: 45 minutes

Distinguished by their creamy, yet crunchy, texture, these lemon bars make a light, refreshing dessert. Bake them in a glass baking dish for crisper crust.

2¼ cups unbleached all-purpose flour
¾ cup confectioners' sugar
¼ teaspoon salt
1 cup (2 sticks) chilled unsalted butter
4 eggs
1½ cups granulated sugar
⅓ cup fresh lemon juice
2 teaspoons grated lemon zest
1 teaspoon baking powder

Preheat the oven to 350°F.

In a large bowl, sift or stir together 2 cups of the flour, ½ cup of the confectioners' sugar, and the salt. Using a butter knife, cut small pieces of the butter directly off the sticks into the bowl. Using a wooden spoon, mix well until the mixture is dry and has a coarse texture. Transfer the mixture to a 9-by-13-inch glass baking dish or baking pan and press firmly into the bottom to form a crust.

Bake the crust until the edges turn golden brown, about 20 minutes. Let cool on a rack for 10 to 15 minutes. Leave the oven on.

While the crust is cooling, in a large bowl, using an electric mixer, beat the eggs until blended. Add the granulated sugar, lemon juice, and lemon zest and beat until blended. Sift or pour the remaining ¼ cup flour and the baking powder into the bowl and mix thoroughly. Pour over the baked crust.

Return the dish to the oven and bake until the filling is set and a fork or toothpick inserted into the center comes out dry, 20 to 25 minutes. Let cool completely on a rack.

Using a fine-mesh sieve, sift the remaining ¼ cup confectioners' sugar evenly over the top. This will be thicker than a dusting. Cut into small rectangles for easy eating. Store in an airtight container for up to 4 days.

Serves 8 to 10 as a light dessert or snack

Chewy, Crunchy CHOCOLATE Brownies

PREPARATION TIME: 15 minutes   **BAKING TIME:** 30 minutes

These brownies are fairly light and not too rich, but they remain chocolaty and sweet—a winning combination for dessert lovers. Pecan bits serve up the crunch. We find that brownie baking is an ideal weekend activity for the whole family, especially on a cold or stormy afternoon.

---

2 tablespoons, plus 1 cup (2 sticks) unsalted butter

3 tablespoons, plus ½ cup unbleached all-purpose flour

5 ounces bittersweet chocolate, coarsely chopped

¼ teaspoon salt

2 eggs

1 cup sugar

1 teaspoon vanilla extract

½ cup pecan bits

Preheat the oven to 350°F. Grease a 9-by-12-inch baking pan with the 2 tablespoons butter. Add the 3 tablespoons flour to the pan and tilt and rotate to cover evenly. Flip the pan upside down over your sink and tap out any excess flour.

In a small saucepan, combine the 1 cup butter and the chocolate and melt over low heat, stirring often until smooth. Remove from the heat and set aside. In a small bowl, sift or stir together the ½ cup flour and the salt. Set aside.

In a large bowl, using an electric mixer, beat together the eggs and sugar until smooth and thick. Beat in the vanilla, and then beat in the chocolate-butter mixture. With the mixer running, pour in the flour in a steady stream, mixing just until smoothly blended. Turn off the mixer and stir in the pecans with a wooden spoon.

Pour the batter into the prepared pan, spreading it evenly. Bake until a fork or toothpick inserted into the center comes out dry, 25 to 30 minutes. Let cool in the pan on a rack for 15 to 20 minutes before cutting into brownies. Serve warm or at room temperature. Store in an airtight container at room temperature for up to 4 days.

Makes about 20 brownies

Chocolate POUND CAKE

PREPARATION TIME: 20 minutes   BAKING TIME: 1 hour

Buttermilk adds a pleasant tartness to this simple, moist, yet light-textured cake.

---

2 tablespoons, plus 1½ cups (3 sticks) unsalted butter
3 tablespoons, plus 2 cups unbleached all-purpose flour
½ teaspoon salt
¼ teaspoon baking soda
7 ounces semisweet chocolate, coarsely chopped
1½ cups sugar
4 eggs
2 teaspoons vanilla extract
1 cup buttermilk
Confectioners' sugar for dusting

Preheat the oven to 325°F. Grease a 9-inch Bundt pan with the 2 tablespoons butter. Add the 3 tablespoons flour to the pan and tilt and rotate the pan to cover evenly. Flip the pan upside down over your sink and tap out any excess flour.

In a medium bowl, sift or stir together the 2 cups flour, the salt, and baking soda. Set aside. In a small saucepan, combine the 1½ cups butter and the chocolate and melt over low heat, stirring often until smooth. Remove from the heat.

In a large bowl, using an electric mixer, beat together the butter-chocolate mixture and the sugar until blended. Add the eggs one at a time, mixing thoroughly after each addition. Add the vanilla and mix. Add half of the flour mixture and beat until smooth. Add ½ cup of the buttermilk and mix well. Beat in the remaining flour mixture, followed by the remaining buttermilk, mixing until the batter is smooth.

Pour the batter into the prepared pan, spreading it evenly. Bake the cake until a fork or toothpick inserted into the center comes out dry, about 1 hour. Let cool in the pan on a rack for 15 minutes, then turn out onto the rack and let cool until room temperature, at least another 15 minutes.

Place the cake on a serving plate and, using a fine-mesh sieve, dust the top with confectioners' sugar. Serve warm or at room temperature.

Serves 6

Orange POUND CAKE

PREPARATION TIME: 15 minutes   **BAKING TIME:** 1 hour

The balanced sweetness and citrus undertones of this light, pleasing cake appeal both to grown-ups and kids. You may substitute lemon zest for the orange.

---

1 tablespoon unsalted butter, at room temperature,
   plus 6 tablespoons, melted
2 tablespoons, plus 1 cup cake flour
¼ teaspoon baking powder
3 eggs
⅛ teaspoon salt
1 cup sugar
¼ cup heavy cream
1 tablespoon grated orange zest

Preheat the oven to 325°F. Grease an 8-by-4-inch loaf pan with the 1 tablespoon butter. Add the 2 tablespoons flour to the pan and tilt and rotate to cover evenly. Flip the pan upside down over your sink and tap out any excess flour.

In a medium bowl, sift or stir together the remaining 1 cup flour and the baking powder. Set aside. In a large bowl, using an electric mixer, beat the eggs until blended. Add the salt and then slowly beat in the sugar until the mixture is pale yellow. Add the flour mixture and beat until smooth. Mix in the cream and orange zest, and then mix in the 6 tablespoons melted butter.

Pour the batter into the prepared pan, spreading it evenly. Bake until a toothpick or fork inserted into the center comes out dry, about 1 hour. Let cool in the pan on a rack for 10 minutes, then turn out of the pan onto the rack and let cool completely before serving.

Serves 6

FLOURLESS Chocolate CAKE
WITH Whipped Cream

PREPARATION TIME: 15 minutes   **BAKING TIME:** 40 minutes

It's hard to go wrong with this smooth-textured, dark chocolate dessert framed in fluffy white whipped cream. Give the kids a head start by letting them lick the chocolate-covered bowl.

---

1 tablespoon, plus ½ cup (1 stick) unsalted butter
8 ounces semisweet chocolate, coarsely chopped
½ teaspoon vanilla extract
1 cup granulated sugar
4 eggs, yolks and whites separated
2 tablespoons confectioners' sugar
Whipped cream (page 37) for serving

Preheat the oven to 375°F. Grease the bottom of an 9-inch round cake pan with the 1 tablespoon butter.

In a small saucepan, combine the chocolate and the ½ cup butter over low heat and melt, stirring often until smooth. Stir in the vanilla, remove from the heat, and cover to keep warm.

In a medium bowl, using an electric mixer, beat together ½ cup of the granulated sugar and the egg yolks until pale in color. In a large bowl, beat the egg whites until soft peaks form. Slowly add the remaining ½ cup granulated sugar to the egg whites, beat until stiff peaks form, about 30 seconds. Using a plastic spatula, gently stir the egg yolk mixture into the egg whites just until combined. Then gently stir in the melted chocolate until the mixture is a uniform chocolate color.

Pour the batter into the prepared pan. Bake the cake until a fork or toothpick in-serted into the center comes out dry, about 40 minutes. Let cool in the pan on a rack for 10 minutes, then invert onto a serving plate and let cool com pletely. Using a fine-mesh sieve, dust the top of the cake with the confectioners' sugar. Top the individual servings with a dollop of whipped cream.

Serves 6 to 8

CHOCOLATE Pudding

PREPARATION TIME: 25 minutes   **BAKING TIME:** 1 hour 25 minutes

Since the ascendancy of instant pudding, many people have forgotten just how good a homemade pudding can taste. This one, with its rich cocoa flavors and velvety smooth texture, is almost like a cool, refreshing liquid brownie.

½ cup sugar
6 egg yolks
¼ teaspoon salt
4 cups heavy cream
1¼ teaspoons vanilla extract
6 ounces bittersweet chocolate, coarsely chopped
Whipped cream (page 37) for serving

Preheat the oven to 300°F.

In a bowl, whisk together ¼ cup of the sugar, the egg yolks, and salt until blended. Set aside.

In a saucepan, combine the cream, vanilla, and the remaining ¼ cup sugar over low heat and bring just to a boil, stirring to dissolve the sugar. Remove from the heat. Place the chocolate in a large bowl. Pour the hot cream over the chocolate and stir until the chocolate melts. Stir in the sugar-egg mixture. Pour the mixture through a fine-mesh sieve placed over a bowl (to remove any remaining chunks of chocolate or egg).

Ladle the pudding into ½-cup ramekins. Place the ramekins in a baking pan. Add hot water to the pan to reach halfway up the sides of the ramekins. Cover the baking pan with aluminum foil.

Bake the puddings until they are firm (jiggle a ramekin to test), about 1¼ hours. Remove the baking pan from the oven, and remove the ramekins from the pan. Let cool to room temperature, then refrigerate until well chilled. Serve with whipped cream.

Serves 6

"LEFTOVER" Rice Pudding

PREPARATION TIME: 10 minutes

BAKING TIME: 50 minutes

Leftover rice is not required for this recipe, but we find it perfectly suited to this old favorite.

1½ tablespoons, plus 2 tablespoons unsalted butter
2 cups cooked white rice (page 206), at room temperature
½ cup raisins
3 eggs
2 cups milk
½ cup heavy cream
½ cup sugar
½ teaspoon ground cinnamon
¼ teaspoon salt
¼ teaspoon ground nutmeg
1 teaspoon vanilla extract

Preheat the oven to 350°F. Grease a medium-sized baking dish with the 1½ tablespoons butter.

Combine the rice and raisins in the prepared dish and mix well.

In a bowl, whisk together the eggs, milk, cream, sugar, cinnamon, salt, nutmeg, and vanilla until smooth. Pour over the rice and stir until the liquid and rice are thoroughly blended.

Bake the pudding, uncovered, until set, about 45 minutes. Remove from the oven. Using a paring knife, cut the 2 tablespoons butter into 6 equal pieces. Using the same knife, make 6 small, evenly spaced incisions in the surface of the pudding and stuff each slit with a butter bit. Return the pudding to the oven and bake for 5 more minutes.

Transfer the pudding to a rack and let cool for at least 5 minutes prior to serving. Enjoy this pudding hot, warm, at room temperature, or chilled.

Serves 4 to 6

Index

A

B

C

D

TABLE OF Equivalents

The exact equivalents in the following tables have been rounded for convenience.

LIQUID/DRY MEASURES

U.S.	METRIC
$\frac{1}{4}$ teaspoon	1.25 milliliters
$\frac{1}{2}$ teaspoon	2.5 milliliters
1 teaspoon	5 milliliters
1 tablespoon (3 teaspoons)	15 milliliters
1 fluid ounce (2 tablespoons)	30 milliliters
$\frac{1}{4}$ cup	60 milliliters
$\frac{1}{8}$ cup	80 milliliters
$\frac{1}{2}$ cup	120 milliliters
1 cup (8 ounces)	240 milliliters
1 pint (2 cups)	480 milliliters
1 quart (4 cups, 32 ounces)	960 milliliters
1 gallon (4 quarts)	3.84 liters
1 ounce (by weight)	28 grams
1 pound	454 grams
2.2 pounds	1 kilogram

LENGTH

U.S.	METRIC
$\frac{1}{8}$ inch	3 millimeters
$\frac{1}{4}$ inch	6 millimeters
$\frac{1}{2}$ inch	12 millimeters
1 inch	2.5 centimeters

OVEN TEMPERATURE

FAHRENHEIT	CELSIUS	GAS
250	120	$\frac{1}{2}$
275	140	1
300	150	2
325	160	3
350	180	4
375	190	5
400	200	6
425	220	7
450	230	8
475	240	9
500	260	10